NOTHING BUT
THE TRUTH

The Secret Barrister is a junior barrister specialising in criminal law. They write for many publications and are the author of the award-winning blog of the same name. They were named Independent Blogger of the Year at the Editorial Intelligence Comment Awards (2016 and 2017) and Legal Personality of the Year at the Law Society Awards (2018). Their first book, *The Secret Barrister: Stories of the Law and How It's Broken*, was a *Sunday Times* number-one bestseller and spent more than a year in the top-ten bestseller list. It won the Books Are My Bag Non-Fiction Award 2018 and was shortlisted for Waterstones Book of the Year and the Specsavers Non-Fiction Book of the Year 2018. Their second book, *Fake Law: The Truth About Justice in an Age of Lies*, was an instant *Sunday Times* top-ten bestseller on publication.

Also by the Secret Barrister

The Secret Barrister: Stories of the Law and How It's Broken

Fake Law: The Truth About Justice in an Age of Lies

THE SECRET BARRISTER

NOTHING BUT THE TRUTH

The Memoir of an Unlikely Lawyer

PICADOR

First published 2022 by Picador

This paperback edition published 2023 by Picador
an imprint of Pan Macmillan
The Smithson, 6 Briset Street, London EC1M 5NR
EU representative: Macmillan Publishers Ireland Ltd, 1st Floor,
The Liffey Trust Centre, 117–126 Sheriff Street Upper,
Dublin 1, D01 YC43
Associated companies throughout the world
www.panmacmillan.com

ISBN 978-1-5290-5706-5

1 3 5 7 9 8 6 4 2

A CIP catalogue record for this book is available from the British Library.

Typeset by Palimpsest Book Production Ltd, Falkirk, Stirlingshire
Printed and bound by CPI Group (UK) Ltd, Croydon, CR0 4YY

*To all those whose love, support and wisdom got me
to where I am today.*

I hold each of you personally responsible.

Contents

NOTHING BUT
THE TRUTH

Preface

I take off my wig and sink into the sofa in the Crown Court witness suite. The ninety-year-old burglary victim sitting across from me looks up from his newspaper and beams a grandfatherly smile. 'Is there good news? Is it not going to be a trial? Is my burglar pleading guilty?'

I stare into his trusting blue eyes and swallow.

'The thing is . . .' I begin, as I try to formulate my next sentence. 'The thing is, the defendant is saying, and as the prosecution barrister I have to ask you . . . She says that she knows you.' I pause and look across to the Crown Prosecution Service caseworker for moral support. 'Professionally.'

His smile doesn't waver as he crooks a wispy eyebrow. 'Well, I'm afraid I very much doubt that – I've been out of the watchmaking world for twenty years!'

'No no,' I cough nervously. 'Her profession. Not yours.'

'I'm terribly sorry, but I'm not sure I follow.'

I take a deep breath. 'The defendant says that she didn't break into your house and steal from you, but that you invited her in for . . . services. And the money she took was payment for . . . rendering those services.'

He remains unruffled. 'I'm afraid not – I'd never seen that

lady in my life until I caught her hopping out of my window with my wallet.'

He's going to make me say it. The kindly, snow-haired, twinkly-eyed bastard is going to make me say it.

'The thing is, Mr Grace, she can give particular detail about your . . . she says that you have . . . apparently in order for her . . .'

The police officer to my left comes to my rescue. 'Tom, she says that every time she blew you, you asked her to help take off your false leg. And she's happy to tell the jury all about it.'

We all sit in appalling silence for what feels like a decade, nobody making eye contact. Eventually, Tom speaks.

'I think, upon reflection, that there might have been a misunderstanding. If it's all the same to you, I'll be on my way. Please pass on my apologies to Natasha.'

As he shuffles out of the witness suite, the police officer and I lock eyes. Neither of us has told him the defendant's first name.

I don't know what I expected a career as a barrister to be like. As an eighteen-year-old embarking upon a law degree, I knew very little about the nuts and bolts of our criminal justice system. Certainly it never occurred to me that the role might entail days like the above, sweating beneath my thick black gown in an unventilated witness room as the image of the nonagenarian Mr Grace expectantly detaching his prosthetic limb was seared for ever onto my subconscious.

But one thing I did know about the justice system was how I believed it *should* work. My views about criminal justice, in particular, were held more fervently than any others from a relatively early age. And while I don't know how usual this is for an adolescent, surveys regularly tell us that adults, at least, feel more strongly about crime than they do on almost any other social or political issue. It's perhaps unsurprising. Criminal acts, by definition, are wrongdoings against all of us – they are the most serious breaches of our social code, the ones which cannot be left for individuals to privately litigate, but which call for the intervention of the state to dispense justice on behalf of us all. It is inevitable that criminal justice stirs interest and excites emotion, and it is only right – as a matter of democracy – that we all have our say on a system which we collectively own. In which we all hold a stake.

Which brings us to this book. Because, while we will look, through charting my own bumbling journey, at what our justice system is like from the inside, I do recognise that 'anonymous autobiography', if not strictly an oxymoron, does border sufficiently on the ridiculous for anybody claiming to write such a thing to be justly and righteously kicked in the shins. 'Allow me, someone who won't even give you their name, to tell you anonymised details of my professional life and charge you for the privilege' has a vibe which, even for a lawyer, feels exploitative.

So, more than that, I want to talk about what we understand by justice. What we expect our criminal justice system to do. And how well it does that. In doing so, I'd like to consider the following set of propositions:

— The justice system is too soft on criminals

— We should have a little less 'understanding', and a lot more deterrence

— Judges are woolly, out-of-touch liberals pushing a left-wing agenda and making us all less safe

— We waste too much money on ambulance-chasing lawyers, criminals and illegal immigrants

— The rights of criminals are put before the rights of victims and the law-abiding public

— Criminal justice needs less political correctness, bureaucracy and paperwork, and more bobbies on the beat and good British common sense

These are views that I hear a lot when I speak to people about justice. They chime with much of what we read in the popular press, and echo sentiments that we hear from the politicians with the loudest microphones. They are views that I have spent nearly a decade valiantly and self-righteously railing against, from my beginnings as an anonymous, rabbit-avatared Twitter account in 2015, through to blogs, newspaper articles, and, somewhat improbably, two whole books.

They are also, all of them, views that I myself used to hold.

But the things I saw and heard once I took the road to becoming a criminal barrister changed me. Almost beyond recognition. Certainties that had shaped me through my early decades started to subside. Truths which I had internalised as self-evident began to seem so much less obvious. And opinions that I would once have reviled became not merely thinkable, but my new creed.

It may of course be that mine is nothing more intriguing than a tale of subconscious conformity. Of a weak-willed youngster uncritically devouring the ideological gruel of their industry in a desperate search for acceptance, their conversion amplifying their zeal in the time-honoured cliché. A hostage to institutional norms. A freethinker gone native. It is entirely possible that my metamorphosis was not special at all; maybe I was just one of thousands of quiet hang-'em-and-flog-'ems on a long-running ideological production line, bending and melting to identical pressures and forces as we were bashed and moulded into uniform shape.

But, doing my best to look at my transformation objectively, I think it's more complex than trading one starter-pack set of values for another. I think the production-line analogy isn't actually too far from the truth; but rather than those pressures and forces arising in the form of social attitudes and rootless institutional mores, what is acting upon all of us is something blunter: experience. There is something that this job, this industry, does. Daily exposure to the criminal justice system makes certain uncomfortable truths impossible to ignore.

There wasn't a pinpointable Damascene moment. There was no single defendant whose story sent scales sliding from my eyes, or crying a late-night Eureka from the bathtub as I unexpectedly divined the solution to mounting internal conflict. There was nothing more dramatic than a series of experiences, clients, colleagues and immutable realities that forced me to examine and adjust what I thought I knew.

Make no mistake, there is no such thing as a universally held opinion. There will be criminal barristers, solicitors and judges who do hold views close to those I started out with. But if there's not homogeny, there is at the very least a dominant strain of ideology, towards which I, like thousands of others, now lean. It's an ideology which is often at odds with the values of people outside the system.

That is why I wanted to write this book.

I wanted to consider why that is. What happens on the voyage through criminal practice that leads so often to one particular worldview? What happened on mine? How did I transition from an ardent *Daily Mail*-reading undergrad to someone described by the *Mail On Sunday*'s Peter Hitchens as 'a tedious dogmatic liberal'?*

This isn't going to be a lecture, don't worry. It is not a book prescribing how and what you *should* think about justice. It is certainly not designed to mock or embarrass people who hold the views listed at the start of these pages; people with whom I would once have fervently agreed. We all have a stake in our justice system, and are all entitled to a view on the meaning and execution of justice. Despite what social media may sometimes have us believe, there is ample scope – nay, a democratic need – for civil disagreement. I'm not measuring the success of this book by whether I 'convince' you to adopt my opinions. It is intended as an exercise in reflection, not advocacy.

But at the same time, I hope that my experiences can inform that conversation. By retreading my memories, from law school up to my present incarnation, I hope to demystify our archaic legal system, shed light on how our peculiar, wig-and-gown-adorned profession works, and pose, if not satisfactorily answer, questions about what we all understand by justice.

Starting from my year of training at Bar school, I'll draw from my memory bank and decipher the scrawled sporadic entries of my diaries to offer a collection of stories, musings and hard-learned lessons. Many, I warn you now, involve tales of degradation and humiliation (almost exclusively mine). But they've taught me things I wish I'd known when an outsider to the system. I hope they might be of similar value to you.

---

* Tweet by Peter Hitchens (@ClarkeMicah) on 8 April 2019, 'Oh I see @barristersecret has at last unmasked herself as a tedious dogmatic liberal. "Two ferrets in a sack" is dead original as well. Got any actual arguments, Ms Barrister?', https://twitter.com/ClarkeMicah/status/1115240551371218945?s=20

Names, dates and other identifying details have been vigorously disguised. But the contents are all materially true; every misstep, every life lesson, every tear shed, they all happened, either to me, or someone I know.

So let's start at the beginning.

As a teenager, the meaning of criminal justice was straightforward to me. It was an understanding shaped in part by my background, in part by the newspapers we had at home – the *Mail* and the *Telegraph* – and in part by the tenor of what little political debate I occasionally tuned into during my largely apolitical upbringing as a middle-class comprehensive student in the heart of Middle England.

Politics was something that was never really discussed when I was growing up. My secondary-school curriculum placed no emphasis on current affairs, and so very little about the outside world cut through my adolescent bubble of angsty solipsism, unrequited love and Roaccutane. The one reliable exception was crime. A headline in the *Daily Mail* about violent offenders escaping justice or an evening news bulletin reporting an illegal immigrant killing somebody in a hit-and-run, and my attention was captive. The instinctive horror I quietly felt at the harm wrought by the selfish criminal acts of others was magnified by the editorials and columnists I would read, and, for want of any alternative perspectives, my opinions on crime grew to mirror theirs. I had few forums to discuss the views I was learning almost by rote – my friends were resolutely uninterested in what was in the news, and my school was very much *not* the 'debating society' sort of establishment – and so my opinions remained largely private, and almost wholly unchallenged.

If they amounted to a philosophy, those values could perhaps best be loosely filed as 'crime and punishment'. That, for me, was how justice was most purely articulated. It had a number of concomitant principles: Commit a crime, expect to be punished. Punishment means prison, and prison should be sufficiently unpleasant so that once visited you never wanted to return.

Self-reliance and responsibility, the backbone of our national story, lay at the heart of my attitude to crime. You have to take responsibility for your actions. Bleeding-heart sob stories do not absolve you of your part of the social contract. Many people have difficulties in their personal lives; most do not choose to commit crime. Deeper examination of these ideas never seemed necessary. The need to obey the law, and the need to punish those who transgressed, were always self-evident. If there was ever any room for doubt, it was quickly occupied by the certitude of the latest Simon Heffer column.

I grew up during the 1990s in the shadow of the horrific abduction and murder of two-year-old James Bulger in Liverpool. I was a similar age to that of his ten-year-old killers, Jon Venables and Robert Thompson, and as their criminal case occupied the political and media landscape over the years that followed, I could not comprehend the enormity of what they had done.

I did not understand how children my own age could have committed an act so wicked. There were naughty children at my school – those whose disruptive classroom antics and playground bullying made my mother tut about indisciplined parenting – but for somebody my age to *kill*? And in such awful, sadistic circumstances? The only explanation that occurred was that offered by the politicians on the news – these boys were uniquely evil. Irredeemable. To be filed in a category that fitted neatly into the binary model I was building to help me to make sense of the world. I had little truck with any suggestion that they were somehow less culpable because of their age or circumstances. I knew that what they did was wrong. So did they. It was as straightforward as that. As Prime Minister John Major told the *Mail on Sunday* – 'society needs to condemn a little more, and understand a little less'. Some crimes, regrettably, are unforgivable. Some people, I remember telling my classmates during a heated debate in sixth form college, cannot, and should not, be saved.

From everything I read in the papers, our criminal justice system did not stand up for my ideals. It often seemed that criminals' rights mattered more than victims', and that – echoing a rare party political consensus – true justice played second fiddle to legal-aid gravy trains, tricksy lawyers gaming the system and loopy judges failing in their duties to protect the public. The paltry sentences handed out to Venables and Thompson, which were the subject of noisy political and legal wrangles through the years that followed, served as a prime example. That the boys would be released after less than a decade* was the ultimate insult; the hallmark of a system which had lost its way. A little less politically correct handwringing

---

* At the time, defendants convicted of murder were sentenced to life (or 'detention at Her Majesty's Pleasure', for children), with a minimum term, or 'tariff', recommended by the judge. In the case of Venables and Thompson, the judge recommended eight years, after which the boys would be eligible for release if approved by the Parole Board. This tariff was increased to ten years by the Lord Chief Justice, then to fourteen years by Home Secretary Michael Howard, before the European Court of Human Rights confirmed that politicians intervening to set criminal sentences was very much not the sort of thing that modern democracies should have, and the tariff was reviewed once again and set by the (new) Lord Chief Justice at eight years.

over 'the causes of crime', radically tougher sentences and a few more bobbies on the beat were the obvious prescription.

As strongly as I felt, however, I can't pretend that my views on criminal justice had anything to do with my decision to study a law degree. My motives were ignoble and self-serving. After school, I chose to read law at university partly because I got the impression that being a lawyer in court is a fun way to make a good living – like being an actor (my true teenage calling), only you are guaranteed, by threat of imprisonment, an audience – partly because it provided a general career direction in the event that nothing more original occurred to me over the next three years.

University nevertheless offered the first real opportunity to share my views on justice, and to be exposed to perspectives that I had previously only ever heard disparaged. I quickly found that attitudes like mine were not hugely common among student millennials. Even scanter were *Daily Mail* readers. I remember being aghast at reports that the then Lord Chief Justice, Lord Woolf, had publicly called for fewer custodial sentences for burglars, and writing a strident letter to the student newspaper, which I suspect they published for its rarity value ('A sheep in Woolf's clothing', I brilliantly burned the LCJ). I was a supporter of extended detention without charge for terror suspects, as, I reasoned, the police are hardly likely to have arrested someone if they are innocent. Soft sentencing of criminals infused me with fury, and I could not understand why there was not uproar among my cohort – self-defined progressives fighting for a better world – when killer drivers were let off with a slap on the wrist and dangerous violent criminals reoffended with impunity. Instead of letting prisoners out early for supposed 'good behaviour' – the bare minimum, frankly, that should be expected of someone in prison – we ought, I seethed to my housemate, to protect the public by refusing to release prisoners unless and until we were sure that they no longer posed a risk to the rest of us.*

Daily exposure to the study of the law and the prevailing orthodoxies of legal academia did little to soften my convictions. If anything, the perceived liberalism of many of my tutors, particularly in criminal law, confirmed my worst fears, and provoked a reactionary hardening in my certainty in the moral righteousness of severe punishment. Like a Mad Hatter's Tea Party of justice, these self-appointed gatekeepers of the system seemed intent on turning common sense on its head. They believed in fewer and shorter prison sentences, for people who were actively out to hurt the rest of us. Their rhetoric diluted personal responsibility to homeopathic proportions; painting criminals as victims of circumstance rather than autonomous, accountable agents. Energy seemed disproportionately exhausted on safeguarding the interests of the wrongdoers, rather than the people who deserved protection. Concepts of deterrence and punishment evoked squeamishness, and the more I read, the less the latter fit the crime. There was a chasm between the harm caused by criminals and the feeble retribution inflicted by the state.

None of this seemed right. So little of what The System designated 'justice' bore any resemblance to the beliefs that were

---

* Around this very time, the Labour government did in fact introduce new laws for 'dangerous offenders' which did exactly this, providing for indeterminate sentences of imprisonment where an offender posed a significant risk of serious harm to the public. These sentences, introduced in 2005, were ultimately abolished in 2012 after they resulted in defendants sentenced to a few months in prison serving decades, due to the state's inability to provide prisoners with the courses they needed to address their risk.

not just held by me, but which, I was assured by the *Mail*, were shared by millions of my fellow citizens. So it was that I emerged from my three-year undergraduate cocoon as an even angrier, more vengeful butterfly, with a Bachelor of Laws (LLB) degree to add a certified layer of reinforcement to how right about such things I must be.

So now, where this book begins, we find ourselves somewhere in the mid-2000s. I have muddled my way through a law degree at a middling redbrick university, and have successfully staved off the swarm of difficult decisions about the future for a couple more years by holding down an eclectic succession of jobs through an obliging temp agency. The highlight of these has been a placement as PA to a university lecturer who admitted on the first day: 'I wasn't expecting you and I don't need a PA', but who due to glorious Britishness was too embarrassed to tell her superiors and so just sat me in the corner of her office with a book for the month. The lowlight has probably been the week spent standing in the rain in a car park with three strangers handing out flyers for a new cafe, all dressed up as characters from *The Wizard of Oz*.* But £5.50 an hour was not to be sniffed at, and if the time could not be described as well-spent, my experiences have at least persuaded me that, given that I've gone to the trouble of getting a law degree, there is probably some merit in at least trying to put it to good use.

As mentioned above, my decision to pursue law is not born

---

* Technically it was three strangers for the first two days only. On the Wednesday the Scarecrow, having spent the previous two days sitting on a bin chain-smoking spliffs, decided to pack it in. Lord knows why – he was literally being paid to sit and smoke. If he only had a brain etc.

of idealism. Nor is it from tradition. I don't boast the heritage of doughty reforming lawyers or campaigning social justice advocates. I am not the progeny of three generations of High Court judges, steeped in our nation's first legal principles since birth. To the contrary, I have absolutely no family ties to the legal profession – neither of my parents has a university degree, and the closest anyone in my immediate family has come to the justice system is when my parents had to fight the local education authority over provision for my brother's special educational needs schooling. For the nearest brush with criminal justice, we have to reach out to my great-grandfather threatening to shoot police officers before deliberately driving a lorry into an oil tanker, causing it to topple over,* or, on the newer branches of my family tree, my cousin's husband being run out of the county because he dealt on the wrong turf and ended up with a contract on his head.

Crime has always been the area of law that intrigued me the most, ardour undimmed by having aced 43 per cent in the criminal law module of my degree. Even in the years post-graduation, when I was resolved to absolutely not ending up in law and instead doing something artistic and tortured (auditioning for *Big Brother* was on the shortlist at one point), the notion of being a criminal barrister lurked permanently in the recesses of my intentions; a siren to whom I would eventually, inevitably, be lured. Maybe, although it never occurred to me, my interest was subconcsciously enhanced by my strength of feeling

---

* The newspaper report of my great-grandfather's trial records that 'he announced that he was defending himself and carried bulky law volumes and large notebooks into the dock'. So it is possible that I owe my aptitude for courtroom advocacy to him. He got nine months.

towards the political dimension of criminal justice, but I think that the main attraction was that crime just seemed interesting – gritty, macabre, deeply human – in a way which no other area of law ever matched. I was also aware that the criminal courts represented the last vestige of the ostentatious theatre of the law. Trial by jury, wigs and gowns – all the traditional elements of criminal trial that have been gradually removed in the civil (i.e. non-criminal) courts – were still alive and kicking in the Crown Courts.

As a teen, I considered myself a gifted, albeit routinely under-appreciated, actor, and a spellbinding public speaker. As would have been painfully clear to my audience, those opinions were not supported by the evidence. Nevertheless, becoming a criminal barrister, entrancing juries with my wit and erudition, seemed an obvious fit for my self-perceived strengths. I don't think I had consciously placed myself in a particular role; had I been asked the question directly, I expect I would at one time have said I desired to be a prosecutor, styling myself as a rough-housing US-style District Attorney. But then John Grisham happened; in particular, my first reading of *A Time To Kill*, and the oppositional malcontent in control of my ego was also attracted to the romantic ideal of a Jake Brigance fuck-the-system renegade defence lawyer.* Holding both of these ideas simultaneously of course makes no sense, but any cognitive dissonance was resolved by my incapacity for self-reflection. And the joy of the independent Bar, in any event, is that you don't actually have to choose one side. You both prosecute and

---

* I was at that stage blissfully unaware that, in England and Wales, Mr Brigance's heroic antics would amount to serious breaches of the Bar Code of Conduct and would almost certainly result in him being heavily sanctioned, if not disbarred.

defend, although not, unless something has gone very wrong, in the same case (this has only happened to me once).

This, however, is something I will learn on my travels. As, at this moment in time, I don't have a particularly clear idea of what it is that a barrister actually does.

1. The Road to the Bar

The notion of a twenty-something qualifying as a barrister may strike some people as odd. When I set off for Bar school, several relatives expressed surprise, assuming that 'barrister' connotes some degree of seniority. This is an illusion I've heard repeated many times while in practice. To the justifiable disgust of solicitors, I've also heard it suggested that a barrister is a promotion; that if you are a 'good enough' solicitor, you may one day be fortunate enough to be upgraded to a barrister. Let's make it clear for the avoidance of doubt: it's not. Barristers and solicitors are entirely separate species* (albeit there is a wealth of evidence suggesting we are capable of interbreeding).

The truth, as far as I could see, was that for many law students – myself included – our comprehension of the distinction between the two branches of the English and Welsh legal profession was no deeper than the general public's. This is no criticism of the public, by the way. The legal profession has gone

---

* Except for those who decided to confuse things by qualifying as both. Solicitor advocates – solicitors who take a course to obtain the same 'rights of audience' as barristers, and so appear in court looking and sounding like barristers – further blur the divide. But trust me – we are different.

to extraordinary lengths over the centuries to cloak itself in unnecessary mystery and erect barricades seemingly designed to prevent anybody without a degree in Latin understanding the first thing about the justice system. That the public are often confused or mistaken as to how our profession operates is entirely our fault, as we – historically drunk on the myth of our own brilliance and determined to draw our members from as narrow a section of society as possible – have shown no interest in making what we do accessible or comprehensible. *Just trust us when we tell you we're important* has been the bumper sticker of the legal profession for most of its existence.

Boiled down to its bare bones, lawyers in England and Wales are split into solicitors and barristers. Solicitors handle the litigation – taking instructions from the clients, drafting legal documents and managing the administrative trial process. Barristers are then instructed by solicitors as and when the case calls for it, mainly for the purposes of providing advice and advocacy, the latter often in court.

In criminal law, solicitors are the first point of contact with clients, often at the police station following arrest. They cultivate the relationships with the clients, deal with most cases in the magistrates' courts and instruct a barrister to act in the Crown Courts (only barristers* have 'rights of audience' to appear in courts above the magistrates' court). Solicitors tend to be employed by firms, whereas barristers are in the main self-employed, operating out of what are grandly termed 'chambers' (premises in which a group of barristers share overheads and support staff, put loosely).

The oft-made analogy of solicitors and barristers is the relationship between a GP and a consultant. Which solicitors would

* And solicitor advocates, as above.

probably agree with, if the GP painstakingly diagnosed the problem, told the consultant exactly what needed doing and then sat forbearingly in silence as the consultant bragged how his consultancy skills had saved the day.

Fork in the road

The fork in the road for law undergraduates is marked as early as freshers' week, it being assumed that as you have chosen to study the academic discipline of law, you not only have designs on practising it, but know with a fair degree of certainty whether it's the university Bar Society or Solicitors' Society that will be pocketing your £10 subscription fee and never hearing from you again.

Throughout law school we were treated to steady subliminal messaging nudging us towards the chorus line of graduates at corporate law firms in the City. Debates and libraries and moots* were sponsored by these big firms, who would send branded stress balls and key rings and exhausted but obliging trainee solicitors to meet-and-greet events where we were told in exacting detail just how much gold would be stuffed into our tiny mouths in return for seventy-hour weeks if we managed to secure a training contract with them. (To put it in today's money, the starting salary as a trainee solicitor at one of the big 'Magic Circle' commercial firms in London is currently just shy of £50,000. Upon completing your two-year

---

* A form of legal debate that takes place as a sort of mock trial in front of a judge. Often with scenarios charmingly constructed from literature – e.g. 'Should the court enforce a contractual term providing for the extraction of a pound of flesh in the event of breach, having regard in particular to the Supreme Court jurisprudence on penalty clauses exemplified in ParkingEye Ltd v Beavis [2015]' – that sort of lark.

training contract, you can expect to tickle six figures, and it's all uphill from there.*)

These firms ran highly coveted 'summer vacation placements', where for the privilege of a stipend just above minimum wage† you could spend a fortnight in their skyline London offices watching whatever it is that high-rolling corporate lawyers do. I don't know – I had only one interview, and in an attempt to explain a particularly low exam result, caused in part by lack of sleep and in part by lack of effort, I found myself deploying the words 'squirrel sex'. At the end of the interview, the partner shook my hand firmly and wished me luck 'in whatever you decide to do'.

The first time I met a barrister, on the other hand, I was prepared. It was at an event organised by the law school in my second year of university. They were there to give a talk on something or other; the benefit to the barristers was that they got a gooey feeling inside for giving something back to their alma maters, and a free buffet. The benefit to us was that we might speak to a barrister and gorge on their wisdom.

Having identified a rotund pinstriped cliché lurking at the buffet table, I seized my opportunity. I walked up to him as he was taking a bite of quiche and, momentarily losing control of

---

* It's important to emphasise the divide between commercial solicitors – enjoying the delights of contract law, mergers and acquisitions etc. for whacking great pay – and their publicly funded (e.g. criminal law, family law) counterparts, chugging away at much, much lower legal-aid rates.

† Nowadays, these vacation placements pay *much* better and, correspondingly, involve an application competition comprising a lengthy written form, Watson Glaser critical thinking test, written assessment, formal interview and the retrieval of a ring from the fires of Mount Doom.

my modulation, shouted my name at him.* 'Becret Sarrister', I spoonerised. He swallowed his mouthful and politely asked, 'I'm sorry?'

'My name is Secret Barrister,' I said, extending my hand. Warily, he shook it. I smiled and nodded my head. He smiled awkwardly and nodded his head. I nodded mine again. Silence descended as I racked my brain for something to say to this adult human. I'd been focusing on giving my name correctly and shaking hands – that was the hard part. Working out what questions I would ask my quarry once I'd cornered him was something else entirely. When it became clear, after two agonising minutes, that neither of us had anything further to contribute to this exchange, I nodded my head and wandered off home, satisfied that I had had some form of interaction, technically even a conversation, with a real-life barrister.

The secret mini-pupil

Back to the present: my first mini-pupillage† arrives post-graduation, courtesy of my former university tutor who has a friend in a local chambers. (Nowadays there is a formal, and highly competitive, application process for the privilege of following barristers bumbling about our daily lives.)

Some mini-pupillages are assessed, with inscrutable criteria scored and boxes ticked, to be filed away in case you later apply

---

* If you're picturing Brick Tamland from *Anchorman*, you're pretty close to the money.
† Work experience at a barristers' chambers cannot be referred to merely as work experience. Instead, we aggrandise these three- to five-day placements into 'mini-pupillages' ('pupillage' being the twelve-month mandatory on-the-job training that follows completion of the Bar course, 'mini' presumably being a reminder to the individual in question not to get ideas above their station).

for a full pupillage. My first is non-assessed, which is a shame because aside from a descending car park barrier striking me on the head as we leave court, I acquit myself with minimum embarrassment over the course of that week. It is a civil law, rather than criminal law, mini-pupillage, meaning I am following barristers specialising mostly in personal injury work. Ambulance chasing, as I once would have called it.

One, Aaron, is around five years' call. (Seniority among barristers, I am learning, is expressed in terms of how many years it has been since you qualified and were 'called to the Bar'.) After a morning watching him adjourn a hearing for a personal injury claim (it appears that the court has given the defendant the wrong date), Aaron takes me to a fancy restaurant for lunch, so it is clear that he is one of the good guys. Still honing my skills in making conversation with grown-ups, I ask him how he knew that the Bar was for him. His response is unexpected. With disarming candour, he spits out the pickle from his Big Mac and says, 'I don't know that it is. Every day I find that I'm asking myself whether I made the right choice. I don't know. If you ask me whether I'll be here in five years' time, I couldn't, hand on heart, say yes.' He smiles apologetically at me. 'Sorry, I don't imagine that's the reply you were hoping for.'

One afternoon that week I sit in on a conference* with Dianne, a senior barrister who specialises in 'catastrophic injuries'. These are the cases carrying the life-changing multi-million-pound windfalls that make newspaper headlines. Serious, lottery-jackpot wonga for the lucky claimant, as the

---

* Barristers don't have 'meetings' with solicitors and clients. Oh no. Again, we're far too fancy. We have 'conferences'. Or 'cons', in hip legal slang (not to be confused with 'con' as occasional shorthand for 'convict'. Or 'confidence trick').

media often has it. I spend the morning reading lever-arch files of the case papers. Much of the medico-legal procedure and terminology is lost on me, but certain parts are not. I am at least able to understand that an eight-year-old boy, Josh, was in the car with his mum when an oncoming driver ran a red light and lost control of his van. I understand terms like 'life-changing brain and spinal injuries'. I can strip away enough legalese to see that Josh will never walk or speak again, and needs round-the-clock care for the rest of his life.

The settlement that has been offered by the defendant's insurers totals seven figures, and the conference is for Dianne to discuss this with Josh's parents. Most of that figure is what I will later learn are called 'special damages' – money to pay for the cost of adapting Josh's home to his new needs, the cost of his care over the years to come, and so forth. The remainder, 'general damages', reflects 'pain and suffering' and is a few hundred thousand.

Doing the maths in my head, the 'pain and suffering' award works out at something like £10,000 a year for the next few decades. Ten grand for a complete loss of independence from childhood? This isn't what Grisham promised me in *The King of Torts*. Turns out there are no juries in our system awarding giddy claimants payouts far in excess of their losses, with lawyers creaming a delicious 30 per cent of the $100 million bonanza. Our law estimates your financial loss, past and future, as best it can, and gives you just that. Plus a modest sum plucked out of a catalogue* to reflect your estimated agony. Not a penny more. Compensation compensates. It doesn't enrich.

---

* The Judicial College Guidelines for the Assessment of General Damages in Personal Injury Cases, which gives you ballpark figures depending on the type and severity of injury.

I don't ever find out whether Josh's parents accept the settlement or not. But I do know that, for all I've read about personal injury claims being an easy, ambulance-chasing ride to jackpot payouts, this sum – these millions of pounds – doesn't feel like much of a victory. As I sit silently in the corner of the echoey conference room, watching Josh's ashen parents absorb the numbers and respond with barely a murmur, they don't look or sound like lottery winners. They look like a mum and dad who just want their little boy back.

Mark, Marvin and Melvin

My debut as a mini-pupil in the criminal courts doesn't arrive until I have decided to apply for the Bar course. I have been to the Crown Court by myself before, but with mixed results. A courtroom, you see, is a uniquely awkward environment. Any entrant who is not a regular is immediately put ill at ease by the sense of otherness and outsiderdom that the language, dress, etiquette and geography appear designed to engender. This first trip was to one of the newer court centres, where Gothic Revivalism and oak panelling have given way to PFI-backed neomodernism and MDF-backed IKEA chic, and in which each courtroom presents an inscrutable configuration of pine benches and unmarked folding seating. So it was that I, nineteen and demonstrating every year of my accumulated naivety, searching the corridors for some courtroom drama to absorb and regale in my first-year 'What I Saw Today in Court' essay, tiptoed into a bustling courtroom and politely introduced myself to the gentleman standing immediately to my left, asking where one, as an undergraduate law student keenly interested in following Crown Court proceedings as part of my university education, might sit to observe what was to precipitate. The response – 'What the fuck you on about? I don't know where the fuck you

24

sit. I'm the fucking defendant.' – provided my first lesson in practical law: Don't talk like a dickhead.

A major plus of mini-pupillage, therefore, is that somebody tells you, explicitly, with no room for error, where to sit in court. I perch behind Laura, the barrister I am shadowing – a blunt-speaking whirlwind, described euphemistically by colleagues as a 'character' – and watch in awe as she opens the case* she is prosecuting to the jury. The court is a beautiful traditional Victorian affair: deep polished oak benches, cushioned with crimson leather; the jury box within touching distance of the barristers, themselves within spitting range of the judge, all parties dressed in their traditional horsehair wigs, starched white bands and crisp black gowns. The only concessions to modernity are the shirt-sleeved security officers flanking the two defendants in the dock. The case concerns a serious stabbing in the city centre. The two defendants – Sunil and Mark – stand accused of wounding the complainant, Marvin, with intent to cause grievous bodily harm.

Laura's opening speech is a poetic and auditory masterpiece, the depth and variety of language twinning perfectly with the rise and fall of her rich voice, pitched to precision against the acoustic rhythms of the courtroom. The only tiny criticism one might make – and I am of course in no position to make it, not even when she later asks me directly what, in my inexpert view, she could have done better – is that somewhere around the five-minute mark, she starts to mix-up the names 'Mark' and 'Marvin'. At ten minutes, we have a new unexpected addition to the cast, Melvin, who acts as an itinerant substitute for both Mark and Marvin at various points in the speech. By the end, a

---

* The prosecution opening speech, in which the jury are told what the prosecution case is against the accused.

few jurors appear perplexed at what this nice boy Mark is doing in the dock, when he has been so viciously stabbed in the midriff by the star prosecution witness Marvin and the inexplicably absent Melvin.

Nevertheless, as an advertisement for the theatre of the criminal courtroom, this trial, and Laura's performance, is irresistible. Examining and cross-examining witnesses, engaging in machine-gun legal argument with an irascible judge; it is every square inch the romantic painting hanging in my adolescent mind's eye. *The noble barrister, fighting the good fight and having a ruddy good time in the process.*

As we leave court on my fifth and final day, Laura is venting sympathy for the ordeal that the teenaged Marvin has been put through. 'If anyone did this to my child, I wouldn't come to court.' I nod, assuming I know what she means. I am wrong.

'I'd handle it myself,' she continues. 'I know people.' It takes me a few beats to catch her drift, and a few more to realise that she isn't joking. 'That's the thing about this job. All it would take is one phone call to the right person . . .' With that, she winks at me, turns on her heel and strides off towards the station, suitcase clickety-clacking behind her.

By the time I am eventually practising myself, Laura is no longer around, having left the Bar under a cloud not long after our week together. Still, as far as life lessons go, 'get the names of the parties right' and 'in criminal law you will meet people who might, if you ask nicely, whack your enemies' were ones to remember. Even if, in practice, I've tended to rely on one more often than the other.

Throwing good after bad
Universal to all mini-pupillages, it transpires, is a succession of warnings, from every criminal barrister you speak to, not to

pursue a career at the criminal Bar. Decreasing volumes of work and severe cuts to legal-aid rates render it impossible to earn a living, I am told multiple times each day. Almost as universal as the gloom-mongering is the experience of sitting around at court waiting for something to happen, only for the barrister you are shadowing to announce that their case is not going ahead, and foisting you on one of their colleagues. This typically happens two or three times a day. If there is nobody else from the same chambers at that court centre, you might be instructed to sit at the back of a busy courtroom and watch proceedings by yourself, which strikes me as somewhat defeating the point of a mini-pupillage and very much the sort of thing I could do in my own time.

On one mini-pupillage, this happens three days in a row, and by 11 a.m. on each day I have been abandoned to my own devices. On the third day, I find myself in a magistrates' court, trying to follow the parade of chaos and impenetrable jargon as a series of short hearings are whizzed through at breakneck speed. One case I understand all too well is a woman who has pleaded guilty to possession of a class-A drug, heroin. She isn't represented by a solicitor, grunts barely a word at the magistrates when they try to engage with her, and the magistrates sentence her to a fine. I watch agog. A FINE! One hundred pounds! What's more, they deem it 'paid' by virtue of her having been 'detained' in the court that morning – so she literally walks out scot free. How on earth not-really-fining this wretched woman is supposed to achieve anything is beyond me. It is clear as day that, as a drug addict, the best thing for her, and the rest of us, would be a few months in prison to get her cleaned up, teach her a trade and deter her from future drug abuse. The cowardice of the sentencing court is everything I feared from reading the newspapers.

Unimpressed with both the rewards of mini-pupillage and the irrationality of the justice system, I go home at lunch and don't return for the rest of the week.

The Brian Sewell plea in mitigation

A 'plea in mitigation' is the speech that a barrister delivers to a court before her guilty client is sentenced. The purpose is to alert the court to the features of the offence and the personal circumstances of the defendant that make the offence less serious, or the defendant more sympathetic, in the hope of achieving a more generous sentence outcome (sometimes avoiding immediate custody, sometimes just keeping the term of imprisonment in single digits). Even though it's directed towards a judge, and so a certain formality is required, a well-executed plea in mitigation – like all successful advocacy – has a ring of conversationality to it; an injection of humanity, realism and pragmatism, much as you would adopt if trying to persuade somebody of something in the real world.

I, having never heard of a plea in mitigation, let alone witnessed one in action, do not know this. So when, on my next criminal mini-pupillage, I am presented with an assessed advocacy exercise which involves delivering a plea in mitigation for a hypothetical defendant convicted of shoplifting, I am flying blind. I assume that addressing a judge requires the poshest of RP accents and the longest and most archaic of words, and the end result sounds something like a concussed Brian Sewell retching up a nineteenth-century thesaurus.

'*Lo, My Lord! In common parlance, one might surmise that this fellow, who is by habit a gentle knave, exhibits remorse! Look upon him, I beseech thee, with mercy . . .*'

And so on for two sides of A4. Had it been a real shoplifter, I'm fairly confident my efforts would have got him life.

A rake among scholars

The standard route to qualifying as a barrister involves a year studying for a Postgraduate Diploma in Legal Practice at a Bar school.* (Friendly tip: if you know somebody studying at Bar school, ask them if they've been taught how to make a good Pink Negroni. It will definitely be the first time somebody has made a joke riffing on the double-meaning of the word 'bar', and you will be applauded for your originality. Similarly, if you have noticed that 'barrister' is almost a homophone for 'barista', you are a comedy pioneer and it is your public duty to go on Twitter and make a remark about coffee to the first barrister you can find. They won't have heard it before. Promise.)

There used to be a standardised Bar Vocational Course. Now there are a variety of approved courses (the Bar Practice Course, the Barrister Training Course, and so on), but whatever the nomenclature, the constants are (i) the course offers aspiring barristers the vocational training they need to supplement the academic knowledge of the law they've acquired from their law degree (or, if they were sensible enough to avoid undergrad law, their postgraduate law conversion course); and (ii) it costs a ridiculous sum of money. After fees hit close to £20,000 in 2019/20, the training framework was radically shaken up and there are now newer and cheaper ways of completing a qualifying course, but even these options cost between £11,000 and £13,000 for the year, before you even consider living expenses.

Many graduates fund their studies through professional bank loans (Bar school does not qualify for a postgraduate

---

* The typical itinerary is law degree (or non-law degree followed by a twelve-month Graduate Diploma in Law), and then either a Legal Practice Course (if you want to be a solicitor) or Bar Course (for barristers).

student loan). Added to undergrad student loans, it means today's newly minted barristers begin pupillage with debts nearing six figures.

I have resolved to myself that the outcome of my application for a scholarship will determine whether or not I go ahead with the course. I don't want to be a barrister enough to plough myself into tens of thousands of pounds of further debt; I will aim for the scholarship and let fate decide.

Scholarships are awarded by the Inns of Court. All prospective barristers have to be a member of one of the four Inns – Middle Temple, Inner Temple, Lincoln's Inn and Gray's Inn – which have, since around the fourteenth century, served as our professional associations. They are based in central London's legal district* and occupy acres of beautiful green land on which many London chambers are built, and provide ongoing training, support and social events, among other things. The Inns themselves are something like a cross between Hogwarts and Oxbridge colleges, boasting grand dining halls, libraries, chapels and chambers scattered across their substantial gardens.

Membership of an Inn does not (whisper it quietly) really mean anything. It's like being in a house at school, only without a sports day. I choose my particular Inn on purely mercenary principles: they (at the time) offer the highest number of scholarships and guarantee an interview to every applicant. So I pay my £50 subscription fee, lodge my scholarship application and wait nervously for the big interview.

When it arrives, I sit in a coffee shop on Chancery Lane for an hour beforehand, letting latte after latte congeal as I scour my revision guides on criminal law. God knows quite what I am

---

* Holborn, Chancery Lane, Strand – that sort of rough and unappealing neck of the woods.

expecting to be asked; I just know that, despite having been told that the interview was a 'general chat' rather than forensic test of legal acumen, I have somehow convinced myself that knowing every Court of Appeal authority on the interpretation of 'self-defence' is the key to survival.

As it happens, none of the barristers on my panel – all wizened senior members of my new Inn – practise crime. I know this for two reasons: first, they don't blink when, in my confusion, I conflate what I have seen on my mini-pupillages with my experiences doing jury service a few years earlier, and profess to have witnessed something as a juror which, if correct, would have made legal history for all the wrong reasons. (It is the legal equivalent of claiming that a GP once invited you to watch him replace a patient's kidney with a bag of Haribo. If it were even close to true, multiple things have gone exceedingly wrong.)

But the second, and biggest, giveaway is the unbridled bafflement they express when I mention that I am not averse to practising criminal law outside of London. 'Crime? In the provinces?' one of the gentlemen splutters. If we were in a cartoon, his monocle would pop out into his bone-china teacup. The notion of pursuing modestly paid publicly funded law somewhere other than our nation's capital strikes them as so delightfully avant garde that they regard me with studied fascination for the remainder of the interview, even forgiving my catastrophically uninspiring, roadkill-in-headlights answer to the question 'Why criminal law?' ('Because, umm, it seems . . . interesting.')

And that is why they very kindly go on to award me a scholarship that (just about) covers the cost of my course, and how I fall into studying to become a barrister.

That, at least, is how I remember it. There can't, logically, be any other explanation for the panel's decision. Looking back at the person described over this chapter, I find it impossible to see otherwise why the Inn would have squandered a precious scholarship on so average a prospect.

Unless, as I suppose is possible, there's a trick of the memory at play. I think I've painted a faithful portrait of my twenty-something self, but it would be easy to overplay the negatives in my eagerness to show off my intellectual progress. Behold this buffoonish, arrogant caricature, with their strident, half-formed beliefs and their entitled behaviour – walking out on a mini-pupillage! – that I can loftily disown from the safe distance of liberal adulthood. *Look, dear reader, how far I've come!*

I promise I'm not consciously trying to set up Young Me, or my beliefs, as a straw figure deserving of your contempt or disdain, although I accept there's much in these pages that some will dislike. I don't think I *was* dislikeable, if that's worth anything. I think I was naive, and immature, and impressionable, and scared of what I didn't know, and desperate to find my place in the world. These – I won't use the word 'failings', because that seems harsh; these are not-uncommon corollaries of being in your teens and twenties – these *traits* are not attractive when viewed from hindsight, but there will have been good that hasn't made it into my memory's final edit. Maybe I'm not being wholly fair or reliable as a narrator of my younger self.

Likewise, the arrogance writ large in my twenty-something assumption that the Bar would always be there *as a back-up*. If *nothing else better came along*. The claim that I just *fell into it*. Maybe, again, I'm misremembering. Maybe it only feels like I fell into it because that's the story I was telling myself at the time, to manage expectations. To cushion what I believed was likely, possibly inevitable, disappointment. *You're only doing this because you've nothing else on. If you don't get the scholarship, you'll do something different. It doesn't really matter either way.* Maybe I really, really wanted it, from the very first day I discovered what a barrister did, and my inability to excavate those feelings nearly two decades later is a testament to their rawness, and how deep I had to bury them.

Maybe my true feelings can be found elsewhere. Maybe in my reaction upon opening the letter from my Inn offering me a scholarship, when, shaking, I grab my nearest housemate by the hands and dance, in unrestrained, uncontrollable hysteria, on and across the sofas in our living room, voice at fever pitch, letter in hand, screaming 'I'M GOING TO BE A FUCKING BARRISTER!' with tears streaming down my face.

First day at Bar school

Packed into a large lecture theatre and grasping our haul of legal practitioner textbooks* to guide us through the year ahead, we squish up on our folding chairs and chatter excitedly as the course leader surveys the room and waits for quiet. Even when the buzz subdues, there is still a palpable electricity coursing through the student body as we wait for the words of inspiration to propel us into barrister-dom.

'Eighty per cent of you,' she says, with a beaming smile, staring pointedly at a group on the back row who were still whispering, 'will not secure pupillage.'

---

* Practitioner textbooks are the half-tonne tomes that summarise the relevant law and legal procedure for a given area of law, and which are carried by barristers in practice. They are to be contrasted with academic textbooks used for the study of law, which are generally more theoretical. To illustrate, if your client tells the judge to 'fuck off', your practitioner textbook will provide a handy guide to the contempt of court proceedings that are likely to follow, while your academic textbook might offer a history of the development of the law of contempt and a rumination on the various ways in which courts have interpreted the word 'fuck'.

The room falls into instant silence. She pauses for effect, but no emphasis is required. The message – one which had most certainly not been in the brochure when the law school was pitching for our thirteen thousand pounds – is loud and clear. A handful of us, maybe half a dozen, have already snaffled a pupillage offer by ambitiously applying before starting the course.* For the rest, bobbing up and down on the start line, we have it all to do. To make sure the point isn't lost, our motivational speaker elucidates:

'Four in five of you will never practise as barristers.'

What she doesn't add at this stage is that, while the ferocious competition means that the odds for securing pupillage – and then tenancy† – are indeed extremely slim, some of us will go on to practise law by other routes. Many international students return to their Commonwealth home countries and practise there; a number of people cross-qualify as solicitors, before then re-qualifying as barristers; many have successful legal careers away from the Bar. The terrifying statistics omit some important context.

But nevertheless, the stark reality that, between us, we are paying millions of pounds to spin the wheel on entry to a career

---

* A curiosity of the system is that you don't actually have to have completed the Bar course to apply for a pupillage. As pupils are often recruited eighteen months to two years in advance, some people apply in the final year of their law degree, on the assumption that they will pass the Bar course and glide seamlessly into pupillage. Others, like me, apply during the Bar course, affording a slight advantage of having learned some of the practical skills. Lord knows I wouldn't have been ready as an undergrad.

† After you complete pupillage at a chambers, there is a vote among members as to whether you should be granted 'tenancy' – i.e. allowed to become a permanent member of chambers.

that will bounce most of us at the door is sobering. We all knew it would be competitive. But I don't think many of us had internalised what it meant. *I could love this job. I could have paid tens of thousands of pounds to train. I could be qualified to do it. And the likelihood is I may never get the chance.*

Red light fail

The course itself is designed to embed the practical skills needed to transform us from statute-quoting academic lawyers to well-oiled litigation machines.

The core skills deemed necessary to qualify as a barrister – advocacy, negotiation, conference skills, legal research, legal drafting, opinion writing, and professional ethics – are taught over one academic year* in lectures and seminars, alongside the law and procedure governing civil litigation (suing people, basically) and criminal litigation, evidence and sentencing (prosecuting and defending, in essence). The tutors are qualified barristers and solicitors, some who teach full-time and some who squeeze teaching into their legal practice. At our institution, it is apparently an unwritten rule that at least one tutor has to be in a clandestine relationship with a student at any one time.

What motivates and terrifies us most is the red light. Every assessment contains an assortment of carefully laid bear traps, which, if stepped into, result in an immediate 'red light' fail (albeit, disappointingly, without a *Britain's Got Talent*-style flashing red buzzer), irrespective of how otherwise perfectly you may have performed. Red lights include ethical breaches, acting in a way that would put the client's interests at risk, and rendering yourself liable for professional negligence (such as wrongly advising a client that their claim is time-barred by statute).

---

* Or two years if studying part-time.

Surprisingly, I learn that 'getting the law completely wrong' does not automatically lead to a red light fail. In a mock negotiation exam, I completely misunderstand the law, leaving my opponent understandably bewildered as I confidently explain – entirely incorrectly – why my client's case is legally overwhelming. Worried that he has himself not comprehended the law, but one rung below me on the bellicosity scale, he agrees to a far more generous settlement than he probably should have done.

Result? I am given an 'Outstanding', the highest grade possible, as 'despite incorrectly identifying the applicable law, you well demonstrated the core skills of negotiation and secured a favourable outcome for your client'.

While I am thrilled, it later seems clear in retrospect that if there is one lesson that society does not need a cohort of arrogant middle-class narcissists learning, it is that bullshitting will literally get you rewarded.

Three-piece-suit Wankers

Bar school, I quickly learn, is not a good advertisement for the human condition. That isn't because of a dearth of exceptionally gifted and genial young people. It's because, while *they* are quietly and diligently plying their giftedness and geniality in the background, the foreground is surrendered to the very worst kind of people who want to become barristers.

Members of this species share a number of defining characteristics. They are predominantly male, white and anxious to give the impression of legal pedigree.

They are not law students, oh no. They are Trainee Barristers, and very keen too that you should know it. It's not just that their insight into the Bar eclipses yours; they are already seasoned practitioners, boasting countless war stories brought home from a thousand mini-pupillages, and an anthology of second-hand anecdotes that they pass off as their own. They refer to barristers they've met once by first name, as long-standing pals, and bray incredulously when you demonstrate your unfamiliarity – '*You know, Charlie? From Number Four? Surely you know old Charlie? Chalkie, as we all call him. Rahahahaha!*'

It is from their distinctive plumage that they derive their official classification. They eschew the hoodie/jeans combo of their student peers in favour of the uniform that they shall one day wear as a practising barrister, for that destiny is pre-ordained. So it is that they are the Three-piece-suit Wankers.

Neither occasion nor season can quell their fidelity to the softest of bespoke woollen waistcoats and the thickest of chalk-stripes, perfectly cut to display the obligatory public-school tie with full Windsor knot.

For sport, they enjoy raising 'clever' points in seminars to try to catch out the tutor. By so doing, they demonstrate their intellectual superiority not only to the rest of us, but to these *academic* barristers who are proving the maxim by teaching and not doing. (That the clever point almost always arises from the TPSW's own misunderstanding of the law is no deterrent.)

Sometimes the order of the day will call for needless antagonism, sometimes casual misogyny. One of our TPSWs tells a female tutor that, in his considered view, women are 'not natural advocates' and that 'most are taken on for their looks'. TPSWs act too as guardians of the gossip geyser, cultivating an endless spring of rumours and half-truths, from scandalous affairs to substance abuse to who has 'red lighted' in humiliating fashion, which keeps the student body in a resting state of hypervigilance and paranoia.

Snobbery is ingrained; the chambers to which you apply are

a reflection on your character and your breeding. If it's not one of the Tier 1 London sets* nestled in the grounds of one of the Inns, you're really lowering yourself, old boy. Someone in our cohort secures a pupillage with the Crown Prosecution Service's in-house trainee scheme. Instead of congratulations for his hard-won triumph, he enjoys whispers of derision for settling for 'not a real pupillage'.

Hindsight grants the consolation that most of this minority never secure pupillage (aside from those whose lineage make it impossible for chambers to refuse them). The majority find their calling in management consultancy or the City or on *The Apprentice*, allowing themselves to be touted as 'qualified barristers' to provide fodder for Alan Sugar's strained gag-writers.

The Apprentice is in fact not a bad analogy for Bar school. For all the performative camaraderie, there is a pervasive awareness that kinship is only skin deep; that you are all competing for the same job(s), and that prospective chambers will be comparing you side by side after you've submitted yourself to whatever madcap tasks and ferocious interviews they've lined up. While the contestants who have convinced themselves that braggadocio and a loud voice suffice as a substitute for ability will eventually fall by the wayside, it doesn't make them any more tolerable while they're still in the contest. Their desperation fuels your own.

There are good times at Bar school – the normal people to whom I try to gravitate get me through the tough parts – but when I look back, the raw competitiveness and the reek of toxicity are what stand out strongest. While the course arguably

---

* A 'set' is just another word for 'chambers'. There are unofficial 'rankings' of chambers – and barristers – released each year by various publications.

primed us for a career at the Bar, it didn't do much for our well-being. It may have made us barristers, but I don't think it made many of us better people.

Inns and outs

It is a time-honoured tradition that, before you can be called to the Bar of England and Wales,* you have to eat a dozen three-course meals.

Even today, this statement only needs mild qualification. The official requirement is that you attend twelve 'qualifying sessions' at your Inn of Court in London. Historically, most qualifying sessions have taken the form of dining, in the company of fellow students, barristers, judges and honourable guests (we either had an ambitious junior government minister or one of McFly – I forget which). More recently, qualifying sessions can be ticked off by attending training courses, lectures and other educational events hosted by the Inns, but the expectation remains that you travel to your Inn for at least a few subsidised dining sessions.

If you are travelling from outside London, this can be an expensive affair. One of the hidden costs that many friends studying in the north certainly didn't factor in.

The transition when you step into the Inns off Fleet Street, Chancery Lane or Holborn is Narnian. The hum and bustle of the capital instantly falls as you are dropped into a tranquil chocolate box of cobbled lanes winding between immaculate lawns, and green squares bounded by a gaggle of Georgian, Victorian and Gothic buildings stretching to the sky.

I arrive for my first dinner after twilight, and, aided by the

---

* The official term for the graduation-style ceremony that follows passing the Bar course.

glow of the gas lamps, make towards the imposing main hall, where our coats are spirited away and our hot little paws filled with ice-cold flutes of champagne. Sipping our bubbly, we mill between several huge reception rooms, ornately decorated and adorned with portraits of judges from centuries past. A boy around my age wanders up to me and smiles conspiratorially. I don't remember what he says, only that he puts on a hilarious fake upper-class voice as he says it, clearly poking fun at our preposterously opulent surroundings. Sensing a kindred spirit feeling equally out of place, I laugh heartily and join in with the fun, reviving my Brian Sewell impression as I purse my lips in what I imagine is an affectation of a posho and raise my glass: 'Oooh yes indeeeed, these is queet the occasion, nooo? My compleeemints to the Lord of the Manor!' He doesn't laugh back though, more stares at me with curiosity. It turns out that is his real voice.

The dinner itself is a blur. As I try to process the magnificence of the dining hall – its vaulted oak ceilings and formidable panels of heraldic stained glass – catering staff swarm in practised formation, piling the long banqueting tables high with warm bread rolls, butter in funny shapes, soups, steaming meats, buttered vegetables and indecent quantities of wine. The seating plan is designed, like the worst weddings, to divide you from anyone you might know in the alleged spirit of encouraging mingling. I have a Bar student from Newcastle to my left, a commercial barrister opposite me and someone to my right who has as little interest in introducing themselves to me as I have to them. Having blown through small talk before the soup arrives, I sit quietly and listen to the conversations around me, overhearing the wife of a High Court judge politely asking: 'Do they have barristers in Newcastle?'

The rules strictly forbid leaving our seats during the meal, making the occasion a test to destruction of bladder capacity. There are long speeches, peppered with Latin and in-jokes and met with laughter by the seasoned attendees (and of course the TPSWs), and by polite smiles by the rest of us, before dinner is rounded off by the port (THE PORT!). Flagons are charged with the foul claret brew as everybody is incited to take to their feet and toast the Queen, which is the official cue that you are allowed to go and empty your bladder. It is, as a whole, a thoroughly discombobulating experience.

But what strikes me most is the fluency with which so many of my contemporaries are chatting to the adults around them. There is no reticence. No holding back. The confidence oozes out of them. It is like they are among friends, not professionals thirty, forty, fifty years their senior. Almost as if they have attended some special training that I missed. How are they so at ease, so poised, talking to real grown-ups? How are they able to converse with people of such power and influence as equals, while I am struggling to break beyond teenager-making-awkward-chit-chat-with-great-aunt?

The predictable reveal, appreciable only through the lens of adulthood, is that most people in that room have been to private school; their confidence was carefully manufactured, at great cost over many years, in order that, when this day or one like it came around, they would feel it the most natural of progressions. They act as if at home among equals because they are. They have been exposed to the pomp and grandeur, and the scent of raw unadulterated power, from their early years. Born-to-rule sounds provocatively chippy, but they are at the very least moulded to feel level with the people doing the ruling.

And this isn't, I promise, intended to sound snippy, or resentful. But it is insane that somebody from as comfortable a background as me, with all the advantages conferred by a loving, financially sound family and decent comprehensive education, was – still is – towards the bottom of the class ladder in the twenty-first-century legal profession. Someone like me – who has encountered no meaningful adversity on account of my class or my upbringing – should not be made to feel like a working-class hero. But at that very first meal, and indeed, on every occasion I visited my Inn as a student, that is exactly how I cast myself; the outsider at the feast, the normal-o among the aristos. I cannot begin to imagine how alienating that environment must feel to someone from a genuinely disadvantaged background, arriving with a (wholly reasonable) suspicion that the Bar is for a Certain Type of Person.

Some of my alienation may well have been attributable to my own shyness and awkwardness, of course. Others from similar backgrounds may have made more of an effort, or more easily struck a chord, with the grown-ups present, all of whom, it must be said, went out of their way to emphasise how welcome we all were. And the number of outreach schemes that the Inns now hold to try to encourage applicants to the Bar from 'non-traditional backgrounds' demonstrates significant progress even since I was starting out.* But the fact that the Bar still talks in these terms – *traditional and non-traditional backgrounds* – and that they mean today exactly what they meant when I was starting out fifteen years ago –non-private school, non-Oxbridge and non-white – is indicative of how much further we still need to go. And I do still wonder today, much as I wondered at the time, whether the Templar-derived traditions to which the Bar

---

* In Appendix: A Note on Representation and Resources, there is a list of social mobility and outreach schemes now offered by the Inns and by the Bar – if you are thinking of a career at the Bar, I'd urge you to have a look.

still clings are indeed just harmless pageantry, or whether, to many watching us swigging our port from outside the stained-glass windows, they simply reinforce the divide.

The best traditions

Over the Easter break of my Bar course, I embark on a mini-pupillage following a grizzled warhorse called Ned. He is gearing himself up for a legal argument before a Crown Court judge, concerning whether a piece of hearsay evidence* should be allowed to be relied upon by the prosecution. Ned is prosecuting three alleged burglars, and the main eyewitness is too ill to attend the trial, so the prosecution are hoping to be able to read the witness's statement to the jury. The major disadvantage with hearsay evidence is that it is difficult to test its reliability – it's not evidence given on oath, and the witness can't be cross-examined if they're not at court. Therefore the courts developed centuries of case law strictly controlling its use. Not too long before this mini-pupillage, the Labour government tore up that law and passed a new piece of complex legislation making it easier for the prosecution to rely on hearsay evidence.[†] It was highly controversial at the time, but, as far as I could see, anything which made it easier to prosecute criminals could only be a good thing.

Ned rolls up to the courtroom with me at his heel. The three defence barristers are already gathered outside, and nod at Ned, stony-faced. Ned nods back. The tension is palpable.

---

* Hearsay evidence is something said out of court which either the prosecution or defence wish to rely on to prove the truth of what was said. For example, where a witness won't come to court, but a police officer can give evidence of what that witness told them at the scene.

† The Criminal Justice Act 2003, which came into force in April 2005.

'So . . .' one of the defence says.

'So . . .' Ned replies, deadpan.

I can almost hear the war drums getting louder and faster as they stare at each other. Then, as the drums reach their imaginary crescendo, Ned speaks again:

'Does anyone else have the first fucking clue how this new hearsay bollocks works?'

In unison, the defence shake their heads. 'Not the foggiest.'

The four fall about laughing. None of them have argued a hearsay application under the new law. There is very little case law from the Court of Appeal to guide the Crown Courts on how the statute should be applied in practice. All are going in blind. Each having poked fun at their own skeleton argument* and reassured the others that there was an equal likelihood of all of them looking like wallies, they straighten their robes and head into court. The judge strides onto the bench, and I watch in awe as each barrister proceeds to argue their case as fluently and persuasively as if they have written the law themselves.

And what stands out is not just the swan-like grace with which they bluff their way through the hearing in court, but the comradery they share outside it. Unlike on TV, the prosecution and defence lawyers are not at each other's throats or engaging in smack talk or plotting psychological warfare; they are just colleagues – mates – who happen that day to be on different sides. Each is fighting loyally and fiercely for their client's interests, but there is a tacit recognition that ultimately all are there to play a role; beneath the wigs and gowns are normal people just trying to get through the day.

---

* A written legal argument supposedly condensed to its bare bones, to be fleshed out by oral argument. In practice, most criminal barristers' efforts end up not so much skeletal as morbidly obese.

Prison visits

Towards the end of the Bar course, the opportunity is extended to students intending to practise in crime to pay a visit to a local prison for a tour of Her Majesty's facilities. Despite studying law for four years, few of us have seen the inside of a prison, and it makes sense to gain an appreciation of where our clients will be spending their time if we turn out to be not very good at defending them.

Our guide is a senior prison officer, Jim. He has thirty years of service in the prison industry, and so while no stranger to deadpan cynicism, he has accumulated the invaluable kind of experience which the coalition government will target for redundancy when it decides to cut prison staff by a quarter in 2010.*

The physical estate is similar to what I expected: a dilapidated Victorian building patched up with caulk and plasterboard; cells that feel like you are stepping onto a film set where everything is only four fifths real-human-size; a persistent odour of sweat and urine and a permanent cacophony of shouting – whether excitement or anguish it is impossible to tell.

What sticks with me is something our guide says. It is delivered with the fluidity that makes plain it is part of his standard patter, rather like barristers have for their closing jury speeches, and it comes in response to a question, from one of our cohort, relating to a story that has been in the headlines this week about games consoles in prison cells and how prisons are becoming

---

* The greatest savings were to be made by cutting the most high-paid, which meant most experienced, prison officers. See the Insitute for Government's 2019 performance tracker for prisons: https://www.instituteforgovernment.org.uk/publication/performance-tracker-2019/prisons

'cushy'. Jim is asked whether in his thirty years prison has indeed become easier. His response is immediate:

'No. You go to prison *as* punishment. You don't go there *for* punishment.'

That is the part I recall verbatim for years to come. Because it articulates something that I have never really considered before. To paraphrase what follows (and I can't replicate Jim's gruff eloquence), the punishment, he repeats, *is* prison. It is the loss of liberty. It is being unable to see your friends and family, or go to the pub or the gym, or make a phone call without seeking permission. It's the confinement, of being closed in by four walls that you can't leave, with people you can't choose, away from the life that you should be living. That is how our society chooses to punish people. Prison conditions are not supposed to be 'extra nasty' to dial up the punitive element. If you think that having access to a TV or an old-style PlayStation 2,* or being let out of your cell for an hour to exercise in a gym, renders prison 'easy', just try sitting in your own house with your own family for a week, without leaving. A hundred pounds says that by the fourth day you will be going slowly insane.

Of course, my professional practice would confirm that there are some people who don't find prison as much of a challenge as others. It can be tolerable, even comfortable, for certain people; mainly the institutionalised or the select few at the top of the prison food chain who can pull enough strings/bribe enough prison officers to make life bearable. But for the overwhelming majority of criminal clients, desperate

---

* Games consoles that can connect to the internet are forbidden in prisons. Only prisoners who have earned the highest level of 'privileges' are allowed to buy and have a console in their cell.

to avoid a custodial sentence, prison is a very real form of punishment.

'Look around you,' says Jim. 'Look at the size of those cells, look at the bunk beds, smell that food coming from the kitchen, look at those unscreened toilets where you do your business in front of a complete stranger. If this is preferable to your life on the outside – what must your life on the outside be like?'

The Portal of Doom

Applying for pupillage erodes the soul. Most chambers recruit via the 'Pupillage Gateway' – an online portal prescribing a lengthy electronic form in which we have to pitch ourselves without sounding like one of those LinkedIn profiles that goes viral for all the wrong reasons, and provide 300-word answers to inane formulaic questions such as 'Why Do You Want To Be A Barrister?' or (worst of all) 'Why Are You Applying To This Chambers?' (Truthful answer: Because you are a chambers, any chambers, and I would literally accept a pupillage at a chambers run by bees at this moment in time.)

The attrition rate is forever nagging in your subconscious. Roughly 1,500 students start Bar school each year. In 2021, there were 246 pupillages nationwide advertised across the Gateway.* Upon completing the Bar course, you have five years to secure pupillage, or your expensive qualification withers and dies. This means that you are up against not only the 1,500 from your year group, but several thousand unsuccessful applicants from previous years.

---

* Incredibly, there are no official comprehensive statistics detailing the number of pupillages *outside* the Gateway, but it is likely to be significantly lower.

You can only apply to a certain number of chambers each year* – twelve is the limit when I am applying – so selectivity is an art. You don't want to sell yourself short, but there is also no point in splurging your twelve attempts on top-tier chambers if realistically you don't have the grades or pedigree needed to secure an interview. Scouring certain websites, I feel my ego shrivel as I read the profiles of current pupils and junior tenants. In a number of chambers, I struggle to find a single recent recruit who didn't go to Oxbridge. Among those who haven't, the compensatory accomplishments are boggling. Someone has been a highly successful US attorney for twenty years; another has worked as legal counsel for the United Nations; several have lectured at Harvard; somebody is a dual-qualified medic and lawyer who has established a network of clinics in Africa.

I swallow hard and reread my application. All of a sudden my prize for getting the top mark in Employment Law in the second year of my degree and the handful of lowbrow sketches I have written for my friends' comedy troupe don't seem quite the CV gold I'd hoped. Maybe if I underline-bold the words 'Semi Finalist' to emphasise how far I got in that first-year debating competition? I could even italicise 'Finalist'. Still feels lacking, somehow.

The first interview

Incredibly, despite my CV not boasting the achievement of cold fusion, I manage to secure my very first pupillage interview at one of London's leading criminal sets, which sits at the apex of the God Tier on my wishlist of the impossible. It counts among

---

* Through the Gateway, that is. When it comes to the chambers who recruit outside the Gateway, you can apply to as many of those rebels as you like.

its members some of the most famous QCs* in the country; its barristers are instructed in the grittiest and most high-profile criminal cases – winning pupillage at a chambers like this is a sign that you are going to make it far. My ego vacillates between certainty that my abilities know no limit, and conviction that I am the token non-Oxbridge interviewee to satisfy some official checklist.

I arrive ninety minutes early, on one of the hottest days of the year. I kill time by trudging circuits around the Inns of Court, mentally practising my model interview answers, and occasionally looking up and allowing myself to imagine tugging my suitcase laden with court briefs, wig and gown across the cobbles and into one of these famous sun-drenched buildings.

I then wait in the chambers reception area, cruelly packed with other interviewees. Awkward small talk and nervous laughter punctuate the terrified silence, as one by one our names are called and we are led like doomed livestock to the interview suite.

Entering the room, I am acknowledged by two figures sat behind a gigantic mahogany desk. I introduce myself and put out my hand. A fatal error. Barristers, you see, don't shake hands with each other. It's one of those traditions that is generally observed,† but which only obnoxious twits make an issue out of if you forget yourself and extend your paw.

My interrogators decline the shake. And that is it. I am

---

* QC = Queen's Counsel. The kitemark of barristerial quality, awarded upon application to the very finest in our ranks. Also known as 'silks' due to their preferred choice of underwear. Or possibly their court robes.
† I'd give you the Reason, but I've had the Reason confidently explained to me in multiple different and mutually exclusive ways, so let's just say the Reason is, like so much else we do, Just Because.

suddenly back at my disastrous interview for Cambridge University, seventeen years old and in the quarters of some elderly chaplain who, having ostentatiously refused to shake my hand, spent the interview alternating between staring at me impassively and arching his eyebrows towards the ceiling. The questions he had asked were marinated in bored sarcasm. When I finished answering he would silently sneer, prompting me to keep talking until I ran out of words. I had left that interview a sobbing wreck, and never told anybody how awfully it had gone, or how pathetically insignificant that man had made me feel.

Today's interviewers are nothing like that. But the handshake snub provokes an intense and spontaneous regression, and once more I am babbling, babbling, babbling. Unable to form a complete sentence, let alone a coherent one.

When they ask why I have waited a few years between my law degree and Bar school, I try to tell them about Aaron – the young barrister on my first mini-pupillage who was afraid that he had made a terrible mistake with his career choice – and how I want to be sure before committing to the Bar. It doesn't make sense. My words come tumbling out in no discernible order. Something about wanting a bar in which to commit to Aaron.

When they ask why I want to become a barrister, I swing at a Hollywood answer I've been trialling in my head and miss spectacularly. 'I want to defend the defenceless, voice the voiceless and . . .' Time stands still as I struggle to complete the trio. I forget what I eventually alighted upon. Seam the seamstress, probably. That would have made as much sense as anything else I gibber over that half hour. After three minutes, I am desperate to just get out of the suffocating room and back into the safety of the outside world.

'This chambers may not be for you.'

In total, I am invited to six first-round interviews from my chosen twelve chambers, and three second-round interviews. Time blurs the specifics, but the highlights are still retrievable.

The most relaxed interview by far is at a set which I have filtered into my final twelve primarily because the pupillage award* is stonkingly generous. Most criminal pupillages offered £12,000 for the year. This one is in the region of £50,000. I can't understand the disparity. The first question at interview – 'Your application form is impressive, but I note that you don't talk much about why you want to practise family law' – makes it clear. Had I done my research more carefully, and not relied on the Gateway's mercurial algorithms, I would have known that this chambers is a leading private family law set, offering a predominantly family law pupillage, with only a sylphlike prospect of doing any crime. After I confess that I have no interest whatsoever in family law, the formality of the interview disintegrates. 'This chambers may not be for you,' the jolly QC in the middle laughs. I agree, almost giddy in my embarrassment. We all top up our cups of tea and spend the remaining fifteen minutes chatting merrily about where I *should* be applying, all pretending that it is perfectly normal that I should be sitting here, interviewing for a job I don't want at a chambers which in no sane universe would ever have shortlisted me.

---

* Pupillages are funded by chambers. There is a 'pupillage award' which has to be at least the figure set by the Bar Standards Board (currently £18,866 in London, £16,322 outside London). Some chambers enhance their award by offering 'guaranteed minimum earnings' in your second six months (when you are doing your own cases).

The sweet spot

A cruel feature of the Gateway is the absence of notice. Many chambers give barely a few days' warning of interviews, and the dates are non-negotiable. Given that they take place over the summer, it shows a wholesale disregard for students who are working to pay the bills, and who are expected to extricate themselves from their employment at the drop of a wig. Fortunately, I have resigned from my part-time job at a well-known fast food restaurant after they refused me time off for my Bar exams, so, while broke, I am at least unencumbered. One Wednesday, I receive notice of three interviews, all to take place on the Saturday. The complicating factor is that I am on a post-exam blowout in Spain, and will be landing at Birmingham International at 2 a.m. on that Saturday morning. All interviews are in London: at 9 a.m., midday and 3 p.m.

The first one leaves me with literally no memory at all. By the third, I have succumbed to the most violent caffeinated sugar crash and just want to crawl into the corner of the room and peacefully expire. But the second interview hits the sweet spot – that magical place where espresso, adrenaline and hysteria collide – and, darling, I am *magnificent*. I don't say this lightly. In fact I don't say it ever. But I can truthfully promise that I have not, in all my years as a professional advocate, performed as fluently, confidently and convincingly as I did during the advocacy exercise in that delirious pupillage interview for Hallmark Chambers.

The panel are lovely; inquisitive and probing, but also completely, reassuringly normal. A more senior chap called Robert, who has a familiar face I just can't place, takes a particular interest, asking questions well over our allocated time. At the end, he asks me where I want to be in twelve months' time. I say, truthfully, that I just want to be in pupillage. 'Oh you'll definitely get pupillage,' he says with a mischievous grin. 'It's just a question of whether you push yourself into one of the very best sets, or . . . settle.'

Still unable to place his face, I go home and find Robert on the website. He is one of the leading QCs in the country, with a history of cases that read like legal pornography.* At that moment I know I just *have* to get into his chambers. There is no other option. The gauntlet has been laid down.

Welcome to the new pupils!

The invitation to the second interview lands in my inbox within a few days, and less than a fortnight later I am back in the same room, now facing a panel of eight. Having slept for more than an hour and ingested fewer than two gallons of coffee, my performance this time lacks the gripping delirium of my first, but it feels – whisper it quietly – like it might just be enough.

A week later, my Gateway notification 'pings'. Although formal offers through the Gateway have to be made on the same day for all chambers, informal (read 'underhand') tactics are sometimes deployed to steal a march on other chambers and tip the wink to favoured candidates. So it is that I find myself invited to a 'third interview', where there are three candidates – for three pupillage vacancies – and no interview. Instead, we are taken on a tour of chambers, where we are indiscreetly introduced to all and sundry as 'next year's pupils', followed by a slap-up lunch with some of the junior tenants. I am conscious that my new co-pupils are much more talkative

---

* As in, something that would excite lawyers. Not pornography that is legal. There was little mention or imagery of pornography in his chambers profile. Just hundreds of incredible criminal cases.

than me, and I hope that my relative quietness will be interpreted as contemplative zen rather than shyness, social awkwardness and a gnawing sense of intimidation. As we Three Amigos leave the pub, still slightly stunned at the events of the day, we exchange email addresses and bid each other au revoir. 'Until next September!' I shout at my new colleagues as I stroll, heart aglow, towards the station, and take out my phone to ring my parents.

Oh, what a beautiful morning

While formal offers all have to wait until results day, there is no such restriction on rejections. The etiquette for notifying applicants on the Gateway is brutal. Logging on, you are presented with a list of your chosen chambers, with an icon next to each indicating the status of your application. Some chambers reject you out of hand – your status is changed overnight to 'UNSUCCESSFUL' without a word of explanation. Some cushion the blow by notifying you by letter or email before updating the portal.

For me, rejections have been steadily pinging through, but my ego is fortified by the promise of The One That Matters. I have not been able to resist telling friends and family about my impending offer, and have even started trawling for flatshares, a year prematurely but just to see what I might be able to afford. The one obstacle in my way – actually passing the damn course – has been cleared, and on the eve of results day, I log on and survey my eleven Gateway rejections and, honestly, I could not care less. The twelfth application, teasingly still marked 'Interview Stage', is winking at me, both of us knowing that come morning it will burst out of its inscrutable chrysalis and emerge into the sunshine as a fully winged, glorious offer.

I get up at 9 a.m. and log on. There is no update, so I make breakfast and idly browse some flat rentals online. Ten a.m. passes without notification. As does eleven. Come midday, the status remains amber, but an email from the chambers lands. Ah ha! Relief washes over me. Of course they aren't simply going to change the notification to 'OFFER' – they want to do things properly.

I read the email greedily. My smile evaporates, and my heart plunges into my stomach.

'We wish to thank you for attending for interview. We are pleased to inform you that you have been selected as the reserve candidate for pupillage . . .'

Reserve candidate.

Reserve. Candidate.

As I say the words out loud I can taste them, foul and bitter. I want to spit them out, to vomit, to bleach my mouth, my eyes, the screen. All of it. I read the email again. There is no misunderstanding. I haven't been made an offer.

My brain tries frantically to recalibrate the plans that I have hubristically laid down for the next twelve months. I'll have to call my parents, my friends, my course mates, and tell them that, actually, I might not be moving to London after all. That the pupillage I boasted about is not in fact mine. There is no need to start looking for flats next summer. For I am not going to be a barrister in the autumn.

The only glimmer of hope is that one of the three candidates who has been chosen – and who, might I ask, is this mysterious fourth person who hadn't even attended the alleged 'third interview'? – might drop out, and my reserve status would be upgraded. The notion is laughable. This is a pupillage at a premier set. Nobody in their right mind would not accept an offer.

I spend the rest of the afternoon in a daze. Every time I think about the future, I want to cry. How? How could I have been so stupid? Then, that evening, another email lands. It is from Rahul, one of the candidates I met at that damned third interview. He has received his offer. He has also received an offer from another top criminal chambers.

'I need your help,' he writes. 'I thought that as my potential co-pupil, you might be a good source of impartial advice. Which offer should I accept?'

It takes no time for the significance of my reply to dawn. This, right here, gift-wrapped from heaven, is my opportunity. Should I? *Could* I?

I take a deep breath and start typing.

The purple ink letter

The sensible thing to do would be to get straight back on the horse, and fire off applications to all the non-Gateway chambers. But the disappointment has left me not just winded but physically exhausted. The thought of going through the entire process again – more forms, more letters, more stupid advocacy exercises – is more than my crushed spirit can take. I of course have to tell Rahul that, embarrassingly, I haven't received an offer after all, and that I can't in good conscience help him with his dilemma given my glaring conflict of interest in the outcome. And, after giving it careful thought, he does what anyone would do, and my reserve offer is quietly substituted for a rejection. No stranger to melodrama, I tell myself that this is a blow from which I might not recover.

A few weeks later, while I am still wallowing in a fug of defeatism, an envelope drops through the front door, bearing a WC1 postmark. I open it to find a letter on Hallmark Chambers headed paper. It is written by hand in purple ink:

Hallmark Chambers
16 September

Dear SB,
[The head of the pupillage committee] has just told me that you were pipped at the post for a pupillage here. Having interviewed you, I just wanted to say how disappointed I am. You are an outstanding candidate and it was very bad luck that the competition was so amazing. Do not be discouraged! You will have a most interesting, exciting and successful career at the bar . . . do not fear.

I hope to see you around. In the meantime, keep at it.
Yours,
Robert
(Robert QC)

PS. No reply needed or expected. But if a telephone chat would help at any point – do ring.

I won't pretend that I withdrew from my orgy of self-pity straight away. But this unprompted gesture of kindness helped piece the fragments of my confidence back together in a way that I wasn't able to fully appreciate at the time. Only with the benefit of distance can I fully see how important that small act of charity was in yanking me out of my funk, and inspiring me to dust myself down and try again.

I send a polite thank-you note in reply, but never quite pluck up the courage to take him up on that phone call.

I wish I had. I would love dearly, fifteen years on, to thank him again, for everything that has followed, and to tell him he was right; I wasn't discouraged, I did keep at it, and I *did* make it, even if our paths did not cross again before his retirement.

And yes, to be brutally truthful, I may have settled, not pushed myself as hard or as far as I could have in the direction of the brightest lights and the biggest cases, but my career has indeed been more interesting and exciting than I, and I expect he, could possibly have imagined, sitting there in that interview room as I woozily performed to his beaming approval.

Unlike other elements of this book, I have faithfully reproduced that letter word for word. I've done so in the hope that, should Robert read this, he might recognise himself in this tale. And that he might know, how truly, unendingly grateful I am.

The Finkelstein Question

When I finally manage to snare a pupillage, it is down to an unlikely source: *The Times* columnist (and now Conservative peer) Danny Finkelstein.

I don't know Mr Finkelstein personally, nor, aside from a couple of brief exchanges on Twitter, have I ever spoken to him. But on the morning of what will turn out to be my last ever pupillage interview, as I am scouring the news for legal stories that might crop up in questions, I happen across one of his columns. The media has earlier this year been whipped into a frenzy over the saga of former Royal Bank of Scotland CEO Fred 'The Shred' Goodwin, who, having overseen the catastrophic near-collapse of RBS, pocketed an estimated £16 million pension pot when the taxpayer bailed out his bank. Politicians have called for Shred to be 'stripped' of his pension; Shred has defiantly stood by his contractual entitlements. It is a whole thing.

Amid the fury is a characteristically measured column by The Fink, in which he calmly assesses the story and argues forcefully in favour of upholding the rule of law in the face of political interference. While down my wormhole of topical legal research, I happen across this piece, and am quickly sucked in.

A popular pupillage interview device is to ask you to offer three arguments in favour of a certain proposition, and then immediately offer three counters. As fate would have it, the subject my panel has selected for me is Fred The Shred and what his case means for the rule of law. With the Finkelstein column still fresh in my memory, I barely have to pause for thought as I pivot from the 'For' to the 'Against', from the moral to the legal. I imagine that, to somebody unaware that I am regurgitating something I'd read only hours before, it probably looks as if I have pretty astonishing powers of instantaneous panoramic argument. Years later, I find out that it is my answer to this question that nudges me ahead of the candidate who receives the suckerpunch reserve-offer letter.

I was lucky. Really, really lucky. If there's a lesson here, and I'm not sure there is, it relates to the centrality of fortune in getting a foot through the door in this job. Why was I chosen ahead of the equally qualified second-choice applicant? It boils down to the fact that, on the scoring system, one of the panel gave me a 9 in a box where they had given the other person an 8. And that isn't because I *was* a 9. It's because I *looked* like it, on that day, in that very particular context, with those very particular questions and the very particular news environment, and the fact that, on that particular day, I had not merely browsed but stopped to inhale a particular Danny Finkelstein column.

These are the margins. Yes, there will be the standout candidates who were always going to glide their way to across-the-board offers. But for most of us, making it as far as pupillage really does come down to little more than pure, dumb luck.

2. Pupillage: The First Six

You might think that, having spent (at least) four years studying and accruing debts up to £100,000, and after squeezing into the 2 per cent of law graduates who nail down a pupillage,* you would have earned a measure of job security. Alas, pupillage is but the Eliminator in the spandexless version of *Gladiators* that passes for barristerial qualification.

For the next twelve months, you are the subject of a 24/7 job interview, in which not just a panel but all of your prospective colleagues will be scrutinising your every move† before voting on whether you should be offered 'tenancy' – a permanent position as a self-employed member of chambers. Some pupillages – mainly outside London – are awarded 'with a view to tenancy', meaning that as long as you demonstrate a base level of

---

* There are approximately 18,000 law graduates each year, plus 3,000-odd non-law graduates completing the Graduate Diploma in Law (GDL). With roughly 500 pupillages in any given year, you have a strike rate of just over 2 per cent.
† Technically not true. Most people probably won't give the pupils much independent scrutiny – some won't even meet them – and will instead rely on the recommendations of the pupil's supervisor. That said, someone in my chambers voted against me on the basis that they 'couldn't place my face', which struck me as a little harsh.

competence and avoid disgracing yourself in a social media/sex scandal,* you are likely to be OK. But many chambers recruit several pupils intending to offer at most one tenancy, pitting contestants against each other in a ~~brown-nosing race to the bottom~~ virtuous meritocracy. The headline is that around a third of pupils don't receive tenancy offers at the end of the year,† leaving them either scrambling for the life raft of a 'third six' pupillage,‡ or bidding adieu to their abortive career at the independent Bar.

Pupillage is split into a 'first six' and 'second six'. For the first six months, you shadow your allocated pupil supervisor(s) – learning by watching them in court, carrying out research and drafting documents. You subsist on your 'pupillage award' paid by chambers – in my day, £1,000 a month. Your second six is when you are 'on your feet' – technically self-employed in your own right, appearing in court by yourself and doing and billing your own cases, albeit under the supposedly watchful eye of your supervisor.

My immersion into this lobster pot is coinciding roughly with the start of the reduction in public spending that followed

* The apocryphal cautionary tale in our chambers was the pupil in a neighbouring set who had been caught having sex on the Head of Chambers' desk. Not doing this seemed an attainable threshold.

† 474 pupils started in 2016/17; 313 began tenancy in 2017/18. Bar Standards Board, 'Call to the Bar and tenancy statistics', https://www.barstandardsboard.org.uk/news-publications/research-and-statistics/statistics-about-the-bar/call-to-the-bar-and-tenancy.html

‡ An additional six months of pupillage, undertaken either at your current or another chambers, in the hope that chambers will be so impressed that they offer you a tenancy at the end. Some people bounce between multiple 'third sixes' before either snaring tenancy or giving up.

the 2008 global financial crash. There has been a long-running battle between the Bar and the Labour government over fee reductions and the structure of the criminal legal profession, although my understanding of the detail is, at this point, limited.

While I know that solidarity with my new profession demands that I adopt their anxieties, I am quietly unfussed; even (silently) broadly supportive of the government's position. My own experiences of the public sector while temping in the civil service and local government have left me with a strong, if perhaps superficial, impression that efficiency savings could easily and painlessly be made, and there is no obvious reason why the justice system should be any different. I know that criminal barristers complain about money, but I can't recall having seen a poor one. (What I was expecting a poor barrister to look like I'm not sure, but those I had followed on mini-pupillage had all bought me lunch, a decadent indicator of largesse if ever there was one.) Having voted Conservative for most of my enfranchised life, and being sympathetic to the Conservative–Liberal Democrat coalition government, I do not need much persuading of the need to tighten belts and rein in spending.

My views on justice have mellowed slightly since university, the influence of partial exposure to law-in-action at Bar school, and, to no small extent, a wider reading list than I allowed myself as an undergrad. But many shibboleths are unshaken. Justice's purest expression is punishment, and, looking around at our streets – or at least reading what my favourite columnists tell me is happening in our streets – there is not enough of it. My impending complicity with the system that allows this to happen does not denote approval, nor denial of the self-evident truth that we do not jail enough burglars, drug dealers, sex offenders or other (to use a description once offered of my client by a judge in chambers*) thoroughly bad bastards.

Instead, I am looking forward to the professional challenge of both defending and prosecuting those bastards with Swiss neutrality, still wholly unburdened by any deeper sense of mission. This is a job that I think I will enjoy, and which satisfies my ego's need to be doing something that matters. And, of course – and I cannot overstate the importance of this factor – it will ensure a rich seam of fascinating, gory anecdotes primed to be mined should I ever be invited to a dinner party.

This job, whatever else it might turn out to be, will never be dull.

You're a wizard, Harry![†]

Without doubt the most exciting part of being called to the Bar is getting your wig and gown.[‡] It is also yet another reminder of the institutional assumption that all aspiring barristers were

---

* The judge's chambers. Not to be confused with barristers' chambers. Or with 'court as chambers', where the public is booted out of court and the barristers and the judge pretend that the court is in fact the judge's private chambers, for the purpose of dealing with something that legally can't be heard in public.

† This entry is cleverly guaranteed to alienate Potter extremists on both sides. For those who haven't read Harry Potter, most of the references will be meaningless. For the superfans, including the one sitting to my right as I type, I have committed the ultimate transgression by quoting from the film of *Harry Potter and the Philosopher's Stone*, rather than the book, in which Hagrid says, 'Harry – yer a wizard'. So I'm very sorry.

‡ Barristers started wearing wigs in the seventeenth century after Charles II imported the fashion from France, and took to wearing black gowns after Charles's death, when the Bar went into mourning, something from which, apparently, we have yet to emerge in 2022.

born choking on platinum cutlery, as these two essentials – you have to wear them for your call-to-the-Bar ceremony – will set you back nearly a thousand pounds.

Again, there are scholarships and bursaries that can be applied for, but as far as a barrier to entry goes, the expectation that you'll just throw another grand onto your debt before embarking upon a year of earning less than minimum wage is quite the border wall. Not least as, unless you are practising criminal law in the Crown Courts, you are unlikely to wear it again for your entire pupillage, possibly your whole career.*

Nevertheless, the experience itself feels like a genuine treat. In echoes of would-be child wizards shuffling down Diagon Alley to Ollivander's to choose their wands,† each summer a new generation of legal nerds tread the flagstones of Chancery Lane towards Ede & Ravenscroft,‡ the approved outfitter of the legal profession since the seventeenth century, where they are measured and probed by distinguished tailors before being introduced to their own perfectly fitting handmade horsehair wig and black hooded gown.

My grandma, forgiving me for failing to make good on the promise I made aged eight to become a famous magician and buy her a house, insists on paying for my wig. Having arrived in this country as an unaccompanied child refugee, she probably didn't expect her grandchildren to be welcomed into the rarefied, horsehair-headed upper strata of the English establishment, so

---

* Wigs and gowns have been discarded in pretty much every area of law except crime. We love our traditions.
† Yes, I know that the wand chooses the wizard, but I'm trying to do something here.
‡ Or, as I learned later, you can do it a fair bit cheaper online.

merrily dissipates her pension on my absurd head ornament, her only conditions being that I promise to work hard and take care of my wig. And, to my credit, it takes a whole four years before, dramatically sweeping a bundle of papers off a robing room table in a fit of pique, I knock an entire cappuccino all over it.

Being called to the Bar is similar to a graduation ceremony, only with marginally more ridiculous headwear. You attend your Inn of Court with beaming loved ones tugging your robe straight and dabbing your face with spittled tissues, before striding proudly, two by two, down the red carpet in the main hall to collect your certificate from whichever legal luminary has been roped in to oversee the ceremony. My only real memory is of my foot becoming entangled with the foot of my co-graduand as we approached the celebrant, sending us both stumbling headfirst into Mr Justice Somebody like rutting drunks in fancy dress.

I would love to be able to say that there is more to my for-mative years as a lawyer than middling slapstick and social awkwardness, and logic dictates that there must have been. But as I would find with so much of this job, it is the missteps and embarrassments that linger with you, overriding your mind's hard drive and brute-force deleting the occasional, fleeting, precious highs.

Alan's rules

My pupil supervisor for the year was Alan. There are many, many things I could say about Alan – almost all of them glow-ing. He was generous, supportive, fantastically entertaining and an inspirationally unconventional advocate. He also made it his personal mission to deter me from pursuing a career in criminal law, having decided, within hours of meeting me, that I was entirely unsuited to the job, both in intellect and temperament.

Directness was very much Alan's hallmark. There was no

malice – he simply considered life too short for niceties. 'Does being ugly make this job harder?' he once asked a male opponent in court. It wasn't intended as cruel. He was just genuinely curious. His skin was rhinocerine, an evolutionary product of having been a working-class man at the Bar in an era when such social status was not only vanishingly rare, but rendered him fair game for overt snobbery and mockery – among practitioners and judges alike – on account of his accent, appearance and lack of approved legal breeding. Not having a blood relative sitting at the High Court was even more of a hindrance to career advancement in the 1980s and 1990s than it is today, and no doubt there was a greasy streak of jealousy among the landed gentry that Alan had forced his way into the profession without the leg-up on which so many of them had relied.

While on paper we shared a rarity value as non-traditional outsiders, our personalities were strikingly different, and our learning to calibrate his irrepressible ebullience with my quiet nervousness made for an unusual first six. From our first meeting, Alan made plain that he was only acting as a pupil supervisor – allowing me to shadow him and teaching me the ropes, for free, on top of his own full-time practice – because chambers had deemed it his turn, rather than out of any ardent desire to impart wisdom to the next generation.

'They taught us only two things on that useless "supervisor" course,' he announces as I walk into his room in chambers on my first day. 'You're no longer allowed to call yourself a "pupil-master",* and you're not allowed to shag your pupil. In fairness,'

---

* 'Pupil supervisor' is the modern, politically correct nomenclature. In Scotland and Ireland, 'pupils' are called 'devils'. Meaning 'pupilmasters' are 'devilmasters'. That I will never as long as I practise be a devilmaster or devilmistress might be my greatest professional regret.

he concedes after a pause, 'only one of those I already knew.' I don't ask which.

His motivational introduction continues: 'You are the least important person in this building. Remember that. You are the last person the clerks want to have to think about, and the last person whose opinion matters. Keep that in mind and you won't go far wrong.'

With formalities out of the way, he leads me downstairs for a whistle-stop tour of chambers.

Barristers' chambers tend to fall into one of two camps: corporate spaceship or eighteenth-century timewarp. I quickly see that my new chambers leans heavily towards the latter; a Georgian rabbit warren of pastel walls and narrow, thick-pile Escher's staircases spiralling into the ether. Inscrutable unmarked oak doors open variously onto yawning conference rooms and poky, two-desked offices, wherefrom a cacophony of names and hearty welcomes boom, to be instantly forgotten as the next door opens. Near the clerks' room, pigeonholes are embossed with tenants' names and piled high with briefs tied in white or pink ribbon.* Names and faces blur as I do my best to compose a mental map of who goes where and does what. It is largely pointless. Years later, I will still have to ask Alice on reception for directions to Conference Room 4, and won't be able to tell you who of the hundred members of chambers live in which room, or whether somebody I bump into on the stairs is a long-standing colleague or opportunistic burglar. I doubt I am alone. It would certainly explain how and why an opportunistic burglar does in fact manage to stroll into chambers one day in broad daylight and help himself to half a dozen laptops.

And then we are off to our first conference; my first

---

* White ribbon = prosecution brief, pink ribbon = defence brief.

face-to-face encounter with a real, breathing, possibly guilty defendant. At Bar school, we practised with actors bearing rub-on tattoos and doing their best impressions of East End hardened crims; now I get to see one in the flesh. 'Remember what you're doing?' Alan quickly turns to me. 'Sit quiet and say nothing?' I venture. He nods. 'You're doing well.' He marches into the conference room and I obediently trot behind.

Pearls of wisdom

Wesley has been charged with aggravated TWOC* and dangerous driving. This, Alan tells me before we enter, is the type of offence that is beneath his level of practice, but it is a repeat client for a favourite solicitor, so he has agreed to sully himself with a case which would normally be fodder for 'someone like you'.

Wes is an old lag. The sort of likeable rogue that it's easy to romanticise if you're not forced to live on the same estate with him as he rampages from burglary to prison to car theft to prison to drunken violence to prison and so on and on and on in a seemingly unstoppable carousel of criminality.

But for a barrister, Alan has told me, Wes is a desirable client, because he listens. He knows the system, he trusts his solicitor – and by extension, the barristers she instructs – and is receptive to advice.

Contrary to popular misconception, the job of a defence barrister is not to dream up preposterous defences for admittedly

---

* TWOC (*verb*) – Taking a motor vehicle Without the Owner's Consent (or joyriding). You TWOC, I TWOC, he TWOCs, they are TWOCking. Aggravated TWOC is where you not only take someone else's vehicle but go on to either drive it dangerously or cause damage. It's pretty common as, you will no doubt be shocked to learn, the type of person who helps themselves to other people's cars tends to have a flexible interpretation of the Highway Code.

guilty clients. Your overriding duty as a barrister – the closest we have to a Hippocratic Oath – is not to mislead the court. So if a defendant tells you that he's guilty, you cannot positively assert the opposite.* This is a principle in which criminal justice aficionados like Wes are well versed, and so before they give you instructions, they like to hear your professional assessment of the prosecution's evidence.

This all means that, far from my own teenage understanding of the role of a defence lawyer, much of your time is spent advising clients on the strength of the case against them, and of the merits of pleading guilty. And – again, not what I expected from TV – it transpires that many defendants will willingly and sensibly throw their hand in when they receive the benefit of robust legal advice.

As this first, remarkably short, conference shows:

ALAN: Right, Wes, there's no doubt that the driving was dangerous. The only issue is whether they can ID you as the driver.

WES: Can they?

ALAN: Well, two police officers, who say they've known you for years, recognise you as the driver.

WES: OK.

ALAN: And you were found a hundred yards from the abandoned car.

---

* If you have a client who, having admitted his guilt to you, insists that he still wants to run a trial, then you can continue to represent him, but are extremely limited in what you can say to a jury. You can 'put the prosecution to proof' – pointing out the holes or inconsistencies and reminding the jury that they must be sure of guilt before they can convict, but you can't positively suggest that your client is not guilty. It is exceedingly rare.

WES: Right.

ALAN: At 2 a.m. in a neighbourhood some miles from where you live.

WES: Yeah.

ALAN: And you gave the police a false alibi that they were immediately able to disprove.

WES: Go on.

ALAN: And your fingerprints were on the exterior of the car.

WES: Hmm.

ALAN: And inside the car.

WES: I see.

ALAN: On the steering wheel.

WES: Uh-huh.

ALAN: And the jury will inevitably be told about your impressive collection of fourteen convictions for TWOC and dangerous driving.

WES: *NODS*

ALAN: So Wes – and butt in if you think I'm being unfair – but you're fucked, aren't you?

WES: *NODS HARDER*

ALAN: So let's maximise your credit with a guilty plea, get our fourteen months and not dick about with a trial.

WES: Sounds like a plan.

ALAN: Good. We'll see you on Monday at court. Don't forget your bag.*

My first day

My first day in court as a pupil is as terrifying as any day I go on to have in practice, and all I do is sit behind Alan in timid silence. The fear congeals in the realisation, as I observe the list† in action, that no longer am I a mini-pupil clockwatching through obligation. This is something which, come hell or high water, I *will* be doing in six months. There is no guarantee it will last any longer, but for those six months I will have to be able to at least speak words in a courtroom populated by people who know what they're doing, with someone's liberty on the line if I fluff up.

The closer I watch and listen to my colleagues-to-be in action, the greater swells the feeling of dread. Fluent eloquence under pressure is one of those *How Hard Can It Be?* skills that looks eminently replicable until you attempt it yourself, like

---

* Anybody facing a custodial sentence at court is well advised to bring a bag containing the essentials – clothes, toothbrush, family photos, flip-flops (for the filthy showers, not in anticipation of a beach trip) – that they will need to get through the first few days in prison, until they can arrange for family to visit.

† In the Crown Court you have trial courts – where they run trials – and list courts, where all the other, shorter hearings (bail applications, plea hearings, case management hearings, sentences etc.) are shoved. The joy of being in a list court is that standard practice is to give all hearings a timeslot of 'Not before 10 a.m.' and then forcing the parties involved to fight it out with the usher to push their way to the front of the queue. It could only happen in the courts. It would be like telling all patients in a GP's surgery that their appointment is at 10 a.m., and then deciding the running order ad hoc based on who can be most obsequious to the receptionist.

hooking a plastic duck at a carnival or digging a shallow grave. The confident poise with which the advocates make their submissions, sparring with not an 'umm', 'err' or 'y'know' in sight, gracefully leaping into the air like loquacious fish* to catch judicial barbs in their mouths and politely spit them back out again – these are things that the version of me in my head is a natural at but, as I will quickly learn, that the real version is not. The idea that I will be able to slot into this tableau in twenty-six weeks would be laughable were it not spectacularly, deathly unfunny.

And it isn't just the verbal dexterity; it is the language. The idiosyncratic mode of courtroom address, which you are summarily trained for at Bar school but which bears little resemblance to match day – all the *May it please Your Honour*s and *In my respectful submission*s and *M'learned friend*s – combined with the indecipherable choreography of barristers seemingly standing and sitting back down again at random, renders a court hearing at best alienating, at worst completely impossible for anybody not versed in Bar lingo to follow what the hell is going on. Throw in the shorthand, the industry acronyms, the in-jokes, the very particular style of wry humour that is permissible – but only with certain judges and only if you have the experience to pull it off – and you have a spectacle which all the actors understand, but which is wholly incomprehensible to the audience, like performing Brecht to a room of dachshunds.

And this is a problem. It's something which you quickly forget once you're doing it, but courts are by their very nature public forums for the administration of justice. What we do matters to

---

* If 'loquacious fish' remains in the final draft, it is a sign that something has gone very wrong in the editing of this book.

society at large, not just the lawyers in the case. It is essential that somebody stepping into the public gallery – and, not least, the person in the dock whose fate is being discussed – can understand what is being played out before them. As criminal advocates, we are (mostly) aware of this when addressing juries or advising clients, when we cleanse our speech of jargon and reach for hammy pop-culture references to clumsily illustrate our points. But when it's just advocates and the judge talking, it can quickly revert to a lawyers' private affair, where the lights metaphorically dim and we only have eyes for each other.

At such times, a member of the public watching from beyond the perimeter, whether a curious stranger or the defendant in the dock whose liberty is being deliberated by wigged heads speaking in foreign tongues, must find it hard to feel much kinship with our justice system. That feeling of otherness, which I know that most of us feel when starting out, is one which I think we would probably do well to remember, instead of – as I know I was guilty of early on – striving to join the natives in their impenetrable legal culture and leaving the public behind.

The clerks
'You live and die by your relationship with the clerks,' Alan tells me on one of our early morning car journeys to some faraway Crown Court. 'They have the power to strap a jet pack onto your practice, or to fuck it into a lifetime of burglaries and affrays.'*

That doesn't sit easily with my early impressions of Paula, our senior criminal clerk, who has been a model of charm and cheery 'Good morning, Sir/Madam!'s since my first day. But Alan isn't wrong. Clerks are the lifeblood of a barristers' chambers. They

---

* Burglary and affray are two of the less serious – and most poorly paid – offences to grace the Crown Court.

bring in the work, schmoozing defence solicitors and Crown Prosecution Service caseworkers* to send briefs into chambers, while haggling with court listing officers and shuffling barristers' diaries to ensure that all cases are covered[†] and all monstrous barristerial egos are soothed by a healthy workload. As you become more established and develop a reputation, solicitors begin to ask for you by name, but at the start of your career you are almost entirely dependent on the clerks to advertise your services, which they merrily do with all the subtlety of an Amsterdam window.

It's a perverse relationship. Clerks are technically our employees – they take a chunky percentage of our earnings – but they are very much the ones calling the shots.

'Never say no,' warns Alan. 'Especially at your level. "No" equals punishment. Say yes to every request, no matter how inconvenient, no matter how badly paid. If Paula asks you to cancel two weeks in Barbados to cover some crappy mags [magistrates' court] trial for fifty quid, you should be asking yourself why you've booked a holiday in the first place. Two weeks off will put you straight in the little black book.'

'What's the little black book?' I ask.

He grimaces beneath his fresh bronze tan. 'It's why we're up at five a.m. to drive to fucking Truro.'

---

* CPS caseworkers are the glue holding the CPS together. Sometimes in the office managing the administrative side of prosecution files, other times in court to assist the barristers. CPS lawyers, by contrast, are rarely permitted by management to attend court (which I've always thought is bizarre).

† Because cases are often moved – either by the courts or at the request of one of the parties – to different dates, barristers frequently find they have diary clashes, and so often we are asked to cover somebody else's case, either instead of, or as well as, our own.

Under advisement

A large part of first six involves drafting written work for one's supervisor. It's unlikely, certainly at the beginning, that it will be of sufficient quality to be usable in real legal proceedings, but with regular feedback and by comparing your efforts to your supervisor's, you can start to see competence on the horizon. My first piece of work is an advice to the Crown Prosecution Service on a case that Alan is prosecuting, involving the theft of musical instruments belonging to a famous band from a large music venue.

The CPS is the independent body responsible for prosecuting the majority of criminal cases in England and Wales.* The general flowchart has the police investigating alleged crimes, and a lawyer from the Crown Prosecution Service reviewing the evidence and advising on and authorising an appropriate charge.†
Most cases in the magistrates' court are prosecuted by in-house CPS solicitors, whereas in the Crown Courts the CPS will usually‡ contact a barristers' chambers and ask for a barrister, either somebody by name or – my personal favourite and the key to my professional success – 'whoever you've got available'.

As I pore over the papers and carefully distil my semi-professional analysis of the law of non-dwelling burglary, particularly pleased by my inclusion of the wiggy turn of phrase 'five-piece power-pop combo', I apply what Alan has told me, which is the second-best piece of advice I've ever had: *Start with*

---

* There are other prosecuting agencies, including local authorities, Her Majesty's Revenue and Customs and the Department of Work and Pensions. There are also a handful of private prosecutions.
† For minor offences, the police have the power to charge by themselves without referring to the CPS.
‡ The CPS do have their own in-house advocates for Crown Court cases, but most are briefed out to the independent Bar.

what's missing. The brief you receive from the CPS will rarely contain all the evidence that you need for trial; your job is to identify the gaps and omissions, those sly loopholes through which a cunning guilty defendant might wriggle, and to advise the police and CPS on how to close them.

I am not prepared, however, for quite how much is missing. Apparently key witnesses, whose names appear in internal documents, haven't given statements. Police officers have filled their own witness statements with inadmissible hearsay and bad character.* Exhibits which seem obvious, even to me as a burglary virgin – such as photographs of the recovered loot at the defendant's home – haven't been obtained. Fingerprint evidence is mentioned but doesn't seem to actually exist.

This, I quickly learn, is the norm. The resources of the police and the CPS to investigate and prosecute crimes – especially ten-a-penny offences like burglary – are minimal. It often falls to prosecuting counsel to rescue a viable case to present at trial. After seven hours and fifteen pages of incisive factual and legal analysis, I proudly present my (surely perfect) document to Alan.

He returns it two days later, ablaze with red pen and a thick circle of ink around 'five-piece power-pop combo' with the annotation – 'DO YOU THINK THIS IS FUNNY? THIS IS NOT FUNNY. DO NOT TRY TO BE FUNNY.'

That is the best piece of advice I've ever had.

Please come again

My first trial with Alan is his third bite at the cherry. On two previous occasions he has turned up at court to prosecute this

---

* As a general rule, juries are not allowed to be told about a defendant's previous misdeeds unless strict 'bad character' legal provisions are met.

serious section 18 GBH* and robbery in the home. The two defendants have allegedly entered the complainant's home, hoping to quietly discuss the small matter of a drugs debt, reinforced by two large machetes which they used to hack at the arms of the unfortunate creditor, before relieving him of various electronic goods.

Both of the previous trials have been adjourned – i.e. pushed back to a later date – for 'lack of court time'. Courts list more trials each day than there are courtrooms open, in the hope that a listed trial will crack – either the defendant will plead guilty or the prosecution will throw their hand in – and a trial courtroom will become free. In principle, it's a sound idea – you don't want usable courtrooms and precious court time going to waste. In practice, courts list far more 'floating' trials than can ever be heard, and close hundreds of usable courtrooms every day in order to save money,† meaning that thousands of trials each year are adjourned on the day.

On both of the previous occasions, Alan has had to sit down with Otis, the complainant, at the start of the day, go through his witness statement, answer his queries, manage his nerves and then, come 4 p.m. when the trial floated into the ether, send

---

* Section 18 GBH = inflicting grievous bodily harm or wounding, with intent to cause grievous (really serious) bodily harm – max sentence life. As opposed to Section 20 GBH = inflicting grievous bodily harm or wounding (without intending to cause really serious harm) – max sentence five years.

† The Treasury allocates each court centre a fixed number of 'sitting days' per year. So rather than, as logic would dictate, using as many courtrooms and judges as we have to get through cases quickly, the government forces the courts to run at artificially low capacity to save money. Only, of course, it doesn't save money. And everyone, from victims of crime to defendants to lawyers, gets screwed over.

the poor shaking man away and ask him to return in six months.

This time, however, we are not a floating trial. We are a fixture. Two years on from the original allegation, we have an allocated courtroom, a designated judge, and all systems are go go go. Alas, so is Otis. The under-resourced Witness Care Unit have not contacted him until the week before trial, and it has become increasingly clear that he has gone underground, presumably no longer inclined to sit in a draughty Crown Court witness suite for days on end for no purpose. The court has issued a witness summons to compel him to attend under threat of arrest, but the overstretched police have not found time to serve it.

With no witness, no prospect of yet another adjournment and no realistic means of getting the crucial evidence before the jury, Alan is left with no choice but to formally offer no evidence.* And the two defendants, neither of whom have ever offered any explanation for their whereabouts on the night in question, or for Otis's injuries, walk free.

Alan bears this result with his usual indifference. This, he shrugs as he crams his wig into the old Quality Street tub that suffices as his official wig tin, is just another day in the criminal courts. I, by contrast, silently fulminate all the way home about a system so easily outmanoeuvred by such obviously guilty men.

The daily grind

I quickly learn that, for professionals who invariably paint themselves as 'trial advocates', barristers spend a surprisingly small percentage of their working lives actually doing trials. While there is at least one trial in Alan's diary most weeks, they

* The technical term for dropping a prosecution at trial.

are liable to be ineffective for a variety of reasons – usually a crack* or an adjournment for lack of court time – and so holes suddenly appear. Much of the filler in between comes in the form of shorter hearings, such as pre-trial reviews, bail applications, sentence hearings, plea hearings and mentions. And not just on Alan's own cases.

The engine of the courts, it emerges, is the system of 'returns'. I had naively assumed that the trajectory of a criminal case was straightforward: a solicitor asks the clerk for your services, the trial (and any pre-trial hearings) are entered into your diary, you diligently prepare the case and then attend the trial. But because the criminal courts are – and, Alan assures me, always have been – so catastrophically disorganised, hearings are listed or moved at the eleventh hour and trials frequently overrun, meaning that barristers constantly find themselves unavailable for hearings on cases in which they're instructed. So, to save the court system from grinding to an immediate halt, the convention is that if you're not available, somebody else from your chambers will be identified by your clerks to step in to cover your hearing, whether it's a five-minute bail application or a five-week trial.

The advantage to the courts is that it means they can behave as capriciously with their listing practices as they like, safe in the knowledge that, no matter how much inconvenience is caused, every case will be covered. The advantage to barristers is that returns make up a decent chunk of your income (and, junior tenants in my chambers warn me, pretty much all of your income when you're starting out and have yet to cultivate your

---

* A 'cracked trial' is a case that is listed for trial, only for either the defendant to subsequently plead guilty or the prosecution to drop the case.

own practice). The disadvantage, it seems, is mainly shouldered by defendants, who often have to attend multiple pre-trial hearings represented at each increment by a different barrister, each promising that 'your trial barrister' will try to be there on the next occasion.

It all means that the Rumpolian caricature of the swashbuckling, cross-examining jury-charmer doesn't capture how Alan spends most of my first six, which is instead frantically running from courtroom to courtroom from hearing to hearing, juggling his own work and other people's as he flits between clients, the CPS room, the cells and the probation office, gown billowing behind him while he pretends not to hear the court tannoys booming his name.

When we are trialling, court sitting hours are 10 a.m. to 4.30 p.m., but this is only 'stage time'. Alan insists that we get to court at least an hour before kick-off, to meet clients or the CPS, and we often don't leave the building until after 5 p.m. As we can find ourselves being sent by the clerks to any corner of England and Wales, the journey home often takes several hours, and upon setting foot through our respective front doors, our evening routines begin. For Alan, this involves preparing his cases for the next day, responding to mounting paperwork, attending to urgent work required on future trials. For me, mimicking Alan's case prep, so that he can compare my amateurish opening speeches and plodding witness questioning with his own professional versions and offer constructive pointers.

A typical working day therefore is 6 a.m. to 11 p.m., with all-nighters not uncommon. We often don't find out our movements for the next day until 6 p.m., after the courts have confirmed the final court lists and the clerks have completed their frantic shuffling to ensure that all hearings are covered, so coordinating family responsibilities or social lives presents certain complexities.

On an entirely unrelated note, Alan tells me over coffee in the court canteen, the criminal Bar has a long-standing concurrency with alcohol abuse, divorce, debt, mental ill health, addiction, burnout and sociopathy.

Home truths (Part 1)

Following Alan into the court cells to visit a freshly sentenced flasher, I bump into Alicia, who was one of the other final-round applicants for the pupillage that I lucked into. She is now a pupil at a chambers across town, and we swap cheerful congratulations before being dragged apart like excitable cockapoos by our respective masters. Clocking Alan's furrowed expression as Alicia scurries away, I remind him that she was one of my co-interviewees. Recognition clicks. 'Of course!' he says, absent-mindedly. 'She's the one I voted for.'

The bullshit conveyor belt

'Another thing they don't teach you at Bar school . . .' should be the advertising slogan for a criminal pupillage. While Alan would never be as frightfully clichéd as to utter the phrase himself, he does reserve an especially acute curve of the eyebrow for occasions when I try to contribute to a discussion by referencing something I learned on the Bar course.

To a large extent the discrepancy between theory and practice is unavoidable. The actuality of dealing with severely malfunctioning human behaviour in conditions of unpredictable, high-stakes, time-pressured turmoil is difficult to replicate in a classroom environment. But a handy primer which I think could have at least been included in one of our seminar hand-outs would be: Everybody Lies. All The Time. About Everything.

Defendants lie, of course. That much, at least, I expect. But any young naïf* expecting to be able to take at face value what they are told by anybody in the system is in for a rude awakening.

Whether it is a witness flatly contradicting their own previous account, or police officers denying something captured on their own body-worn video camera, or a prison claiming that a defendant has 'refused to leave his cell' to attend court (the default excuse when HM Prison has cocked up and forgotten to put a prisoner on the van), untruthfulness pervades the criminal courts. While many inaccuracies can be attributed to genuine mistake, there is a healthy churn of bullshit being pumped through the arteries of the criminal justice system.

Commonly – and most frustratingly when prosecuting – I find that there is an inherent truth to a complaint, but that for their own reasons a witness hasn't been completely honest. It is not always as straightforward as outright malicious fabrication; sometimes they change or omit key details out of embarrassment; sometimes they embellish an account to twist the knife into the defendant – say, claiming an assault involved more blows or caused greater injury than was really the case; sometimes the complainant is simply a compulsive liar with a criminal history to prove it.

It's probably why we place such a premium on honesty between lawyers, and why – I am repeatedly warned by Alan – the suggestion that a barrister is sharp or untrustworthy can leave an indelible mark in the eyes of her colleagues. The ubiquity of deceit also gives the lie to the idea of the criminal process as an independent guarantor of truthfinding. The rather less satisfying reality is that 'truth' is often scripted by the victors.

* i.e. Me.

This much is brought home to me in the court cells as Alan expertly extracts a guilty plea out of a career burglar, Raz, whose astonishing record of being caught and imprisoned – this will be his sixteenth conviction for burglary – might persuade a sane man to try his hand at a different type of criminality. Or to at least wear gloves. Nevertheless, what Raz lacks in – to use the Probation Service* argot – 'thinking skills', he more than makes up for in candour, as he invariably pleads guilty whenever he's hauled before the courts. Today, however, Raz is peeved by the witness statement provided by the victim, who has listed all the items that Raz has allegedly stolen, a list which will be submitted in support of any insurance or compensation claim.

'I'll plead to it,' he says, 'cos I know with my record no judge is gonna believe me at a Newton,† but that list is fucking bullshit. You know my graft, Alan. Electronics and gold. Course I took the laptops and the iPads and the phones and the jewellery. But

---

* Before a guilty defendant is sentenced, the Probation Service will usually prepare a Pre-Sentence Report, which often contains a proposal for an alternative to immediate custody – either a community order or a suspended sentence (a prison sentence which you only have to serve if you further misbehave). Frequently a 'Thinking Skills' programme will be recommended to help those in need.

† Sometimes a defendant pleads guilty, but on a 'basis' (version of the facts) that the prosecution doesn't accept. Where the difference between the prosecution and defence versions would make a material difference to the sentence that the court passes, the court will hold a Newton hearing, which is a short trial that takes place in front of a judge, usually involving the defendant giving evidence. The judge will then decide whether or not they are sure that the prosecution version is correct. Any doubt is exercised in favour of the defendant. Career burglars like Raz tend not to present as the most compelling or creditable witnesses.

you've seen the tiny rucksack I was carrying. How the fuck is it I'm also supposed to have taken . . . what is it?'

Alan glances at the statement: 'A pair of men's Alexander McQueen leather ankle boots valued at £650, some Tom Ford cashmere boxer shorts valued at £900, three Rouge Hermès limited edition twenty-four-colour lipstick piano sets each valued at £1,300, and [squints] a black silk Versace evening dress worth £7,500.'

Foul play

'Roast,' Alan mutters to himself as I walk into his room. 'It was a fucking roast.'

Assuming this is some sort of legal jargon with which I am supposed to be familiar, I nod knowingly. Yup.

'What kind of moron charged this? Do you know?' he thunders as he tosses his brief across the desk towards me. 'You're a bright spark – you tell me whether this offence is made out in law.'

I scan the charge sheet and the police case summary (officially known as the MG5). Intercourse with an animal, contrary to section 69 of the Sexual Offences Act 2003, in that Wayne Hemsby on 14th day of December 2008 intentionally penetrated with his penis the anus of a living animal, namely a chicken.

'Now look at the CSI* photographs,' Alan barks.

I flick through the bundle with trepidation. A neighbour saw Wayne in the act and immediately called the police, who arrived with uncharacteristic alacrity and stormed into the garden mid-coitus. The plucky recipient of Wayne's unlawful urges was duly photographed by the attending officers.

* Crime Scene Investigator

As I reach the victim's mugshot, Alan's bemusement becomes clear. I nod. 'Not an offence contrary to section 69 as far as I can see, Alan.'

'Exactly. He may be a voracious predatory pervert,' Alan says, gravel in his throat and steel in his eyes, 'but if an Englishman cannot in the privacy of his own garden buy and shag a roast chicken, why are we even bothering to get out of bed?'

Home truths (Part 2)
It takes the best part of five months, but I finally extract some much-hungered-for praise from my supervisor. Apropos of nothing, during a long drive home from court, Alan declares: 'I think you would be quite well suited to being a prosecutor.' Having been repeatedly assured, since the first day, that my future lies away from the criminal Bar (in no small part because Alan, like many men of his generation, has mistaken basic IT literacy for unparalleled genius, and is convinced that I should be making 'proper money' doing commercial law), this represents a welcome show of faith in my aptitude for crime.

'Prosecutors have to be organised, and logical, and able to construct a case. Whereas defending is pure destruction. I think prosecuting would suit you.'

I nod and smile to myself.

'Plus,' he adds, 'it's not as big a problem if you don't have much of a personality.'

Rio (Part 1)*
'Do you find sex cases more . . .' I ask Alan as he swings his Volvo into the prison visitors' car park.

* I've discussed Rio's case before. For full details of Rio's story, see Chapter 3 of *The Secret Barrister: Stories of the Law and How It's Broken*.

'More what?' he deadpans. 'Titillating?'

'God no,' I hurry. 'No, more . . . challenging. Or upsetting?'

He raises an eyebrow. 'No. It's just another type of crime, isn't it? Just a different way in which people can inflict dreadful harm on each other.' He pauses to reflect. 'I mean, some of the offences are objectively more disgusting, and perverts present their own challenges as clients – they're manipulative fuckers – but it makes no odds to me whether I'm defending an alleged stabber or an alleged rapist.'

Today's latter is Rio, a twenty-something man whose ex-partner, Lori, has at the acrimonious conclusion of their relationship made allegations that Rio regularly raped her throughout their time together. Rio, having dispensed with his previous barrister, now has Alan acting for him, and is desperate for bail pending his trial next month. Alan's task at today's conference is to explain to Rio how unlikely that is.

Having passed through the layers of invasive prison security checks (photo ID, shoes and coats off, full body rubdown, fingerprints – the whole Champneys experience), Alan, our solicitor Denise and I pile into the boxy legal visit room. The opposite door is unlocked by a squat prison officer, and Rio slinks in. He is not what I expect from my first accused sex offender. He is my age, for one. And, his antecedent record shows, he was born in the same small town as me. Which sounds an odd thing to be surprised about, but there's something about the realisation that he could have been in my class at school that brings home that this prisoner, visibly othered by the high-vis vest slung over his grey tracksuit, doesn't exist on some imaginary separate plane. I've met plenty of defendants in my first five months with Alan, but I've so far managed to maintain the hermetic seal between me – law-abiding young professional – and the clients – hooded troublemakers from neighbourhoods that I, thankfully, will never have to visit. The illusion is for the first time pierced by the realisation that, but for the circumstances that have brought Rio here, he would be walking the same streets and visiting the same shops as me.

While he has a long criminal record, Rio is surprisingly frank and easy to talk to. Maybe it's the effect of our shared birthplace, but I find myself warming to him, in spite of the horror of what he is alleged to have done. He wants to vent, not about the case, but about his life on the outside. How, after years of cocaine-fuelled violence and disorder, he has a new partner, Jade, who has straightened him out, dragging him off the class A and into legitimate paid work as a delivery driver. He hasn't grafted* for nearly a year – a personal record. It was all falling into place when Lori, having discovered the overlap in Rio's relationships with her and Jade, called the police to report what Rio describes as 'bullshit that I haven't done this time'. For the first time in his adult life, he'd got things together. Then one morning a knock at the door has led to his immediate return behind bars, his life put on pause and his liberty snatched away and placed beyond his reach. Now his job has likely gone to somebody else, he hasn't seen his three-year-old son for five months, and he is terrified that Jade, the best thing to ever happen to him, is tiring of waiting. Listening to his fears of what he stood to lose on remand while his life carried on outside without him, it is difficult not to feel sympathy. This, needless to say, is not on the shortlist of things I expected to feel on my first face-to-face encounter with an alleged serial rapist.

The next month, Rio's trial has to be adjourned after last-minute complications arise. The CPS apply to extend the Custody

---

* Stolen. Rio liked to steal things, particularly cars.

Time Limits* to keep Rio inside, but Alan, fiercely critical of police and prosecution delays that have led up to this stage, persuades the judge to grant Rio his bail. Wiping away a tear, Rio raises a hand in thanks from the dock as he turns and walks down the stairs to the cells with the Serco security officer, only this time he will not be going on the van to the prison; he will be processed for release, and will return to his family. And in six months' time, after telling a jury what he has told us, he will be acquitted of the charges against him.

But we'll come back to that later.

The legal dictionary

After a few months of daily court-watching, I have cracked the code. The stock-in-trade phrases that roll off the tongues of practised criminal hacks do not, it transpires, take long to absorb and regurgitate. For the benefit of future generations, I record my lawyer-to-layman translations thus:

WHAT BARRISTER SAYS	WHAT BARRISTER MEANS
In my respectful submission . . .	Listen up, yo.
I am specifically instructed that . . .	My client, contrary to my sensible advice, is insisting that I say that . . .

---

* The law limits how long a defendant can be kept in custody on remand awaiting trial. In the Crown Court, it has long been 182 days (six months), until Covid-19 provided an excuse for the government to increase it to 238 days (eight months) in 2020. But this period can be extended, repeatedly, if the prosecution show a 'good and sufficient cause' and that they have acted 'with all due diligence and expedition'.

WHAT BARRISTER SAYS	WHAT BARRISTER MEANS
My client has had the benefit of robust advice.	I have told him how utterly rubber ducked he is.
Your Honour may be aware that I am not trial counsel.	Your Honour should be aware that, whatever it is, it isn't my fault.
If Your Honour is with me on that point . . .	Please just say you agree so I can sit down and stop talking.
If Your Honour is against me on that point . . .	I infer from the ten minutes of puce-faced shouting that we've all just enjoyed that you might – *might* – disagree with me, so let's move on.
I mean no criticism of my learned friend . . .	But my learned friend's solicitors and/or client are incompetent/dishonest/kick puppies for fun.
It may be that in due course I seek assistance from Your Honour . . .	I'm going to ask you to confirm that my client won't go to prison if he pleads guilty, and then we can all stop messing about.
I concede that the proposal in the Pre-Sentence Report is unrealistic.	Lord alone knows why the Probation Service think that a community order is appropriate for this rabidly stabby armed robber, but please don't think I don't realise how crazy that sounds, because I do.
With respect . . .	Without much respect . . .
With the utmost respect . . .	With no respect at all.

WHAT BARRISTER SAYS	WHAT BARRISTER MEANS
I am instructed that the Crown intend to proceed to trial, although I will of course faithfully reflect any observations that Your Honour might have.	The CPS are insisting on pursuing this hopeless case, and I need you to tell them to drop it.
Of course, Your Honour, although I note that on a previous occasion Your Honour's brother judge observed . . .	But Mummy, Daddy said . . .
This is a matter that the Crown Prosecution Service initially dealt with in-house . . .	. . . before realising what a hog's bumcheek they had made of the case and briefing it out to Muggins here at 6 p.m. last night.
Perhaps the strongest feature in mitigation, notwithstanding that it arrived late in the day, is the defendant's guilty plea.	The only positive thing I can say on this man's behalf is that after two years and three aborted trial dates, having dragged the victims to court multiple times, he has finally – FINALLY – admitted the overwhelming case against him.
Your Honour well knows that sentencing guidelines are guidelines, not tramlines.	See those guidelines that are designed to apply to cases just like this? The ones that tell you to send my client to prison? See them? Well just ignore them. Please.

WHAT BARRISTER SAYS	WHAT BARRISTER MEANS
It's a matter for Your Honour.	I don't give two hoots.
So be it, Your Honour.	Fine. Be like that.

A *family affair*

Law is a highly heritable disease. The children of lawyers are apparently seventeen times more likely to become lawyers than those whose parents did not work in the law* and, meeting other pupils as I roadied for Alan on his tour of England and Wales, it shows. While you don't have to be the offspring of a barrister or judge to work here, it helps. Even allowing for the confirmation bias that doubtless skews my perspective, the frequency with which somebody is introduced with a sotto voce rider '*He's the son of . . .*' all compounds my initial impression of the Bar as a swamp of inbreeding.

Everybody, it seems – barristers, solicitors, judges,[†] CPS staff – is either related or wedded to each other. Forgetting this and injudiciously sounding off in the robing room carries an obvious hazard, as we've all mortifyingly witnessed at one time or another [SAMPLE DIALOGUE: 'Christ, have you ever appeared in front of that bigoted old twat who sits in Court Five?' 'No, but I have married him.']

I suppose that it is partly inevitable that in an all-consuming profession which demands eighty-hour weeks, your putative

---

* CJ McKinney, 'Children of lawyers 17 TIMES more likely to become lawyers themselves', Legal Cheek, 22 March 2019, https://www.legalcheek.com/2019/03/children-of-lawyers-17-times-more-likely-to-become-lawyers-themselves/
† In case you are wondering/worrying, judges cannot hear cases involving barristers to whom they are married or related.

romantic interactions will largely be restricted to snatched conversations with others in the industry. And, trying to ease the chip off my shoulder, it's probably likely that somebody growing up in a household in which the legal profession is demystified and you are exposed from a young age to lawyerly modes of discussion will confer benefits which give you an unavoidable advantage in scrupulously neutral recruitment exercises. It's not always stark-naked nepotism, at least not these days.

But even if explicable, this entrenched dynastic element is something I still struggle with a decade after first seeing it in action. I know that there is a similar – apparently greater* – generational dimension in medical careers, but doctors don't appeal to democratic legitimacy to justify their existence. The justice system, on the other hand, is precariously dependent on public faith, both in its structure and its purpose. The more it is seen as controlled by a narrow set of elites, the less we can expect people to engage with it, and a justice system which in real terms serves only certain strata of society is not a justice system at all.

I don't have a ready answer. It may be insoluble; unless we start forbidding intra-Bar breeding or actively discriminating against those with legal heritage, I think that the best we have may be the old (or, to the Bar, the new) familiars – fair and open recruitment; name-, age- and gender-blind paper applications; aggressive outreach programmes to attract a more diverse pool of candidates. If we can make the Bar more reflective in terms of ethnicity, sex, disability, sexual orientation and social background, it perhaps matters less that Lord Justice Whatshisface has two daughters as judges and three sons as QCs.

* Medicine was the one profession deemed more inheritable than law, according to that study.

But I do still think, for all the welcome statements of intent about increasing diversity at the Bar, there remains this blind spot. Whether born of defensiveness or defeatism, I sense a stubborn institutional reluctance to look closer to home, and to ask ourselves whether it's right, in the justice system in 2022, that blood remains thicker than water.

The pupil's tale

Bumping into pupils from other chambers, as well as allowing me to spin a vital network of contacts for emergency legal/pastoral support, also affords the opportunity to do what every barrister loves most – tell stories about ourselves.

As every chambers is different in its structure, ethos, composition and how much it pays its pupils, nobody's experience of pupillage is quite like anybody else's. The common perennial thread is pupillage as a rite of passage, but each chambers' interpretation of that cliché varies. The Bar Standards Board publishes a checklist of things you are supposed to see and do in order to complete first six, but aside from paying pupils the minimum pupillage award there are few mandatory obligations on chambers and even less regulatory oversight. From talking to my peers, I learn that it is very much pot luck whether a pupillage represents a supportive vocational training experience or a frat-house hazing.

The ad-hoc, late-night wine-and-Domino's therapy sessions that our cohort of pupils arrange at each other's flats is the closest thing to a social life that we manage. Drawn from an array of chambers across the city, we make for a ragtag bunch, but it seems to work. The chancery* and commercial pupils – with

---

* Chancery generally covers the law of property, trusts and contracts. It is very much where the money is.

their calm, measured wisdom and quietly ferocious intellect – offer a much needed balance to the hypermanic egotism of the criminal pupils and the violent cynicism of the family law folk. While those of us with other pupils in the same chambers, all scrapping for a single tenancy, can never quite put out of our minds that grinding, exhausting sense of competition, there's a tacit acknowledgement that therapy nights are sacred. They are what get us through.

I look on with envy at what some of them are doing. While Alan has a strong practice, he's not doing the huge cases – the murders and terrorisms and international drug rings – that fixate the legal community. My fellow pupils at more prestigious chambers are involved – albeit vicariously – in precisely those trials. Junior briefs* and jury trials will be lain at their door the moment they start second six. I try to choke down this feeling, hoping it will dissolve once I'm doing my own cases, but it turns out that this is anything but transient. To the contrary, over the coming years, it grows. As a junior tenant, I will find myself constantly comparing diaries with others of a similar call, constantly fretting that they are getting more work – and better work – while I toil in the mediocrity of the magistrates' court. Forging a glittering career in their own names, while I service the returns of my colleagues.

However, other pupillage experiences of my new friends do not inspire jealousy. Quite the opposite. One reveals that she has been conscripted as her supervisor's de facto housekeeper,

---

* In complex and lengthy cases, the courts sometimes grant a defendant 'certificate for two counsel' – meaning that they have the benefit of two barristers. The more senior barrister 'leads' the junior. Being a led junior is a fantastic way of gaining exposure to the big cases at an early stage of your career.

expected to respond 24/7 to ad hoc demands, from cat-sitting to putting the bins out. Another tells us he was instructed to dress up as the entertainment for a children's party thrown for the offspring of senior members of chambers. Two criminal pupils at a large set were sent out to buy fifty bottles of Dom Perignon for a silk's celebration party, the promise of future reimbursement not really a solution to footing the upfront cost on an income of £800 a month. One chap has been hauled before his chambers' disciplinary committee when word got out that he offered a senior QC 'a brew', such crass northern informality having occasioned gross embarrassment to the poor delicate silk.

For all Alan's quirks (his latest theme for long car journeys is his sincere concern that I might 'look too child-like for any solicitor or any client to ever want to instruct you'), I realise that I have it very good indeed.

The art of cross-examination

One of the hardest skills to master as an advocate is cross-examination. At trial, a witness will be asked gentle, open questions by the party calling them ('examination-in-chief'), and will then be asked slightly trickier, closed questions by the other side. Libraries are stocked with books on the art of cross-examination; how to hone the skill of layering perfectly weighted leading questions, one atop another, until a witness suddenly realises they have no choice but to agree with your final, devastating proposition. Cross-examination, I'd learned at Bar school, is not about eliciting truth from witnesses, as much as extracting the answer that you want, and, most importantly, the answer you expect (the cardinal rule being never to ask a witness a question to which you don't know the answer). No cross-examination outside a courtroom scene in *Hollyoaks* will end in a witness falling to their knees and admitting through heavy sobs that they're a dirty rotten liar, but by teasing out inconsistencies and carefully putting your client's case, you can at least hope to cast their evidence in the most convenient light. Week on week, I watch and learn from Alan in action as his clipped questions masterfully shred the evidence of witnesses and defendants like pulled pork, one day conjuring doubt where none appeared to exist, the next sledgehammering the nails into a lying swine's casket.

No cross-examination I ever see, however, by even the greatest silks, turns out to be as effective as that of our chambers' most junior tenant, Cain, as I trail him around the Youth Court towards the end of first six. Prosecuting a trial where the teenaged defendant is charged with breaching his ASBO by entering a prohibited road, Cain takes to his feet to cross-examine.

'You've just told the court that you didn't go on Hartfield Road, yes?'

'Yes.'

'Well, I'm going to suggest that you did.'

[PAUSE]

'OK, yeah, I did.'

The innocent man

One of Alan's final cases of my first six involves a Polish client, Lukasz. The prosecution case is pure tabloid-bait: Lukasz is one of three Eastern European migrants who have come to the UK to embark upon a spree of burglary and miscellaneous thieving, working their way from town to town over the course of a week relieving anyone they encountered of anything that wasn't screwed to the floor. After the judge found substantial grounds to believe they would disappear if granted bail, they have been remanded for six months prior to trial. Now they are benefitting from taxpayer-funded legal aid to wriggle out of their deserved fate.

Alan, picking this up as a late return, meets Lukasz for the first time on the morning of trial. Lukasz's case is simple: he knows the co-defendants, but wasn't with them, or indeed anywhere near the crime scenes, over the week in question. The identification evidence relied upon by the prosecution is mistaken. It isn't the strongest ID case – a couple of witnesses were a bit equivocal during the VIPER,* one gave an initial description that didn't quite match Lukasz. There is enough to work with, Alan notes, to raise reasonable doubt, which when you're defending is all you need to do.

But as it turns out, Alan doesn't need to do anything. Upon entering the robing room, he is accosted by a red-faced prosecuting counsel. The police have, this morning, mentioned the existence of a cell-site report† based on Lukasz's phone. This is news to everyone, as no such report appears in the evidence, nor on any of the schedules of unused material.‡ The prosecutor

---

* VIPER = Video Identification Procedure, the standard way that ID parades are conducted in England and Wales. The witness is shown nine moving video clips, each of a person matching the description of the suspect that the witness gave. One of the nine is the suspect. The witness is asked whether they can identify anybody in any of the clips, and their response is recorded.
† Cell-site analysis involves looking at the cell masts used by a mobile phone, which can allow an analyst to plot the location and movements of the phone and, by extension, of the person possessing it.
‡ All relevant material generated in the course of the investigation which doesn't end up as evidence is 'unused material', and must be listed on a 'schedule of unused material'. Anything on the schedule which may reasonably be capable of assisting the defence or undermining the prosecution case must, by law, be disclosed to the defence. Each item on the schedule must therefore be reviewed by the police and CPS and marked either 'disclosable' (i.e. of potential assistance to the defence) or 'not disclosable'.

demanded to see it and, quite properly, is now immediately disclosing it to Alan. The report shows, beyond doubt, that at the time of the offences Lukasz's mobile phone was exactly where Lukasz has said he was – hundreds of miles away. It was in frequent use over that time, and it is clear from the content that Lukasz was the person using it. He isn't merely not guilty – he is positively innocent. The prosecution has no case.

When Alan walks into the cells with the interpreter to deliver the good news, Lukasz is completely calm. He simply looks at Alan and, before Alan can say a word, asks: 'You are my barrister? So can I go home now?' His tranquillity is stunning. There has not been any doubt in his mind that he will be going home. He has to – he is innocent. It is, he has apparently been telling himself, just a case of waiting for his barrister to make the system do the right thing. It is a pity it has taken this long, but still, all's well that ends well.

While I promised earlier on to avoid a catalogue of lightbulb moments and Damascene conversions, I do have to single out this case as being the first time it had occurred to me – physically struck me in the gut – that in this job we might be dealing with genuinely innocent people. It's a realisation which I am sure many if not most of my colleagues will have had long before they embarked upon a career at the criminal Bar, but for me, Lukasz's case exposed an assumption I had apparently been carrying for years. It's an assumption that I think prevails not only outside the system, but also among certain actors inside: that all those drawn into the criminal justice system are guilty of *something*. It's just a case of the prosecution lining up their ducks and avoiding witness problems or evidential pitfalls, or attaching the correct label to the criminality. Defence lawyers are there to expose holes in the prosecution case and keep the Crown honest. The verdict you seek from the jury is, after all, 'not guilty', not 'innocent'. Criminal justice is how we deal with criminals.

And I'm aware of how this sounds; the preposterous naivety of a trainee criminal barrister expressing surprise that they would be dealing with innocent people, like some sitcom medical student expressing shock at having to treat the sick. I don't defend it. It *was* absurd.

Even now, I can't explain how I came to internalise that idea. Since teenagehood I had been exposed to a steady feed of miscarriages of justice. Our university-taught case law was built on the backs of real victims of wrongful convictions. My go-to fiction of choice was crime, my favourite book a paradigm of a broken system. I was fluent in the language of the ideals of our criminal justice system – *convict the guilty, acquit the innocent* – and had filled Christ knows how many pupillage application forms and interviews with my – honestly sincerely held – pontifications about the importance of defence lawyers upholding justice. I had my standard response to the dinner-party classic *How can you defend somebody you think is guilty?* down to a pithy one sentence: Because they may be innocent, and it is not my job to judge them.

But apparently, I'd not been understanding the language I was speaking. I had been harbouring an inability to transfer this academic awareness to the very system in which I was working. These, I must have reasoned, were problems which existed in America, or which *had* existed here, but didn't really feature in twenty-first-century Britain. Miscarriages of justice were a relic, or a stain on the conscience of other nations, like torture or shell suits. British exceptionalism had seen to that.

That, obviously, is simply wrong. While not every defendant who swears their innocence will be innocent – indeed, the vast majority may well be guilty – to believe that it is vanishingly rare for the twenty-first-century British justice system to fall into error is recklessly complacent.

Because Lukasz would have been one such miscarriage. In fact, he was. This man had spent six months in a foreign prison for something that he absolutely did not do. Worse, as Alan – the angriest I ever saw him – had raged all the way home, the state had known, or had at best been in possession of evidence proving, that this man was innocent. Reverse the roles, place a photogenic middle-class British lad in an Eastern European prison for half a year, with the state sitting on evidence proving his innocence, and you have a newspaper campaign that will cause diplomatic phones to ring off the hook.

But there was no campaign. No public outcry. Lukasz released from court a free man to a wall of silence, just grateful that our strange foreign system – thanks to the honest diligence of the prosecutor – had belatedly, at significant human cost, got the right result.

3. On My Feet: The Second Six*

A peculiarity of first six is how much time I spend watching my veteran supervisor conduct cases that I am not going to be getting near for years. The exposure to seniority is doubtless valuable, but Alan's practice of sex and serious violence† bears no resemblance to my diary as a pristine second sixer, which is a paleo diet of magistrates' court lists.

The magistrates' court is the first port of call on the criminal court production line. All cases start in the magistrates' courts, and around 95 per cent are tried and sentenced there. Only a tiny sliver of the criminal pie – the most serious cases – makes it as far as the Crown Courts, where barristers do most of their work.

Magistrates are volunteers. They require no legal qualifications and receive only a few days' training, but exercise the powers of the formal legally qualified judges (District Judges, or DJs) who also sit in the magistrates' courts.‡ These include the

---

* Second six is when you are said to be 'on your feet'. Although a more accurate description of my early days would involve landing on a different body part.
† Professional practice. Let me be clear.
‡ This section offers a whistlestop tour of how magistrates' courts work. For full detail, including the miserable stats and stories that

power to imprison people for up to twelve months. Unlike in the Crown Courts, where you have legally qualified judges deciding questions of law (such as bail, whether certain evidence is admissible, sentencing) and lay juries deciding the facts of a trial, magistrates do it all. They sit in a 'bench' of three, and get to make all the legal rulings as well as to decide the outcomes of trials. They have a qualified legal advisor to assist, but the magistrates are to all intents and purposes judge, jury and executioner.

The history of the magistracy stretches back to the fourteenth century, and the modern justification is that having local volunteers dispensing summary justice keeps justice rooted in the local community. In practice, notwithstanding recent diversity drives, the magistracy has long been overwhelmingly dominated by middle-aged white people from a certain background. Needless to say, the type of person over whom they sit in judgement tends to have experienced a very different life. Perhaps the more compelling reason for the government's enthusiasm for magistrates is that they cost far less than Crown Court judges and juries.

I'd already learned that there was a fair degree of scepticism at the Bar towards magistrates.* Throughout first six I'd been subjected to countless horror stories by junior colleagues of their early years in the mags, and the attendant ludicrous decisions, legal fluffs and passing remarks straight out of the Bernard Manning school of equality and diversity. I'd also

---

support my pessimistic view of their operation, see Chapter 2 of *The Secret Barrister: Stories of the Law and How It's Broken.*

* And, correspondingly, magistrates often have a dim view of barristers, thinking us smug and superior. I may not have done much to dissuade them from this view.

shadowed a couple of juniors at the mags for a few days, so had – I thought – a fair idea of what to expect.

I was wrong.

Learning by drowning

Some cases at the magistrates' court are prosecuted by in-house CPS lawyers. But much of the work is outsourced to 'agents' – independent barristers and solicitors. Typically, agents will be given the trial lists, and allocated to a single courtroom in which the optimistic listing officer has stuffed anything between three and eight trials, in the hope that at least some of them will be tried, and that the others might crack. It is a cheap way of ware-housing cases and rushing them through the production line – an agent cost £200 a day,* and, unlike civil servants, was expected to remain in court as long as the magistrates wanted to keep the building open. Eight p.m. is my record.

For reasons that were not explained to me as a pupil and have not been explained since, the CPS do not provide the papers to agents until the very last minute. When I was in pupil-lage and files were literally paper, this was typically 9 a.m. on the day;† you would rock up at court and be handed an enor-mous bag of thick cardboard files, each containing several hundred randomly assembled pages, and be expected to read and prepare the contents for trial in time for court starting at 9.30. You had no idea which ones would be called on, so had to do your best to get on top of every case.

This, it is fair to say, is not the ideal way to prepare trials

---

* Increased in 2019 to £300 per day.
† Since the criminal justice system discovered email in the mid 2010s, briefs have been emailed to agents the night before. They are, how-ever, just as voluminous, incomplete and disordered.

which could result in someone's imprisonment. Prepping a trial is not just reading the papers. It requires detailed analysis – what are the witnesses saying? Where are the conflicts? What legal applications do we need to make? What am I going to say in my opening speech? What questions will I ask when cross-examining the defendant? Is there anything that has been over-looked that should be disclosed to the defence to ensure a fair trial? To prepare the simplest trial properly takes at least an hour. A trial with any factual complexity requires two to three hours minimum.

In a list, I typically had around five minutes' prep per trial. In which time I would also need to visit the witnesses, deal with queries from defence solicitors asking for disclosure,* and chase missing evidence by calling a CPS duty lawyer sitting in an office and praying they picked up the phone. As I say, less than ideal.

My first day is slightly different; the court to which I am being sent is next to the CPS office, which opens at 7 a.m., so I am allowed to attend early to collect the files. Whereas in a standard case, counsel would be sent a brief by the solicitor, containing written instructions about the case and carefully ordering the relevant evidence, prosecution lists involve picking up the entire CPS file, placing it into some sort of coherent order and picking out the bones. While I've watched a couple of lists in first six, this is my first attempt at making sense out of a file

---

* The prosecution are under a continuing duty of disclosure – that is, to hand to the defence any material in the prosecution's possession which is capable, reasonably, of undermining the prosecution case or assisting the defence. A huge proportion of miscarriages of justice arise out of disclosure failings – and successive reports over the last decade have shown this to be a problem in – incredibly – the majority of criminal cases.

by myself, and my eyes blur in a whirlpool of witness statements, exhibits, internal police and CPS documents, reviews, unused material, MG3s, MG3As, MG5s, MG6s, MG6C, D and Es, MG10s, PPI logs – the acronym soup gets gloopier the more I read. I fire off text messages to junior colleagues in chambers, begging their advice at what feels like thirty-second intervals.

In order to decipher what has happened in the case previously, I am reliant on the hand-scrawled endorsement of the preceding advocate – itself a mash of spidery contractions. 'DNA. PIA refused. WNBFB. Adj 10/4.' [Defendant did not attend. Application to proceed to trial in absence refused by the magistrates. Warrant issued for the defendant's arrest. Trial adjourned to 10 April.] Two hours to plough through the three trials I have been given (I have been handed a mercifully short list as it is my first day) flash by – I could easily have spent twelve. There is no time to stop and appreciate the solitude – the first day in six months that I have not been under the watchful eye of Alan or another senior colleague – but I am continuously, sickeningly aware of my lack of stabilisers. The training wheels are off. I'm flying without wings. And it feels inevitable that I will crash.

When the court building opens at nine, the bedlam begins. Not a second is spared; the magistrates' court is the A & E of the justice system – scores of desperate and/or intoxicated people poured into waiting areas, a new unforeseen problem arising every five minutes, police officers randomly sprinting across concourses to break up fights. There's nothing quite like it.

Reliving that first day conjures violent flashbacks. It will suffice to summarise it as including three full trials, two solicitor opponents far more experienced than me, one unrepresented defendant, two contested legal arguments, one absent interpreter, one fake interpreter attempting to persuade me to grant him access to the cells, ten phone calls to the CPS duty lawyer,* a broken photocopier, ten witnesses unable to access their witness statements, two absent complainants, reams of missing evidence, one police officer who has been told to attend in error, three very forbearing magistrates and no time to stop for a sip of water between 9 a.m. and 6.30 p.m.

No day has ever been as daunting or overwhelming as that first list. The only people keeping me alive were the legal advisor and the usher, patiently and kindly midwifing me through what they knew was my first day. Without their kindness, I have no idea how I'd have survived. I often tell pupils in what I intend as reassurance: if you can get through a mags list, everything else is easy by comparison. And that may well be true for the professionals, but is this really what we want for the 95 per cent of criminal cases dealt with in these courts? Should we be settling for a system where prosecutors are given minimal notice of the cases they are running? In which trials are stacked on top of each other – even less realistically than in the Crown Courts – with witnesses compelled to waste a day of their lives waiting for a hearing that is never going to be called on? What faith are the people involved – defendants, victims, witnesses – supposed to have in this? It was the way for years before I started, and remains the way years later. And my own perspective has remained static since that very first day: *If I were a victim of crime, or accused of a crime, this is the very last place I would want my case to be tried.*

---

* As an agent, you are powerless. So if the defence offers a sensible alternative plea, or you spot a giant hole in the evidence that can't be filled, you can't take the obvious decision yourself. You have to find somewhere with phone signal and call the CPS lawyer on duty, who will know nothing about the case, and take your instructions from them.

Long haul

In my second week of baby barristering in my own right, I am treated to my furthest-flung mags list, which calls for a furry-eyed 4.30 a.m. start and a three-hour bus ride to the coast. I wait outside in the rain until 9 a.m. (court security won't let agents into the building before nine) and sprint in to find my files. The CPS messenger hasn't yet delivered them, and doesn't stroll in with his overflowing rattan bag until shortly before 10 a.m. Begging the magistrates for time, I am granted fifteen minutes to read and prep four trials, containing approximately 500 pages of documentation. Somehow – it can only have been largely by guesswork – we manage to crack two trials and blitz our way through another by 4.30 p.m., the end of the court day.

Or not. The magistrates – knowing how far I have to travel but observing that, as they live locally, they can stay 'until nine if need be' – decree at 4.30 that we are starting the fourth trial, which has an estimated length of four hours. Mercifully, I am saved by our star witness, who, when told of the mags' plans, responds succinctly: 'They can get to fuck if they think I'm staying all night. What are my kids supposed to do?'

The magistrates having reluctantly agreed to adjourn, I get home at 8 p.m., to start on a (unpaid)* written advice I need to do for a solicitor. I have my first meal of the day at 10 p.m. The next morning I wake to a phone call from my clerk, Paula. The CPS have complained about me for 'having kept the magistrates waiting until 10.15 a.m. to start the court list'.

---

* Pretty much any time you see reference to written work in publicly funded criminal law, it will be unpaid. That's the superb deal we fat cats managed to strike for ourselves.

Missing in (red)action

A few weeks in, one of my list trials includes a man charged with fraud who, frustrated with what he perceived as unsatisfactory parking by his neighbours, has allegedly printed hundreds of official-looking penalty charge stickers and posted them on the windscreens of those he deemed to be transgressors, reasoning that if he could not improve the parallel parking of the residents on his street, he could at least inveigle £75 a pop out of them. He is not legally represented – the means test for legal aid being absurdly restrictive in the magistrates' court,* forcing many people to self-represent – and so hasn't had the benefit of the robust advice he would have received to plead guilty. So here we all are – me, standing in the witness suite with a dozen prosecution witnesses, each seemingly with a dozen supporters each trying to ask a dozen questions.

The statements are all handwritten by the police,† and so almost entirely illegible.‡ What is clear, however, is that each

---

* It is a hideously complex formula, but put simply, if you and your partner's combined gross annual income (marginally adjusted to reflect the number of people in your home) is £22,325 or more, you are not entitled to a penny of legal aid in the magistrates' court. The Crown Court is not much better – if your joint household disposable income is £37,500 or more, you are ineligible for legal aid. Worse, if you are acquitted, you are unable to reclaim your private legal rates in full. It means that many households who are far from wealthy – say those including teachers, nurses or (whisper it) legal-aid lawyers – would not qualify for financial assistance, and could be left bankrupted if wrongly accused of a crime.

† Witness statements are written by the police based on their interview with a witness, and the witness then reads and signs the statement to confirm that it is true and accurate.

‡ It is completely hit and miss in the mags as to whether witness statements have been typed up. It basically depends on whether the police

statement carries on its face the witness's home address. This is standard practice; however, unless a witness's address is relevant to the case (e.g. in a burglary, where the parties need to know which property is said to have been burgled), the police or CPS will redact it from the witness statement before it is served on the defence. For obvious reasons. Few witnesses wish to place their home address in the hands of someone they might be assisting to convict.

In this case, it transpires, no such redaction has taken place. The witnesses' addresses have been left in, and, because the defendant doesn't qualify for legal aid, the prosecution papers have been served directly on him.

It is one of the witnesses who first spots this when I hand out copies of their statements for them to review before the trial begins. 'Excuse me – should my address appear on this? The defendant won't have seen this, will he?'

Rarely have I felt as impotent as I did standing there before those twelve horrified people, offering sincere vicarious apologies and meaningless words of reassurance, but no explanation at all as to how this had happened. Whether any of those twelve would ever cooperate with the police again in future, should they witness a crime, is probably an easier question to answer.

No latecomers

I soon learn that adjournments are actively discouraged in the mags. Speedy summary justice means that most cases should be concluded in two hearings – the first appearance, and the trial (and sentence for the losers) a few months later. Applications to

---

typists have had enough time. Some officers are issued with tablet computers, allowing them to type witness statements as they take them, but many are still reliant on pen and paper.

push a trial back to a later date because one party isn't ready seldom succeed. In principle, encouraging the prosecution and defence to get things right first time by withholding second chances sounds sensible enough; in practice, a lot of innocent people get punished on the altar of expediency.

No adjournments means that if the prosecution encounter a witness problem on the day of trial or a piece of evidence has been missed (one of which happens in almost every mags case), you have to crack on with what you've got, or, if what you've got isn't enough to string together a viable trial, offer no evidence. In 2017, a DJ* refused to adjourn a trial when a complainant in a sex case couldn't attend because five members of her family had been killed the night before trial.[†]

For the defence, no adjournments holds that if the defendant doesn't turn up, he's unlikely to be given a second chance – the prosecution will apply to proceed to trial in his absence (PIA), and the defendant will inevitably be convicted.

My first exposure to PIA comes when prosecuting the alleged – and achingly vintage – theft of a car stereo in a mags list. By 10.30 a.m. the defendant has not arrived. His solicitor having no explanation and being unable to contact his client on his mobile, I apply to proceed in absence, and the trial begins. Ten minutes in, the defendant arrives, pink-faced and out of breath. The bench announce, in the face of both lawyers' protestations, that he is to wait outside the courtroom until the trial is over, nose pressed up against the soundproof glass and screaming into the void as his fate is determined without him.[‡]

---

* District Judge, remember? Not Disc Jockey. Never Disc Jockey.
† R (DPP) v. Birmingham Magistrates' Court [2017] EWHC 3444.
‡ You may be relieved/even more horrified to know that this was not only grossly unfair, but also spectacularly unlawful. Viva les mags!

My first client

As a second sixer, I am at the very bottom rung of the chambers ladder, and so the very first port of call for the least desirable cases. If a defendant who is on the run has been arrested and taken to court, I am the lucky bunny schlepping forty miles to court to defend or prosecute that lucrative (£30 after deductions) hearing. If the clerks miss a case in the court list that needs immediate cover, I am the one whose empty afternoon, conscientiously set aside to tackle a mound of case preparation and written advices, is whipped away at a phone call's notice.

It sounds like a lament (and it is), but this is also the way that, as a newbie, I accrue the opportunities to forge connections with new solicitors and impress new clients and demonstrate myself to the pupillage committee as being the Right Sort of Person, so, remembering Alan's wise counsel, the word 'no' never escapes my lips.

The first papers day* I have lasts until 10.16, when my phone rings and Paula breaks the good news: 'A solicitor has just collapsed at court. The magistrates have refused to adjourn, so you've got yourself a nice defence trial, SB! Get your skates on – they want to get started.'

On arrival, I am handed the solicitor's hulking file. The defendant, Majid, is charged with harassment of his cousin, a baker's dozen of alleged incidents stretching back over many months. Getting my head around the case will take a few hours. Majid has been remanded in custody, and so taking his instructions involves locating the Urdu interpreter and battling my way to the cells. Before I can do so, the magistrates call the case on. They thank me for stepping into the breach, and I explain that I will need at least the rest of the morning to get to grips with

* Literally a day set aside to do papers, as opposed to being in court.

the case. They nod, confer at length and eventually deliver their considered judgment: 'You have fifteen minutes.' I tactfully choose not to scream 'HAVE YOU DUNDERHEADS THE FAINTEST NOTION OF WHAT PREPARING A DEFENCE TRIAL ACTUALLY INVOLVES?', nor to point out that, in the time they have taken to make this very simple decision, and to get it wrong, I could have had an invaluable extra half hour with my client, and instead I fawningly thank them for their benevolence before legging it to the cells.

What follows is a panicked maelstrom of skim-reading and mangled half-interpreted dialogue as I do my level best to process the evidence, take Majid's instructions and formulate a vague strategy for cross-examining the three prosecution witnesses. When the trial is called on, I improvise through my stumbling cross-examination, manage to elicit a vaguely coherent account from Majid in the witness box, and treat the magistrates to a circumlocutory forty-five-minute closing ramble about the burden and standard of proof,* and somehow, as the clock turns 6 p.m., Majid is gloriously, improbably acquitted.

I step out of court into the driving twilight rain, feeling utterly invincible. *This* is what being a barrister is about. Seat-of-your-pants, thinking-on-your-feet, buccaneering advocacy, safeguarding the little guy against the machinations of the state. I have arrived.

But while it was a valuable learning curve and gives me a

---

* The so-called 'golden thread' running through our criminal justice system: The prosecution have to prove the allegation (the burden of proof), and to prove it they have to make the magistrates/jury 'sure' of guilt (the standard of proof). As a rule, the more a defence advocate refers to this in their closing speech to a jury, the more overwhelming the evidence against their client is.

passable war story to take back to the other pupils, even as I am polishing my ego on the bus ride home it is hard, objectively, to exonerate – much less justify – the way in which that trial was handled. My client has been acquitted, which was the top and bottom line for him. But we can't assess justice solely by outcome; for one thing, none of us, except the people present when the alleged offence was committed, knows the truth of our cases. I have no idea whether, as I put to the tearful complainant, her accusations were malicious fantasies born of a family dispute over money, or whether Majid was indeed a vindictive and obsessive menace. Even I, green as I am, cannot equate a professional victory with justice.

So much of our system is built on the idea of procedural justice; of rules fairly and equally applied, and evidence fairly and independently assessed. And while I know that there are those who say it's not our place to worry about such things – our role is simply to represent our client to the best of our abilities, to take the playing field as we find it – I do again question whether this stack-'em-high, production-line style of justice in our lower courts is fit for purpose. Had Majid been convicted and imprisoned in those circumstances – represented by a lawyer-in-Pampers who hadn't even been given time to read the evidence – I would have considered it an outrageous injustice. And therein, I guess, lies my answer.

I'm grateful to my friend

During a nightmare mags list, I spot that a fingerprint expert, whose evidence is disputed by the defence, hasn't been warned to attend trial. If a witness statement isn't agreed between the parties, and if the witness doesn't attend court, you don't have any evidence. Panicking that my application for an adjournment will be refused by the magistrates and I will have to drop the case – and that this will somehow be my fault – salvation arrives in the form of a kindly defence solicitor, who reassures me that, if I apply to adjourn the trial for a few months to get the fingerprint expert to court, he will not object.

Had I had more than a few months' experience and more than two hours' sleep, I might have spotted that our case is overwhelming even without the fingerprint evidence. And that the proposed agreed adjournment would mean that the case went off until after Christmas, with the defendant on bail. Add a crystal ball into the mix, and I would have seen that, at the next hearing, when there was no route of escape, the defendant, having had a very merry Christmas with his nearest and dearest, would plead guilty to the theft and receive his eight weeks' custody.

Instead, overcome with gratitude, when making my application to adjourn I publicly thank my opponent for his 'kind and generous agreement', telling myself that I must be imagining the Mutley-esque sniggering from the dock.

Keres & Co

As the pages of the calendar fly off in the montage of my budding magistrates' practice, the composition of my cases is split roughly fifty-fifty – half of my cases are prosecuting lists, the other half defending first appearances, trials and sentences for the defence solicitors who entrust me with their (often long-standing) clients. Keres & Co are one such firm, and might most charitably be described as incorrigible shysters. They send a lot of heavyweight work into the senior bods in chambers, and in return for this loyalty have the pick of the junior end to handle their magistrates' work. Their business model – encouraged, it becomes clear, by the low fixed-fee model of payment under legal aid – is to get the client signed up, sit back and do the absolute bare minimum. Either the client will end up pleading guilty, or, if it has to be a trial, the case can be briefed out to counsel at the eleventh hour for us to sort out. There are never any written instructions from the clients; no witness statements will have been taken, no disclosure chased. The very practice of law is apparently alien to them, and the gleaming, pinstriped Mr Keres can more likely be found in the pub on a weekday afternoon than in court.

The first file for my first Keres client, delivered at 5.55 p.m. the night before trial, is virtually empty. There is a police summary, a laughably named client care letter, and that is it. I thus turn up to the trial the next morning and as my first order of business have to beg the prosecutor to give me a copy of the evidence. (In what remains the finest example of officious prosecuting I have seen in my career, the initial response is: 'We've already sent a copy to your solicitors, so I don't *technically* have to give you a copy.')

Once in the cells, it is obvious that something isn't right. For one, my client is fixated with the notion that I have been sent by the Labour Party and am in league with the prosecution. For two, he keeps asking me why I am carrying a firearm.* Taking meaningful instructions is impossible – the man is plainly severely psychiatrically unwell. He is in obvious need of an assessment, treatment and specialist intervention. A competent firm of solicitors would have recognised this and addressed it months ago. I explain the position to the magistrates, who, despite the objections of the prosecutor ('I've known Mr Keres for many years, and I can't believe he'd miss something as obvious as this.') agree to adjourn the trial for medical enquiries to be made.

---

* For the avoidance of doubt, neither of these were accurate.

That marks the end of my involvement in that case. I later learn that upon receiving my attendance note, Keres had taken the case back under his wing, arranged for it to be listed the next week, and attended court himself to button his jacket and smooth his lime-green tie and calmly assure the magistrates that his client was absolutely fine, that the inexperienced baby barrister had become 'panicked and overwhelmed', and that his completely well client would, after all, be pleading guilty.

Putting Keres's flagrant professional malpractice to one side, he was inadvertently right about one thing – I absolutely was panicked and overwhelmed. While I had been taught the procedural law concerning defendants with mental ill health, I had never been one on one in a confined environment with somebody exhibiting serious mental health problems, bearing – in that moment, at least – sole responsibility for their welfare. I had no clue how to talk to him, how to reassure him, how to help him. This simply isn't in the Bar school training. It would be akin to presenting a psychiatrist with a patient who has a legal problem and expecting her to advise on litigation procedure. Given the prevalence of mental ill health across the criminal justice system – rare is the defendant with no reported history – this seems an obvious, potentially dangerous, shortcoming in our profession.

And while there has been progress over the past decade – the courts are far more attuned to recognising vulnerable defendants and witnesses, and making adjustments at trials and providing intermediaries – and while diligent practitioners will undertake their own training for communicating with vulnerable defendants, it all still feels piecemeal; somehow lacking.

I regularly speak to police officers who report similar unease at the ubiquity of mental ill health among the people with whom they have the most contact, and the relative sparsity of training. 'We're not medics or social workers' may be a clichéd police complaint about the roles they are expected to fill, but it is true. A police officer's lot in the twenty-first century properly involves more than slapping handcuffs on stripey-topped felons, but it is not fair on them, nor the people they serve and protect, to fail to equip them with what are, increasingly obviously, essential skills for anybody involved in front-line criminal justice. The same principle, it is equally increasingly obvious, must apply to barristers too.

First hearing in the Crown Court

Learning at 6 p.m. that I am to debut my wig and gown the following morning at my very first Crown Court hearing* freezes the blood in my veins. The clerks have apparently identified me as suitably proficient/available to stand in for a senior colleague at a faraway Crown Court, and the junior tenants sitting with me in the criminal common room† all chirrup their support as I absorb the news. It's happening – I am going to be dressing, and possibly even acting, like a real barrister.

That night, as I carefully fold my black robe into my suitcase, trying not to overthink the momentousness of the occasion, my phone chirps with a missive from Alan. He's obviously been told by the clerks about my impending ascension, and wishes to impart his own words of support: 'COURT IS A SHITHOLE. PARK IN BUS STATION. DON'T FORGET CHANGE.' I appreciate the sentiment, even if I don't have a car.

The day itself spins past before I can really take it in. The

---

* Wigs and gowns are not worn in the mags.
† The room in chambers where we gather to procrastinate once we've finished in court, waiting for the clerks to confirm our diaries for the following day.

prosecutor applies for the confiscation order* that has been agreed by the barrister whose case I am covering, the judge asks me if the defence agree, and I squeak, 'Yes, Your Honour' with sufficient confidence that an onlooker may have mistaken this for my second or third ever appearance in court, rather than my first. If I hadn't left my papers in the robing room, or if I had realised before I was two hours into my train journey home, I dare say it would have been the perfect day.

Judges

I quickly adjust to the mild stage fright of appearing in front of magistrates. After all, my mother told me, Mrs Rathbone who had lived opposite us growing up was a magistrate, and her son Tim once stole my Casio watch when we were both five and she and her husband used to hold special adult parties on 'Bonus Tuesdays', so they're just ordinary people, really. Crown Court judges, on the other hand, absolutely terrify me. Even the nice ones. It takes me at least a year until I feel even semi-confident contradicting them, let alone standing up to them, which no doubt makes me an entirely ineffective barrister.

When you start, you notice senior practitioners (or junior practitioners trying to sound senior) referring to judges by their first names. A sign of ageing is when you start to see people you knew as barristers appointed as judges, and find yourself doing the same thing. Suddenly judges are not petrifying vessels of legal omnipotence, but people you once shared an outrageous joke with, only sporting a new costume (and, in the worst cases, a new personality disorder – Judgeitis, the symptoms of which,

---

* If you gain a financial benefit from your crime, the prosecution can confiscate potentially everything you own – and anything you *will ever* own – to recoup your illicit gain.

to borrow from Alan, are 'acting like a cunt to everybody in sight').

However, one thing I do manage to nail pretty quickly is Modes of Address – the proper way to refer to a judge in court, depending on rank. For the benefit of future generations, I offer the following handy refresher:

Modes of address:

— Magistrate/District Judge – Sir/Madam (or collectively 'Your worships')

— Circuit Judge (Crown Court) – Your Honour

— Honorary Recorder, High Court Judge, Lord/Lady Justice of Appeal/Supreme Court Justice – My Lord/Lady or Your Lordship/Ladyship

— Minor royalty – Your Highness

— Queen – Your Majesty

— Pope – Your Holiness

While it is unlikely that you will encounter any of the last three sitting in court, I have heard all those honorifics deployed by defendants addressing judges, and, when it happens, it may just be one of the finest things about this whole job.

The robing room
The Crown Court robing room is literally that – a room in which barristers unzip their suitcases and put on their court robes, collars, bands and wigs. It's also the social nerve centre of any court building, serving as a bubbling hub of frantic

last-minute written prep, pre-match inter-counsel haggling, viral gossip and improbable-story one-upmanship, as well as offering a crucial pool of wisdom for anybody stuck with a tricky legal problem. It is at its busiest and bustliest first thing in the morning as barristers pile in and ready themselves for the morning list, and at lunchtime as frenzied trial advocates work through the legal issues for the afternoon's session, but bodies swill in and out throughout the day, in gaps between hearings or when juries go out,* so the room seldom falls silent.

Desks will be informally reserved, German-tourist style, by coats or paper bundles proprietarily strewn. Depending on your luck, you may have access to a small law library and a canteen hawking tea, coffee and hot breakfasts, or you may find no books and a kettle that was last PAT tested in 1992. You are guaranteed at least one locker stuffed with files and a men's suit jacket that have been in situ as long as anybody can remember, but which nobody has any intention of reclaiming or removing. Think of a sixth-form common room, but with cheaper furniture and less angsty prog rock, and you're getting close.

For a first-timer, it can be an overwhelming, sometimes intimidating environment. Even when you've been doing the job for years, entering a robing room in a new city where everybody knows each other can spin you back to New Kid At School mode, as you quietly survey the raucous action, gauge the personalities on display and try to work out who your opponent is.

But even hundreds of miles from home, what marks the robing room is the collegiality. The way in which opponents who have spent the entire day loudly and publicly demolishing each other's arguments would take off their wigs and kick back

---

* 'Jury out' = a jury which has retired after a trial to deliberate on its verdict(s).

as colleagues, rather than adversaries, was something I'd seen on mini-pupillage, and had obviously witnessed from the side-lines in first six, but it was only on transitioning from observer to participant that I appreciated its value.

It is such a strange dynamic. Sometimes tempers flare when a bad tackle or the occasional deliberate foul is made, and some players are known for their intentionally dirty or confronta-tional style, but largely our adversarial system is notable for the undercurrent of collaboration, among the advocates at least. Partly it's a coping mechanism. Partly, I think, it's attributable to independence; the fact that we are instructed on a case-by-case basis, taking whichever brief, prosecution or defence, that comes our way, means that it is probably easier to maintain a sense of objectivity, to hover at least a few inches above the fray. The atmosphere certainly defied my US-TV-generated expect-ations, with death-penalty-chasing District Attorneys pitted in personal, existential combat against dyed-in-the-wool public defenders.

I expect it runs counter to most people's perceptions of crim-inal lawyers. I think we sometimes forget how unnerving it must be for clients when the bonhomie leaks out of the robing room and into the public areas. Seeing your lawyer joshing with the prosecutor intent on convicting you is unlikely to inspire you with confidence as you psyche yourself up to be cross-examined. And the explanation – that we're all part of the same machine, with the same overarching ephemeral goal (justice), who just happen to be competing for entirely opposite outcomes – pro-vokes more questions than it answers.

It would help to have an analogy, but I don't think that one exists. In a hospital, all the professionals want the same result for the human being lying in front of them. Whereas in the courts, for every 'patient' there is one doctor trying to save them, one trying to finish them off and one much more experienced consultant largely ambivalent about their fate but anxious to ensure that the doctors play by Queensberry rules in their life-or-death tug-of-war.

Witness handling

Something which I don't think is widely appreciated by those outside the system is just how uncontrollable a live witness can be. While all witnesses provide a witness statement in advance of a trial, so the parties know what the witness is *expected* to say, it is what is actually said from the witness box that stands as evidence in a criminal case.* Until studying ethics at Bar school, I hadn't realised that it is forbidden for either side's lawyers to 'coach' witnesses, or the defendant, on what to say or how to present. I remember reading something in a trashy American crime novel involving acting coaches being hired to hone witnesses into paragons of sympathetic, trustworthy jury-bait; over here, aside from general advice (talk loudly and clearly; don't lose your temper; take off that NWA T-shirt) we can't intervene to improve a witness. We are reliant on our skill of questioning to elicit the best evidence; the rest is in the lap of the gods.

Which brings us to my first taste of contested advocacy in the Crown Court, involving a fifteen-year-old boy called Adeel.

Adeel has been convicted by the Youth Court of breaching a curfew imposed by the court for a previous offence. The Youth Offending Team (YOT) say that when they went round to Adeel's address during curfew hours, he was not present. Adeel maintains that he was; he was in the bathroom, and his mum

---

* Unless your evidence is uncontentious, in which case to save time the parties will agree to your witness statement being read to the court.

told the YOT officer as much, but they refused to listen and reported him for breach. He has been convicted in absence by the magistrates having failed to turn up for his trial in the Youth Court, so he is availing himself of his automatic right to a fresh hearing before the Crown Court.*

The YOT officer's evidence is straightforward. He knocked, mum answered the door, he asked where Adeel was, mum didn't know, a quick look around the house yielded no Adeel. My cross-examination doesn't really make a dent. This will all hinge on Adeel's credibility in confidently assuring the court that he was at home at the time of the visit.

I call him to the witness box and ask him where he was at 7 p.m. on Saturday 15 June.

'I can't remember.'

This, of course, is not what appears in the proof of evidence† that Adeel has read and approved twenty minutes earlier. Proof of Evidence Adeel can clearly remember where he was. He was

---

* Anybody convicted and sentenced in the mags has an automatic right to appeal to the Crown Court and have a completely fresh trial, although in front of a Crown Court judge and two magistrates, rather than a jury. This automatic right of appeal from the magistrates is the systemic corrective – and frankly a bald admission – to the chaos that prevails in the court below and the widespread scope for injustice. By contrast, to appeal a Crown Court conviction or sentence, you need permission from the Court of Appeal before they'll allow you to darken their doorstep. (Technically you can also be granted permission by the Crown Court judge who presided over the decision you're appealing, but surprisingly enough it's pretty rare for a judge to say, 'You know what? I think you're right. We've probably ballsed this right up.')

† 'Proof of evidence' = a witness statement taken from the defendant. It is not served on the prosecution, but is used by the defence lawyers as their guide to what the client is saying.

in the bath, writhing in ecstasy amidst the bubbles as the YOT officer failed to heed his mother's pleas. But Live Grinning Witness Adeel, blinded into inanity by the stage lights, has gone violently off-proof. With experience you learn to hide your surprise when this happens. Right now, I do not have that experience. After a pause of approximately four years, I stammer a rephrased version of the question.

'Would . . . where . . . were you at home or were you out of the house?'

'I can't remember.'

'Do you remember an occasion when you heard a YOT officer at the front door?'

'I can't remember.'

I release Adeel from his torment and he trots, with inexplicable unearned confidence, back to his seat. It is OK. This is salvageable. I still have mum. My ace in the hole. Her witness statement is clear – she told the YOT officer that Adeel was in the bath. Mum, I am sure, will reverse us out of this cul-de-sac.

If you have ever watched Baldrick give evidence at Blackadder's court martial, you will have a pretty clear vision of how mum's evidence went:

'Were you at home at seven p.m. on Saturday fifteenth?'

'Yes!'

'And was Adeel at home at that time?'

'No!'

[PAUSE. SHUFFLE PAPERS.]

'Do . . . you know where he was?'

'He must have been out!'

'Umm, are you sure he wasn't in the bathroom?'

JUDGE: 'You have your answer. He was out. Now do you have any further questions?'

He doesn't even try to hide his amusement. I sit down, defeated, wishing I'd paid greater heed to Alan's maxim against calling defence witnesses ('However good you think they will be, they will find a way to fuck up your case.'). The prosecutor has no further questions for this manna-from-heaven-case-winning witness. I am then forced to make a closing speech in which I have literally nothing to say, beyond four or five babbled iterations of the Burden and Standard of Proof (Sample: 'The prosecution have to make you *sure* of guilt – can Your Honour and Your Honour's colleagues really be *sure*? I mean, *sure*? The burden is on them. The standard? *Sure*. You must be sure. You can't be sure. Can you? Sure.') The judge and magistrates don't even retire. They literally stand up, walk to the door and immediately loop back and return to their seats to dismiss the appeal. Adeel is given an extra twenty-eight days on his curfew.

Money money money

Every single one of my mini-pupillages involved at least one conversation in which a weary veteran delivered a sombre warning: Don't Do Crime. There's No Money In It.

Naturally, I, like the rest of my cohort, took such warnings with a punnet of salt. 'No money', although framed as an absolute, is usually relative. 'No Money' to somebody wearing nice clothes and able to put a roof over their head is likely to involve Some Money, Actually, In Fact Probably Quite A Bit, Just Not As Much As They'd Like. If our comparator is the (not inaccurate) stereotype of the commercial barrister, draped in Savile Row and rolling in a six- or seven-figure income, one could still be comfortably off and feel very much the poor relation.

Throughout pupillage, senior colleagues would occasionally hark back to the halcyon 1980s and early 1990s, when publicly funded criminal law really did pay extremely well. 'Time was,' I was told with a sigh during one trial, 'that after a piddly little case like this, you'd stick your bill in and go and buy a terraced house in the north.'

But decades of cuts to legal aid and a twenty-year freeze on prosecution rates had radically altered the landscape. The first clue was in the level of pupillage awards on offer for criminal pupillages. Pupillages used to be wholly unfunded – if you didn't have the means to support yourself for a year, the door to the Bar was immediately closed to you. In fact, that's not quite right; up until 1975, pupils would *pay* their pupilmasters 100 guineas for the privilege. It was only in 2003 that chambers were required to pay a minimum pupillage award. While some criminal sets go beyond that sum, some – especially in London – do not. This isn't simply parsimony; pupillages are funded by chambers, so by barristers. If the barristers collectively aren't bringing in much, there's a knock-on effect.

And there's no obligation on chambers to offer pupillages at all. If barristers decided overnight en masse that they were not going to fund pupillages any more, or found themselves unable to, there's no national back-up plan. The government would suddenly find that the pool of advocates for prosecuting and defending criminal cases had dried up.

That, it transpired, was a very real risk. The rates of pay during pupillage, once you were undertaking your own work, could be dismal. A defence trial in the magistrates' court, which could involve four or five hours' prep, plus four hours' travel, plus eight hours at court, would pay £150 if you were lucky. Chambers take around 20 per cent of that, and once you've deducted travel, professional insurance, practising certificate fees, sundry expenses and tax, you're taking home around £50 for sixteen hours' work.

Prosecuting in the Crown Court was not much better. A committal for sentence – a case in which the defendant has pleaded guilty at the magistrates' court and has been sent to the Crown Court to be sentenced – might involve reading hundreds of pages of evidence and preparing an extensive written opening – potentially three or four hours' work – and you could find yourself stuck at court waiting six hours for the case to be called on, all for the gross sum of £85 plus VAT.*

One of the added perks of second six is that you will also be called upon to do work for free, in the promise of future, paid briefs being sent into chambers. These won't necessarily be briefs for *you*, of course. But we're a team and freebies for solicitors who instruct your senior colleagues are all part of being a team, so you obligingly shut up and eat your gruel.

Many criminal pupils and junior tenants literally can't survive in the job. Those who can usually have the fallback of family money or an unusually busy practice. I was exceptionally fortunate to fall into the latter – not, I emphasise, through my own ability, but that of my clerks to funnel more work my way than my talents warranted.

Nevertheless, as the years passed, more and more of my criminal co-pupils sidled into better-paid areas of law, or left the Bar altogether. Today, I only know of one other of my peers still in full-time criminal practice. It's a pattern replicated across the country; the attrition rate at the five- and ten-year mark, particularly among women looking to start a family, is frightening.

---

* In 2019, these fixed prosecution fees were increased for the first time in decades, so that a mention hearing – a hearing listed because either one of the parties or the court wants to discuss something that has arisen – pays £91 and a committal for sentence pays £150. The *Daily Telegraph* breathlessly reported it as 'Criminal barristers win doubling in fees', which, while technically correct . . .

There's an unhappy mirroring with the belated efforts being made by the Bar to increase diversity; just as we are finally opening the profession to those without entrenched material privilege, the government is driving them out the second they set foot through the door.

Media darling

It takes only three months for me to make my first appearance in the press. After a trip out of town, a local paper runs with 'Drunk thug banged up for racist singing' on page 22, reporting the sentence of a client, Dave, who received sixteen weeks' imprisonment from the magistrates for a very unpleasant incident outside a pub. And I am mentioned by name!

Alas, the report contains two technical errors. First, it wrongly states that Dave has been imprisoned for a racially aggravated 'section 5' public order offence* (singing a famous Al Jolson song at the victim), whereas he was in fact fined for that offence and imprisoned for affray (threatening to 'kick the shit out of' the crowd of onlookers trying to break up Dave's impromptu performance). Although this sounds like legal pedantry, it's actually a rather important distinction, as a racially aggravated section 5 is punishable only by a fine – not prison.

Second, in the course of my mitigation, I realistically conceded that, because Dave was in breach of an existing suspended sentence, he would have to go prison, and, in an effort to illustrate

---

* Section 5 of the Public Order Act 1984 provided (at the time) an offence of using threatening, abusive or insulting words or behaviour to cause harassment, alarm or distress. A 'racially aggravated' version of the offence was created by section 31(1)(c) of the Crime and Disorder Act 1998, although, for reasons I have never understood, carries the same type of maximum penalty – a fine – as the non-racially aggravated offence.

Dave's contrition, I assured the magistrates that he would take advantage of whatever drug and alcohol support was available. This is reduced in the news report to me pronouncing that Dave 'wanted' to go to jail.

What this means, in short, is that to any prospective solicitors googling my name, my only reported court appearance for the whole of that year is one where I have successfully begged for my client to be locked up for a non-imprisonable offence.

The art of shutting up

There is often an overriding temptation to talk in court. One of the most important rules of advocacy, I quickly learn, is when to say nothing. That extra question asked of a witness to try and ram home your point can offer them an opportunity to wriggle out of the concession you had painstakingly extracted. Thickly laying on mitigation after the judge has tipped you the wink that she is minded to give your client what you're asking for is likely to serve as a judicial irritant. We know this – it is hammered home from Bar school and beyond – but the dissonance between being paid to speak and staying silent can overwhelm.

Covering a mention hearing in a serious multi-handed robbery case, and having listened attentively as the senior players around me quibble over dates for legal directions, I succumb to the temptation. My client deserves to at least hear my voice. Feeling pretty confident that the judge has misspoken when formally adjourning the case to the trial date, I stand up and respectfully point out that the trial is in fact on the twelfth. With slightly less respect, and to hoots from the public gallery, the judge points out that the twelfth is a Sunday, and asks whether my sole contribution to this hearing is really to invite him to open the court building and relist the trial on a weekend.

What's in a name

I'd not given criminal judges much thought before starting pupillage. Aside from a rootless certainty that they weren't sending criminals to prison for long enough, my impression was that they were all much of a muchness; a beige collage of staid middle-aged white men with little to differentiate them. Judicial impartiality, I'd assumed, left scant room for quirk or personality.

I was swiftly disabused. *Who's your judge?* is one of the first questions a colleague will ask if you're discussing a case, because while Lady Justice may be blind, the way your case will go often hinges on the views and idiosyncratic temperament of her understudy.

As a pupil, the uncertainty is nerve-shredding. You can say something in front of one judge without an eyelid being batted which, when repeated in front of another, provokes an eruption of judicial fury. Learning how to navigate the divergent judicial personalities is like attempting to Riverdance in a minefield. Your first time in front of certain judges can be an exercise in disabling a highly temperamental car alarm, randomly shrieking at you out of nowhere as you weep, *What have I done to deserve this?*

Today's appeal, before General Melchett soundalike HHJ* Cartwright, is one such treat. 'SB!' thunders the judge as I embark upon my examination of the first prosecution witness. 'I don't know what your pupilmaster taught you, but it is entirely improper for you to refer to witnesses by their Christian names. The gentleman you are asking about is "Mr Kane".' *Pupilmaster* and *Christian names* give a flavour of the epoch in which this judge is operating.

* His/Her Honour Judge

But . . . but . . . I want to cry out . . . *it's a punch-up at a family wedding. They're all called 'Kane'. The whole family. Forenames are the only way to distinguish them.* Too cowed to even consider answering back, however, I comply. Or at least, I try to. I resume my questioning.

'Mr Kane, when your brother Mr Kane hit your son Mr Kane, did you immediately tell your father Mr Kane?'

Mr Kane stares at me blankly. I look to the bench. Far from any recognition of the farce that he has instigated, Melchett is beaming with approval. And throughout the tortuous three hours that follow, he continues to beam every time I say 'Mr Kane', and to bark every time I slip and inject an illicit forename, in what he no doubt considers a formative lesson for this young pupil in the importance of fidelity to tradition. A tradition which, I learn upon returning to chambers that evening and reliving the day with some of the more senior juniors, Melchett has apparently entirely made up.

Girls and boys

My first trip to Southwark Crown Court is an eye-opener. Not so much because of its glorious setting, perched on the Thames with sweeping views of the capital's skyline and ready access to the delights of the South Bank, nor for its reputation as the Place to Be Tried for heavyweight white-collar crime, nor because, covering a pre-trial hearing for Alan, I am appearing in a very serious fraud case and feeling like a very serious barrister. Rather, Southwark stands out for its policy of banning women from the main robing room, redirecting them to two smaller, female-only rooms down the corridor.

While the tendency to refer to each other by surnames only and the NSFW gallows humour can sometimes lend a robing room the vibe of a locker room, nobody actually gets undressed,* so there is no need at all for separate quarters. Southwark's state of affairs, in place since the 1980s, not only ensured that the men got the biggest room with the best facilities, but excluded women from the vital wheeling and dealing taking place between the lads. If you were a woman in a multi-defendant case, it meant that crucial conversations about your case might be taking place between your co-defending male counsel and the male prosecutor in your absence.

Southwark's gender segregation was ended in 2017 by a (female) senior judge, but it is replicated in several courts across the country. Again, it bears the classic hallmarks of one of those Bar traditions that are unthinkingly tolerated as 'harmless', but which do absolutely nothing to counter the impression that the legal profession is most comfortable in the 1950s.

Toil and trouble

Since the early 2010s, we haven't had court stenographers in the Crown Courts. Nowadays, everything in court is digitally recorded and the records are retained for seven years before deletion. Which is a pity, because it means that there is no longer any earthly record of my effort to finalise the terms of a restraining order in front of an elderly and very hard-of-hearing judge:

SB: And finally, the prosecution seeks a prohibition on the defendant attending the victim's place of work, the Hobble Bobble Soft Play Centre.

JUDGE: Hobble hobble?

* Or nobody *should* get undressed.

SB: No, Hobble Bobble.

JUDGE: Wobble bobble?

SB: Hobble Bobble.

JUDGE: Ah, Bobbly Wobbly.

SB: Hobble Bobble, Your Honour.

JUDGE: Hobble BOBBLE! Not Bobble Wobble.

SB: Not Bobble Wobble, no, Your Honour. Hobble Bobble.

JUDGE: Very good. Hobble Wobble.

The only way is ethics

At Bar school, the professional ethics component of our assessment was built into the other, skills-based, modules, such as advocacy or conference skills. An ethical problem would magically present itself – like a 'client'* in conference casually mentioning that he was guilty but wanted you to lie to the court for him – and if you leaped over the elephant trap you'd get your tick for professional ethics. The unmissable blatancy was a running joke among the students, who even at our zygotic stage of development were pretty sure that the ethical quandaries that arise in practice would be slightly more nuanced than a gravel-voiced opponent offering to bung you some cash to throw your client's case.

So the examiners would presumably feel vindicated to read

---

* Clients were invariably played by drama students or resting actors. Or sometimes neither – one of my many pre-Bar school temp jobs involved playing a 'patient' for trainee doctors. My efforts at feigning kidney stones were, though I say so myself, Olivier-worthy, but sadly they must have lost my phone number for the next round of exams.

that, four months into second six, I am approached by my gravel-voiced opponent and offered a bung to drop the case I am prosecuting. It is a barrister I have never encountered before, and will never encounter again (a quick scan of the Bar Standards Board website a few years later confirms he was disbarred for failing to keep up with his Continuing Professional Development obligations – presumably an Al Capone tax fraud-style prosecution). He is instructed by a spangly firm of private criminal law solicitors with a proud record of acting for celebrities, and is representing the daughter of a soap star in an appeal from the mags.

Having exhausted the standard template for bouncing pupils* – feigned outrage at the prosecution; spurious legal argument; obsequious compliments; veiled threats – he shuffles right up to my face, the choking scent of stale tobacco and ale assaulting my sinuses, and growls: 'Look, Mr [SOLICITOR] has a lot of very lucrative briefs. If you can see your way to making this all go away, I know I can get him to push a few your way.'

I squeak the firmest 'No thank you' that my shock permits, and we trot into court to fix the date for the appeal four months hence. It never goes ahead, as it happens; the appellant deciding to accept her guilt and abandon the appeal before the next hearing.

What did I do? I'd like to tell you I immediately reported him to the Bar Standards Board and sparked the investigation that ultimately led to his disbarment. But I did what so many young juniors do when faced with abuses of power by their seniors; I questioned my judgement, doubted my instincts and allowed myself to believe it was all in my head.

---

* Bouncing = using your experiential advantage to pressure someone more junior into doing what you want them to.

Stranded

Packed off to prosecute a mags list in the back of beyond, I am given strict instructions to ensure that my six trial files are returned to the local CPS office at the end of the day, rather than, as is usual practice, locked in the CPS room at court for the messenger to collect the following morning. Having left court at 5 p.m., I duly stagger with the two-metre-high stack of files to the CPS office two miles across town in the driving evening rain. Forty-five minutes later, I arrive a bedraggled mess to find the lights off and the building shut down. With nobody answering the phones and no other point of contact, there is little option but to leave the files at court. Or there would be, were court, by the time I make it back at 6.30 p.m., not also locked up for the night.

I have felt the heat of public opprobrium several times during my professional career. Defending killers, rapists and child abusers as enraged shouts rain down from the public gallery can be unsettling; meeting the eyes of those same people as you leave the court building even more so. But never have I felt more vulnerable to immediate physical harm than on that rammed rush-hour train home, with my sprawling, sodden files occupying three precious seats as fifty standing commuters plotted my destruction.

Will the mini-pupil

I feel terrifically grown-up having my own mini-pupil shadow me for a mags list. But any sense that Will – six foot three, public-school tie, Prince Charming hair – feels correspondingly awed in my presence is quickly dispelled when, during my pre-trial introductions with the witnesses, he holds up his palm to stop me answering a question from the complainant, announcing with a toothy smile: 'I'll take this one'. It is a move that had

I, an actual qualified barrister, attempted with Alan, would have resulted in an Archbold* being thrown at my head. It is reassuring to learn that the Three-Piece-Suit Wankers were not unique to my generation; as Jesus said, they will always be with us.

As I scramble through the afternoon's trial papers in the CPS room over lunch, a reclining Will tells me that he has an entire summer of mini-pupils (or 'min-pups', as he bizarrely insisted on calling them) lined up. When fair and open competition did not bear fruit, a quick phone call from Daddy straightened out any misunderstandings, he haws.

My first thought is *How on earth can he afford not to work over the summer?* Actually my first thought is unprintable, but my second thought motors towards the financial mechanics of being able to take a whole two months of unpaid placements. Such unassuming privilege is astounding.

The station that that particular train of thought does not reach, however, is the relativity of privilege, and in particular my own. For while I had worked every school and university holiday to keep myself afloat, I was lucky enough to have the support of my parents to meet accommodation and tuition costs, and so while not able to take an entire summer off, was at least in a position to forego a week's wages in order to undertake my own min-pups. The notion that I wouldn't be able to afford to do them did not enter my head.

Nor, it seemed, did it trouble the minds of those who organised the profession. The assumption that all young people could afford to take an unpaid week – or, if you had to travel to a distant city, to pay hundreds of pounds in expenses – in order to get this necessary experience onto their CVs (it being

---

* The giant leaden criminal practitioner textbook that barristers had to lug around courts until we discovered electricity in the mid 2010s.

expected that applicants for pupillage undertake multiple 'minis') was prevalent. I don't think it was malicious; it was just that – an assumption. If money has never been a problem for you, a status historically applicable to the vast majority of the Bar, such things just don't cross your mind.

Lack of malice doesn't neutralise the assumption's perniciousness. Because it constructs yet another potentially insuperable barrier for people good enough to do this job, but not wealthy enough. And not having to jump that barrier was a privilege that I couldn't see until it was light years in the rear-view mirror. The privilege not to have to fret about the cost of a train fare, or about buying suitable attire to attend court, or having to negotiate time off from precarious part-time employment; the privilege not to have to think about whether you could *afford* to accept an irresistible career opportunity – this privilege was not just Will's, not just the TPSWs', but mine. And honestly, when I appraise my ability, my drive and my motivation as objectively as I can, I don't think I'd have made it to the Bar without it.*

The golden thread

'And when London is but a memory, and the Old Bailey has sunk back into the primeval mud, my country will be remembered for three things: the British breakfast; the *Oxford Book of English Verse*; and the presumption of innocence.

* Fortunately, there has been sufficient momentum, especially among the junior Bar, that many mini-pupillages are now funded, so that expenses are paid, and there are many organisations geared at assisting young people with grants, bursaries and other financial aid. See Appendix: A Note On Representation and Resources.

That is the golden thread which runs through the whole history of our criminal law. So that, if a man is murdered on the Old Kent Road, no man shall be convicted if there is reasonable doubt as to his guilt.'

Thus spake John Mortimer's Horace Rumpole, in one of his virtuoso courtroom addresses that brought the founding principles of our nation's criminal justice system onto the bookshelves and the TVs of generations of future criminal lawyers.

Or, in the melodic Welsh tones of a magistrate to a defendant in the trial ahead of mine in an idyllic rural town one sunny July morning:

'Well, we've had a pretty good think, and we reckon you did it. You did, didn't you? You did! No? Well, we think you did.'

A holiday miracle

'Four section thirty-nines* for you at the seaside, SB!' grins my clerk as she hands me tomorrow's defence trial. My client, Cory, has pleaded not guilty to assaulting the pub landlord, the security staff, the barman and a random punter who made the mistake of trying to act as mediator and received a (fortunately unbroken) pint glass to the face for his efforts. Glassed are the peacemakers, or something.

Cory's not guilty plea appears optimistic in light of the seven prosecution witness statements attesting to his rampage and his resolute 'no comment' police interview; once I've arrived at court and the CPS deign to serve the CCTV from

* Section 39 of the Criminal Justice Act 1988 – common assault or battery. The least serious type of assault, causing minimal or no injury – maximum sentence six months' imprisonment.

the pub,* it is untenable. The only course of action open to him, we agree, is a late guilty plea in the hope that belated and full-throated candour might persuade the magistrates to suspend the inevitable custodial sentence. It should also ward off the prospect of the CPS realising how woefully under-charged this case was.

The case is called on, I ask that the charges be put to Cory again and he duly pleads guilty. I ask for a Pre-Sentence Report (PSR),† and the legal advisor and the prosecutor stifle a laugh. 'I don't think SB is familiar with this defendant,' the prosecutor says knowingly to the bench, and they all share a conspiratorial smile. Cory, apparently, is something of a local legend, and not the good kind. While I have seen his lengthy record of previous convictions, I have not quite appreciated its significance in a small town; unlike in the big city magistrates' courts, where nobody remembers anybody and names and numbers blur into insignificance, in this cosy community everybody knows each other – including magistrates and defendants. Cory's reputation for drunken violence and public disorder well and truly goes before him. Twelve times he has appeared before the magistrates for offences like this, and twelve times they have sent him to prison for between two and six months. The outcome today, it is clear, is pre-ordained.

Nevertheless, I persist in my application for a report, just in case it yields something that points towards an alternative to custody. To my surprise, the mags relent, and four hours later

* The prosecution serving vital evidence on the morning of trial is par for the course, I'd learned.
† A report prepared by the Probation Service to assist the sentencing court, setting out all relevant information about a defendant as well as recommendations for sentence.

we are all reconvened and scouring the PSR swiftly compiled by the on-duty probation officer.

Several things stand out. Cory, it doesn't need saying, is a very troubled man. Now twenty-nine, he has been brawling since he could walk, drinking since he was eleven and, following his exclusion from school at thirteen, bouncing from state benefits to brief cash-in-hand labour and back again, punctuated by regular sojourns at Her Majesty's penal establishments whenever his temper gets the better of him, which is pretty much every time he drinks.

But the chink of light that catches the attention of the Probation Service is that now, for the first time in his life, Cory has a full-time job. And, while it has only been eight months since the ill-fated night that brought him here today, he has not been in trouble since. Half a year without committing a crime may not sound a boastable achievement, but in the context of Cory's record, this represents serious progress. These two factors, Probation observe, are clearly linked. After three decades without direction, Cory has something he can take pride in; a purpose, a reason to avoid trouble. He still drinks, but knowing he has to be up at five each morning, coupled with his bail condition to avoid the town centre, means he has found a level of functional alcoholism; he is learning his limits and ensuring that, whatever chaos envelops his personal life, he attends work sober and impresses his employer. For the first time in his criminal career, the Probation Service feel that he is motivated to change his ways, and that they can work with him. In the 'recommendation' box on the PSR, where a dozen times previously appeared the words 'The Probation Service is unable to recommend an alternative to custody', there now reads a comprehensive suite of conditions to attach to a suspended sentence, including alcohol treatment, supervision, a curfew and two specialist rehabilitative programmes.

The sticking point, of course, is that Cory deserves to go to prison. Really really really deserves to go to prison. This was an appalling act of drunken violence, the latest of many, and Cory is fortunate not to be facing even more serious charges. There is no doubt that as a member of the public, hearing the prosecution facts, I would expect him to be imprisoned. If I read about this drunken thug on MailOnline, and watched the CCTV and read the Victim Personal Statements of those affected, and then heard that this man had acted in this way a dozen times before, I would be swinging my online weight behind the below-the-line comments calling for immediate custody.

But there is, I urge the magistrates in mitigation, something genuinely, identifiably exceptional on this occasion. Probation are able to offer something that looks as if it has a very real chance of succeeding where a repeat prescription of short custodial sentences – twelve in a row! – has failed. It is the type of intensive work that simply couldn't be achieved in custody – there wouldn't be time, for one thing, given that the maximum sentence that can be passed is six months. Prison, while fully deserved, will simply mean the end of his employment and, on his release in three months, an inevitable descent back into the same old patterns. The long-term benefit to the local community of a sober, rehabilitated Cory far outweighs the temporary respite of yet another ineffective prison sentence.

Cory's was a paradigm case of those that make newspaper headlines and Twitter storms; where a defendant convicted of a serious offence 'walks free from court', in the favoured cliché. As with Cory, there is almost always something compelling in the circumstances of the person that drives a court to suspend a prison sentence and give an offender a chance to prove their stated intentions. Sometimes the court's faith will be misplaced; the compact will be broken and the offender will be back before the court for breaching the order or reoffending, at which point the court will have little choice but to send them to prison.

But where it is possible to piece a broken life back together, our system will usually try. Punishment is just one of the aims of criminal justice; not, as I had long believed, its raison d'être. Rehabilitation, public protection, restitution and reduction of crime (including by deterrence) also sit on the scales as the court measures how best, on the facts of that individual case, to justly deal with someone. Sometimes somebody, like Cory, richly deserves to be sent to prison, but the public deserve for him to get better.

I am proud of that final line, which I deliver with a flourish of what I think might be pathos before I sit down and the magistrates retire to discuss sentence. I still look back on that plea in mitigation as one of my best, raw and unpolished though it was. Somewhere in my meandering submissions, I lost my professional detachment; the sensible course seemed so damn *obvious*, and I felt my blabbering earnestness pierce the certainties of the magistrates, whose froideur thawed into slow, receptive nods as I urged them to try the one thing that hadn't been tried. *What do you have to lose?* I implored. *If a suspended sentence doesn't work and he reoffends, he goes straight to prison. But if it works . . .*

I have no idea where Cory is now or what he's doing; whether he's a reformed sober warehouse manager climbing the career ladder, or hurtling into his forties as an institutionalised mess. But I'll always remember the thud in my stomach as the magistrates re-entered, accompanied by a dock officer, who made a beeline for Cory so that he was in position for the frog-march to the cells when the bench announced six months, minus 10 per cent for Cory's guilty plea.

Rio (Part 2)

As second six draws to a close, I am seeing less and less of Alan in person, although his sporadic all-caps text messages make plain that he has spies reporting to him on my progress.* One evening he calls me about the report he is due to write for chambers ahead of my tenancy vote. 'I'm basically going to be recommending you, but I don't have time to write it all down. If you want to knock something up, I'm happy to sign it.' As ever, I struggle to discern whether he is joking. When I tentatively suggest that writing my own glowing reference might be an ethically sketchy way to secure tenancy, he ends the call with what sounds like disappointment, only to ring back half an hour later. This time, however, there is something else on his mind.

'I've had a call from the solicitors in the case of Rio.' Taking a second to scan my mental database of the scores of clients I met in first six, I locate the relevant entry: Rio – rape, long-term partner, custody time limit extension refused, bail.

'Let me guess?' I venture with affected world-weariness, an old hand now at predicting the vagaries of client behaviour. 'He's breached his bail by contacting the complainant?'

'Actually,' Alan replies, 'he's been as good as gold with the ex. Kept well away. No, he was out last night past his curfew.'

I sigh. 'So after all your efforts, he's going to be remanded for a single breach of his curfew? His girlfriend's going to be livid.'

'No no no!' says Alan. 'No. The new girlfriend's long gone.

---

* Throughout pupillage, other barristers, solicitors and judges will sometimes take it upon themselves to contact your pupil supervisor if they are particularly impressed/horrified by something you have done.

No, he's going to be remanded because while out past his curfew, high on coke, he's wandered into a pub with a carving knife and stabbed some random chap to death. The silly boy.'

Alan's insouciance dulls the immediate impact of his words. I am still processing as he holds forth about the unexpected dividend of a murder brief, and sets me some homework researching case law on the issue of intent and self-induced intoxication.* But what is plain, and what will no doubt be plain to the family of the deceased once they learn Rio's history, is that this historically violent man was released onto the streets as a direct result of Alan's efforts. By doing his job to the best of his professional ability, using the law to argue that the prosecution's failures required the judge to grant Rio bail, Alan had set off a chain reaction culminating in an innocent man's death.

You can't think this way, I hear Alan's voice booming in imaginary retort. *You just can't.* You have to distance yourself from the flesh and blood of the subject matter, maintain the clear divide between what we do in court and the aftermath out on the streets and inside private homes. We are not the decision makers; we merely present arguments on behalf of those who cannot make the arguments themselves. The rule of law requires that we do this; in an adversarial legal system – prosecution versus defence – those accused of crimes, and those who have committed crimes, must be treated fairly and lawfully, and defence lawyers are integral to establishing that safeguard. We cannot be held accountable for choices that judges make; much less the choices our clients make.

---

* If you get voluntarily drunk/drugged, you may have a defence to murder if you were so intoxicated that you couldn't or didn't intend to kill or cause really serious harm. You would, however, still be guilty of manslaughter.

Take the doctor, my hypothetical interlocutor suggests. If she saves the life of a man who leaves the hospital and kills, she bears no moral culpability. Nobody would sensibly say that she should. But as with every time I recline onto my medical analogy, it buckles. Nobody in the medical system was arguing for the patient *not* to be saved and let out onto the streets. Everybody in the hospital was in agreement that the only proper course was to treat him and discharge him as soon as was medically safe. Whereas in the dark, woody corridors of our world, there were loud prosecutorial voices urging that Rio be kept behind bars, to avoid this very thing from happening. And the reason that those voices did not win out, is you, Alan.

We protect ourselves with our certainties; comforted by our first principles that tell us it is a necessary function of justice that we do these things. *We merely present arguments.* Except we don't, of course. We *advocate* for those arguments; in the words of our professional Code of Conduct, we 'promote fearlessly and by all proper and lawful means the client's best interests . . . without regard to the consequences to any other person'. We don't neutrally tender the available options to the court; we urge, we cajole, we persuade. We fight to secure a particular outcome, irrespective of what that means in the real world. *Without regard to the consequences.* That, Alan, was what you did. Properly, lawfully, entirely in accordance with the best traditions of the Bar. And somebody died.

No moral culpability attaches to you for that; both your actions and the rules by which you – we all – play are fully justified. It has to work this way, I know. But as a matter of pure causation, were it not for your positive, deliberate act, that man would probably still be alive today. We apologise instinctively if we bump into somebody even when it's not our fault. Can it really be so easy to disown our consequences when the harm caused is so high? If we struck a pedestrian who ran out in front of our car, would absence of moral blameworthiness permit us to dust down our bonnet and carry on as if nothing had happened?

A better philosopher, probably a better lawyer, might have the tools to unpick all this. I have been fortunate, if that is the word, that while many of my clients have gone on to reoffend, none, as far as I know, has taken a life in circumstances immediately traceable to my professional 'success'. I've never asked Alan how he carried that; whether it drilled even a millimetre below the armour he wore so proudly, or whether, as with all else, he was able to compartmentalise it, lock it in his pigeon-hole with the case papers and leave it behind for the night as the door to chambers slammed shut.

4. Becoming a Barrister

For reasons best known to my chambers colleagues, but probably attributable largely to sympathy at my having spent a year in Alan's mercurial company, they have voted in favour of offering me tenancy, meaning that I am officially a fully qualified practising barrister, with rights of audience in every court in the land, from the dinkiest magistrates' court up to the Supreme Court of the United Kingdom.

The occasion has been marked by a celebratory night of excess in the pub across the road from chambers, only slightly tinged by the awkward absence of those of my fellow pupils who weren't so lucky, and who now face an uncertain future of third sixes and squatting.* The relief at having actually made it – not merely passed a course or secured an insecure pupillage, but actually barged my way through the door and barricaded myself inside – is not as awesome as I had anticipated; instead, as I sip my fruity cider my mind fixates on a colossal fuck-up I

---

* Despite the temptation not to explain this term and just leave this sentence to the reader's imagination, 'squatting' is essentially an informal arrangement whereby someone who has failed to be offered tenancy is permitted to remain in chambers for a short period – a few months or so – while they try to find somewhere else to apply.

made the week before when I had misread an email from a solicitor and inadvertently agreed to a judge issuing a warrant for my client's arrest.*

It follows that, on some days, I still do not have the slightest clue what I am doing, but unless three quarters of my hundred co-tenants muster the enthusiasm to call a meeting and vote me out, I am here for life, or at least until the ever-increasing legal-aid cuts cause our chambers to collapse in on itself.

My practice for the first few years of junior tenancy charts a steady graduation from the magistrates' court to the Crown. Bail applications, committals for sentence,† appeals from the mags, covering plea hearings and mentions for senior colleagues – all coalesce into a relentless avalanche of full days in court and near-full nights doing written prep. At the beginning, I don't receive many cases in my own name; a new tenant's bread and butter is servicing the returns of established colleagues. The juicy carrot dangling perennially just out of reach is the promise of a Crown Court jury trial – of actually getting to do the thing that I've spent five years training to do.

My black gown is still neatly creased and my wig a brilliant white, the two sartorial signs that immediately mark me out as brand new. These neatly complement the permanent tremor of uncertainty in my voice and rabbit-in-headlights style of court-room advocacy which, I'm pretty sure, strikes fear only into the hearts of those I'm defending.

Certain aptitudes, however, accumulate quickly. I develop a

---

* Thankfully remedied before the warrant was issued, and before the client ever found out.
† Where a defendant pleads guilty or is convicted after trial at the magistrates' court, and the magistrates consider their sentencing powers inadequate to deal with the offence, and so 'commit' it to the Crown Court.

(I'm told, disconcerting) familiarity with the production, preparation, nicknames and street values of our country's most popular illegal drugs (knowing the import purity of cocaine,* or that a tenner will get you a shot of W, one rock or a wrap of B,† may not be on every pub quiz, but is still useful trivia to throw out once in a while). I amass a running order of the most salacious, extreme and unusual cases that cross my radar in court (sitting in a Crown Court list to hear the sentence of a defendant charged with blackmail after threatening to expose a married man who had been advertising himself on specialist websites as a 'human toilet' is one that will always live long in the memory).

But I also start to internalise some of the industry attitudes. Fairly quickly I have my stock answers up my sleeve for the stock dinner party/Wetherspoons questions. How do you defend someone you know is guilty? *Well, I only know they're guilty if they tell me. If they tell me they've done something, I'm not allowed to suggest to a court that they haven't. If they say they haven't done it, it is not my role to judge them. I'll advise them on the strength of the evidence against them, but the history books are replete with miscarriages of justice where 'overwhelming' evidence of guilt turned out to be fatally flawed, so to minimise that risk we ensure that there are lawyers to present the defence case, however unlikely it may look at first glance. If you were wrongly accused of a crime, you wouldn't want your lawyer to be judging you, would you? And even when people are guilty, it is still vital that they are treated fairly*

---

* Generally over 80 per cent purity, which is then diluted to street purity using bulking agents such as benzocaine and paracetamol.
† Respectively, a 0.1 gram deal of cocaine ('white'), crack cocaine and heroin ('brown').

and lawfully, and that all relevant facts – including mitigation – are put before the sentencing court. Again, if you made a mistake, wouldn't you want the court to know everything about you, not just the worst version of yourself presented by the prosecution?

That sort of thing. High and mighty principle, served in a mild marinade of lemon-and-herb sanctimony, becomes a second language. I quickly transition from an advocate for my client to an advocate for the virtue of the profession; of the tradition of a cadre of independent advocates available to prosecute or defend any criminal case, irrespective of popularity or public sentiment, in order to ensure that our fellow citizens are as fairly and robustly defended as they are prosecuted.

On the subject of prosecuting, again, the principles underlying English and Welsh prosecutorial culture, as opposed to caricatures inherited from American crime fiction, are seeping in. Prosecuting, I am learning, is not about obtaining a conviction at any cost. Sometimes, it is not about obtaining a conviction at all; it can be about forming a humane and compassionate view that, even if there is evidence of a crime, the public interest is not served by prosecuting somebody.

Prosecuting is also not about vengeance or pushing for the longest possible sentence. You obviously have to present the prosecution case robustly and persuasively, and ensure that sentences passed are appropriate in accordance with the law and sentencing guidelines, but your guiding principle, Alan has drummed into me, is fairness. Politicians often threaten 'the full force of the law' against the social malady du jour, but this is not merely empty; it runs counter to the duties our system places upon both the police and prosecutors. A sense of proportion and humility, and an acute awareness of the risks to people's lives and liberty if the wrong person is convicted, are indispensable. As with defending, no matter how strong the evidence may look, you have to maintain the detachment that recognises the scope for error. Prosecutorial desperation to convict is the leading cause of miscarriages of justice across the legal world.

The prosecution suffers no defeats nor glories in victory, as the adage goes. There should be no elation in winning a prosecution case; there may be a sense of professional pride, and sometimes an exhalation of relief that the public might now be protected from a provably dangerous person. But, experience teaches, there are rarely any winners with a criminal conviction. Whatever damage has been wrought cannot be undone.

But while such certitudes may serve as a worthy touchstone for negotiating metropolitan dinner parties,* I'm learning that navigating the practicalities of the day job – living, breathing, screaming criminal cases, in an overfilled pressure cooker of a system with no time, resources or working Wi-Fi – presents a very different sort of challenge.

The first mags list of tenancy

Magistrates' court, Reception Desk, 9.34 a.m.
'Hi, I'm the agent prosecuting the trial in Court Four. Can you let me into the CPS room? It's locked and I need to make photocopies of these witness statements. The CPS file doesn't have any copies for the witnesses and the trial starts in eleven minutes.'

'I'm afraid I don't have the code. You'll have to ask someone from the CPS.'

'There's nobody else from the CPS here, and the switchboard

---

* In my case, Nando's and Lambrini, mostly.

keeps ringing out. Do you have a phone number for the local CPS office?'

'I'm not allowed to give that out.'

'But . . . OK . . . fine. Is there any other way I can get these statements photocopied?'

'You could ask the usher.'

'Thank you.'

'Although the court's photocopier broke yesterday and under the service agreement the technician has fourteen days to come and fix it.'

'Is the technician coming today?'

'No.'

[CHECKS WATCH. PANICKED. INSPIRATION STRIKES] 'OK, what if I scan them onto my phone and email them to you? Can you print them?'

'I can, but it will cost you five pounds for the first ten pages and one pound every page thereafter. We're not here to provide a free printing service.'

'Even though I'm . . .? Fine. I have three one-page documents.'

'That will be fifteen pounds.'

[SILENTLY WEEPS] 'What if we say it's one three-page document?'

'Go on then. That will be five pounds.'

'Thank you. Can I pay by card?'

'No, cash only.'

[RETURNS WITH CASH TEN MINUTES LATER AFTER INSANE DASH TO ASDA CASHPOINT]

'Here you go, five whole pounds.'

'Oh, I'm afraid our printer has just run out of ink. The new cartridge won't be here until Monday.'

Dillon (Part 1)

Dillon was born the sixth of seven children, and was the sixth of seven to be taken into care at birth. He was never told the identity of his father, whose surname he carried, and only knew his mum by her first name. A revolving door of state care, foster homes and temporary reunions with his mother and her latest violent, heroin-addicted boyfriend slowed to a halt in Dillon's early teens, leaving him a permanent resident in local authority accommodation. Instability was also the hallmark of his schooling; his undiagnosed autism and ADHD manifested itself in behavioural problems, the easiest solution to which was to spring him out of mainstream education and into pupil referral units, from which he would truant with the older lads from the care home, who had older brothers with nice cars and all manner of intriguing things to smoke.

When Dillon, using the only language in which he had been taught fluency, lashed out with his fists against the chaotic disciplinary regime of his care home, he found himself the beneficiary of the local authority's Prosecute First, Ask Questions Later childcare policy. Kick a door? Charged with criminal damage. Shove a member of staff? Charged with assault. Throw a chair? Add an affray. All unpleasant behaviour in need of correction, for sure, but the kind of acting out which, at certain types of private school or world-leading universities, might be quietly rectified by a hastily written cheque from the bank of Ma and Pa and a discreet course of therapy, rather than a criminal prosecution.

So it is that, by the time I meet Dillon at the age of seventeen, he has been before the Youth Court over a dozen times, with a list of convictions growing exponentially in length and seriousness. Today's trial is an allegation of knifepoint robbery; that Dillon and a mate turned up unannounced on the nineteen-year-old complainant's doorstep at 1 a.m., ragged him around and stole his phone. *I didn't know either of these men,* the complainant has told the police. *They just knocked on my door and I stepped outside to have a conversation with them about something . . . No, I can't remember what, it was just general chit-chat, like one is wont to engage in when menacing hooded strangers arrive outside your house in the middle of the night.* A curious allegation rendered slightly less curious by the subtext that in fact he knows Dillon and the other lad very well indeed, and this impromptu knock-on was enforcement of a cannabis debt.

The Youth Court is designed for defendants aged under eighteen. It carries less formality (defendants are referred to only by their first names), and there are restrictions on who can watch proceedings and what can be publicly reported. The principal aim of youth justice is rehabilitation – trying to prevent young people coming back into contact with the criminal justice system – in contrast to the adult system in which rehabilitation sits alongside punishment, deterrence, compensation and public protection as just one aim of criminal sentencing. The most serious offences will still be tried in the Crown Court,* but most allegations of crime against under-eighteens are dealt with by specialist magistrates and District Judges in the Youth Court, where custody is very much a measure of last resort. The Youth Offending Team (YOT) will usually exhaust all non-custodial options, repeatedly, before youth detention is imposed.

However, when a case does call for custody, although the Youth Court is essentially part of the magistrates' court, it has far greater sentencing powers – it can pass custodial sentences

---

* Also, sometimes if a youth is accused of committing an offence with an adult, they can both be tried together at the Crown Court.

of up to two years. Because the sentencing regime for under-eighteens is generally much lower than for adults, it means that Youth Courts frequently deal with extremely grave offences, including rape, sexual assault and serious violence. All of which makes it particularly disconcerting that, for years, Youth Courts have been served by the most junior lawyers,* who are shunted into this world of damaged children, byzantine legal procedure and appalling pay as something of a training exercise. By far the most serious cases I prosecuted and defended in my early years were those in the Youth Court, where the stakes for defendants, and arguably society, are probably the highest.

The Youth Court's efforts at rehabilitating Dillon have so far not succeeded. Programme after programme with the YOT has ended either with Dillon withdrawing his cooperation, resulting in youth detention, or with his being charged with a new offence, resulting in a remand in youth detention. Every time he goes inside, he meets new, more sophisticated young offenders, who further normalise his disrespect for society and expand his criminal toolkit, which he puts to use the minute he is released back into the alleged care of the local authority. Theft of cars progresses to burglary, drug possession to drug supply, common assaults to violence with weapons. He is, in the jargon of youth justice, a prolific young offender. Or, in the timeless vernacular of the tabloids, a yobbo; a lout; a thug; the archetypal urban hoodie that I, like New Labour, mocked David Cameron for supposedly wanting to hug in the mid 2000s. And the system is rapidly running out of ways to deal with him.

* In the past few years, there has been an overdue shift towards requiring specialist training for barristers undertaking Youth Court work, but this was not in place when I started out.

And while Dillon must ultimately take responsibility for his actions – he's old enough to know right from wrong – he is at the same time a near-inevitable product of his background. When you take a child from a violent, drug-ridden home, put him in a violent, drug-ridden care system, bounce him out of education and around the country, touring four different care homes and three different Young Offender Institutions, exposing him at every stage to older youths who themselves have known nothing but crime – if you were consciously programming somebody to defy social norms from birth, would this not be a near-perfect formula?

We hold in the highest disdain the parental and state failings that visit such misfortunes on children like Dillon. Most of us would have the most urgent sympathy for newborn Dillon in care; five-year-old Dillon being beaten by his stepfather; seven-year-old Dillon being misdiagnosed as not having any special educational needs; eight-year-old Dillon preyed upon by gangs who lurk outside the care home knowing it to be a ripe source of cheap, impressionable drug-and-weapons couriers; nine-year-old Dillon being given his first taste of cocaine. Yet the moment they turn ten, the age of criminal responsibility, and transgress the law, the oasis of public sympathy is exposed as a mirage; we zero in on that word – *responsibility* – and demand that these children take it. As they progress through teenagehood and into young adulthood, we hold them not just legally but morally to the same standards we expect of those who have been nurtured with love and constancy, as if once they hit the age of majority they can immediately assume the behaviour of a supported and well-adjusted child from a stable and loving family.

Often our contempt for these young criminals is justified by the convenient case studies of those few who survive Dillon's sort of upbringing to function in society's mainstream. *See? You can choose to knuckle down and make something of yourself, or you can choose to be a criminal.*

It's like watching twenty people swim through a lake of crocodiles, condemning from the safety of the riverbank the feebleness of the nineteen who get eaten because there was one who 'didn't let it do them any harm' and who 'took a bit of personal responsibility for their decisions'.

And I say 'we', but really I mean 'I'. These were my certainties before I came to the Bar. I can't give you a time and date of departure – as I say, there was no Damascene conversion – and I still understand, and share, the instinctive boil-over of anger when I read in the news of the very real and lasting harm inflicted by wild young offenders. I would not for a minute underplay that harm, nor suggest that youth absolves them of culpability. But the Dillons – and there have been thousands – whose stars crossed mine, have gradually colourised the monochrome portrait of criminality and personal responsibility that I wore like a sandwich board in my early twenties whenever the subject of crime was broached.

And maybe that is why, after our trial in which the complainant's eagerness to deny knowing Dillon dilutes the prosecution identification evidence to homeopathic concentrations, to the extent that the judge throws the case out at half time,* I allow myself a fleeting fantasy. It's a fantasy which has still not been entirely blanched by a decade's accumulated cynicism; it still pops up uninvited in certain cases with certain young clients, a breathy seductive whisper: *I might just be the person to turn his life around.*

---

* Half time = the end of the prosecution case. If a judge, in any court, considers that there is insufficient evidence for a court safely to convict, s/he is required to direct a finding of not guilty.

This case, our case, could be the chapter in his memoir when everything changes. A fortunate acquittal and the return of his liberty – could this ignite a recognition within him that his life doesn't have to be what he currently seems destined to make it? Might the patrician words of a middle-class legal professional with no real idea of what his life is like possibly spark the epiphany that there is still time for him to turn his back on his criminal peers, to work with the YOT to learn a trade, to live a good and upstanding life – to deliver on all the clichés that we, when delivering a plea in mitigation on behalf of a client, assure the court are sincerely intended?

As we sit on the stiff folding chairs in the court conference room, me doling out unsolicited and unqualified life advice while my charge stares captively at his phone, are we perhaps moments away from Dillon leaping onto the screwed-down desk to declare: 'O captain! My captain!'? Will we see each other next in twenty years' time, not negotiating the awkward imbalance of our roles as criminal lawyer and client, but embracing each other as equally empowered law-abiding peers?

To hubris, solipsism, naivety and self-importance I plead unequivocally guilty. But those charges are mitigated, I hope at least to some extent, by optimism.

I accept Dillon's fist-bump as he spins on his heels and strolls off to greet the taciturn hooded twenty-somethings who have been marshalling the court corridors for the duration of the trial.

Penury

A long morning mitigating before a famously punitive judge concludes in a suspended sentence for my dangerous-driving client, Barney. The central plank of my mitigation, as per my written instructions and reiterated by Barney to probation in the Pre-Sentence Report, is built around the loss of employment that has left him penniless, depressed and unable to afford his rent. Custody, while deserved, would simply compound his financial woes when he is released. The judge accepts that Barney should be given a chance to work with probation and get his finances in order. As we walk out of court, Barney is complaining about his feet hurting. 'I'm gonna take these trainers back. They cost me two hundred quid – fucking outrageous.'

Filthy rich

A staple of the junior criminal barristerial diet is private road traffic law. As most driving offences carry a maximum penalty of a fine at the mags' court, they are not serious enough to qualify for legal aid; however, the powers of the magistrates to disqualify offenders from driving makes it a very important area of law indeed for people anxious not to be parted from their wheels. Hence there has long been a thriving boutique industry in the supply of specialist road traffic legal representation, often aimed at high-income clientele willing to pay literally whatever it takes to save their driving licence. The junior criminal Bar are the trickle-down beneficiaries, receiving a slice of the pie – tiny relative to what the solicitor is billing, but hearty by comparison to legal-aid rates.

Road traffic lawyers built their empires on 'technical defences' – spotting procedural failings by the police or prosecution which charitable High Court decisions of the 1970s and 1980s had ruled afforded an apparently guilty defendant a complete defence. The style of combat, particularly in cases of alleged speeding or drink driving, was guerrilla; the defence would say absolutely nothing until the prosecution had closed its case at trial, and would then jump up to point out some flaw which, it was said, meant that the prosecution hadn't proved its case. Such 'ambush defences' have been deprecated by the courts in more recent years, and defendants are now required to positively identify the issues before trial, in order to give the prosecution fair notice/teach them how to do their jobs.

Where no procedural point arose, standard defences included challenging whether a speed camera met the statutory definition of a 'prescribed device', or whether the intoximeter in a drink-driving case was working reliably – strategies which involved bombarding the prosecution with speculative requests for disclosure of years' worth of calibration records. If all else failed and a conviction or guilty plea was unavoidable, a Hail Mary would be launched at sentence, either in the form of an exceptional hardship* argument for those facing twelve points on their licence and thus a six-month ban, or, in extremis, a special reasons† claim for drink drivers staring at a minimum one-year disqualification.

A specialism of one particular firm serving celebrities and international sportsfolk involved setting up shell companies which were listed with the DVLA as the 'registered keeper' for the client's vehicles. If the client committed a speeding offence, the Notice of Intended Prosecution requiring the keeper to identify the driver would be sent to the 'company' – usually just

---

* If you can show that, despite totting up twelve penalty points on your licence, disqualification would cause 'exceptional hardship', the magistrates can choose not to disqualify you. You'd be surprised how often courts are persuaded to find such hardship for millionaires who can easily afford their own chauffeurs.

† A twelve-month ban for drink driving is all but unavoidable. 'Special reasons' not to disqualify is a tightly restricted category of exceptions, such as where the car was driven in an emergency, or where a driver's drink is spiked.

a PO Box. An individual who fails to identify a driver is liable to six penalty points. But a company? Just a modest fine.* No reply = £600 fine = 1/100th of a Premier League footballer's weekly wage.

For the most part, whatever view one might take on their approach, there was little doubt that these firms were giving their clients an excellent service. But there were exceptions. Some firms, the Keres of the commercial world, simply milked their cash cows for all they were worth. One reportedly charged a premium fee for the senior partner to 'personally' handle the case, which amounted to subcontracting the legal work to a paralegal and simply adding the partner's signature. Others were known to advise on – and charge for – a trial, irrespective of the absence of any possible legal defence, only to brief the case out to counsel the night before trial so that the last-minute, negative advice would come from our lips, not the solicitor's.

A case that remains with me is that of my colleague, Andrea, who was briefed to defend a firefighter charged with drink driving after being found to be fractionally over the limit the morning after a work party. Conviction would mean the loss of his licence, which would mean loss of his job. He was a father of young children with an exemplary record of service. Andrea had to break the news to him that, despite the assurances of his solicitor that 'the barrister will find you a defence', there was none to be found. He broke down in tears, telling Andrea that he had exhausted his family's life savings on this false promise of salvation. When the magistrates came to disqualify this

---

* In theory, if the police can identify an individual at the company to pin the failure to, that individual could be prosecuted. But, at the time I was starting out, they often settled for prosecuting the company.

...oken man, they said that they sincerely wished they could avoid it – but the law in these cases is clear. Their sympathy was abundant, but there was no alternative. The next day, Andrea received a call from the solicitor. 'The case of Mr Jackson yesterday – just FYI, his daughter walked into the garage this morning to find him swinging from the rafters. Good thing we got payment upfront, eh?'

It may be because my perception is jaded by the horror of this case, and of others like it, but road traffic law as an industry never sat well with me. On the most superficial level, it represented everything that most people believe is wrong with the system: rich, guilty people trying to buy their way out of justice.

But superficial such protestations undoubtedly are. Because forced to drill a little deeper, what is my actual objection here? That most road traffic clients are likely to be guilty? The same goes statistically for most people accused of crimes that I won't bat an eyelid when defending. That these people are not advancing any sort of positive defence, trying to eke out a lucky escape in the face of overwhelming evidence? That too, is hardly unusual in crime. Dillon, for instance, never advanced an alibi for where he was during the robbery. He just said that he hadn't been correctly identified, and kept his fingers crossed that the case would somehow go his way. Is my problem with the solicitors? Maybe in part, but the grasping, profit-maximising caricature does not apply across the board. Many traffic firms offer proper advice, charge reasonable commercial rates and represent their clients ferociously but entirely professionally, giving the type of Rolls-Royce service that should rightly be granted to everybody accused of a criminal offence, but which due to the paucity of legal-aid rates (where it is available, it can pay a tenth, sometimes a twentieth, of standard private rates) is simply unattainable. Unpalatable though it is that wealth confers advantages in the legal system, that is the fault, surely, of the system, rather than those accused?

When cleaved from the unrepresentative dishonest practices of the minority and coldly dissected, I'm not sure that my objections are sustainable. Deploying the law in favour of one's client is literally the name of the game. *Promote fearlessly and by all proper and lawful means the client's best interests.* My lofty dinner-party disdain for those who would quail at defending somebody accused of child sexual abuse was – is – rank hypocrisy. Because I too, apparently, can identify clients and causes which make me recoil. They just fit a different profile. And while I would never – could never – refuse to act in such a case, it was clear, even at that early stage, that my newfound certainties were no more certain than my old ones.

The language of love
'I'm sorry?' I say. 'He's what?'

I like to consider myself closer to the modern end of the barristerial spectrum. I'm under thirty. I am computer literate. I have a working grasp of pop culture. I think I'm able to communicate with clients and juries in a way that doesn't sound like I'm sneezing out a nineteenth-century legal textbook. But I have to admit ignorance when the mother of my eighteen-year-old client, Darin, bolshily inserting herself into our conference to offer her own perspective on the allegations of harassment against his on/off girlfriend, alights upon a particular adjective to describe her son's inability to let go of this toxic relationship.

As she repeats the word, my poker face slips. I stare at Darin, who nods forlornly in agreement and tries to avoid meeting my eye, with a grimace of familiarity that suggests this is not the first time he has been diagnosed in public by his own mother as 'cunt-struck'.

Breakdown

It was at around the eight-month point of tenancy that I was able to finally articulate how I felt: I really hated this job.

I loved the idea of it – I would tell everyone who would listen that I was a barrister. I revelled in sharing the parables I'd heard in the robing room, and bigging up my own non-events as Rumpolian legends. I adored making casual reference to the grave and weighty criminal cases that I had seen in court, mere proximity to the gritty glamour affording, I thought, vicarious glory. But I hated actually doing it.

I hated being noticeably the least competent person in the room, a jarring culture shock for an erstwhile straight-A student who, PE and art aside, had coasted through three tiers of education. I hated not knowing what I was doing; I hated not having any experience to fall back on and how I felt flummoxed at every turn. I hated standing up to bellicose judges, and having to feign confidence when it was clear to everybody how brittle I was. I hated that, no matter how book-smart I could try to make myself, there would every single day be a situation I had never encountered and that I would have no idea how to handle. I hated that my cross-examination of witnesses felt perpetually ineffective, my legal arguments were laboured and my speeches left me convinced of my opponent's case. I hated that *I* would not want me as my barrister, or, given my all-consuming eighty-hour working week, as a partner, or really even as a friend, and this feeling of worthlessness, of failing in every area of my life, stuck with me for at least the first three years, the daily consciously articulated doubts subduing into a permanent medium-level anxiety.

My escape came in learning to embrace the ignorance; at the risk of sounding like an inspirational Facebook meme, to run towards fear, rather than from it. There is simply too much to possibly absorb in five years of training. This bizarre existence depends 10 per cent on knowing the law and 90 per cent on judgement, something for which there's no shortcut. You can only ever acquire it through experience. It follows that you *should* be learning every day. You should be continually confounded and searching for new answers to new questions; if you aren't constantly craving to be better, you're probably not doing it right. You will make mistakes daily, and that isn't cause for shame, it isn't failure. Failure is not spotting those mistakes, and not acting to put them right.

I say 'escape' as if it connotes permanence; it doesn't. Perhaps 'itinerant coping mechanism' is a better fit. A decade in, I still slip back into a despondent fug on grey days. It doesn't necessarily take much. A difficult trial. A hostile judicial remark for something that's not my fault; worse, something that *is* my fault, and that I should have sorted earlier. The encumbrance on any sort of healthy personal life is a perennial weeping sore. Most days I question whether this job is right for me; whether I'm right for this job. There was a time when this was every day. To that extent, I suppose this is progress.

Good cop, bad cop

One preconception that criminal practice did not change, and has not changed, is that the police have an impossible and invariably thankless job. The willingness of individual officers to lay their personal safety, frequently their lives, on the line day after day, keeping the public safe while we throw brickbats from the cosy safety of counsel's row or social media, is something that is often lost. Without in any way seeking to minimise the very real problems that exist in our policing culture, the majority of the officers I encounter, whether prosecuting or defending, are honest, hardworking, civic-minded and inconceivably brave. Walking into a barely lit crack den armed only with a torch and a baton, not knowing whether you'll be stumbling into an empty room or over a dead body or onto a psychotic zombie wielding a machete, is a scenario from *Resident Evil* in most people's lives, rather than a daily occurrence.

The use of force is a similarly frequent occupational requirement. Not everybody reacts peaceably to the idea of being arrested, particularly those who know they have done something legally impish, and exercising lawful, reasonable force in self-defence or to apprehend a suspect is something that the police, like the rest of us, are entitled to do. There is something enduringly fascinating about reading police witness statements and seeing the sanitised forms of wording approved by the College of Policing to describe such physical encounters:

'*I deployed a Home Office-approved distraction strike.*' = '*I punched him in the face.*'

'*I was compelled to implement a balance displacement technique and thereafter to adopt a modified ground-pin position.*' = '*I pushed him over and sat on him.*'

'*Apprehending the immediate use of unlawful force, I opted for a repeated foot-led stunning technique to the area adjacent to the femoral pressure point.*' = '*I thought he might twat me so I repeatedly kicked him in the nads.*'

The ubiquity of body-worn video (BWV) cameras pinned to police uniforms has helped to emphasise the incongruity between the written word and the theatre of conflict, like a First World War general's missives from the Western Front. Sometimes the mismatch is jawdropping. One of my clients, Perry, was charged with assaulting a police constable after mouthing off to an officer in the street and dragging him to the floor, the officer only avoiding serious injury through a single well-placed distraction strike. So claimed PC Parker's statement, in any case. His colleague's BWV camera told a slightly different tale, in which PC Parker, pumped up and with 'Eye of the Tiger' presumably playing in his head, strutted towards a wholly unthreatening Perry and shoved him to the chest. As Perry fell backwards and reached out instinctively to grab hold of the officer's stab vest, the officer unloaded a barrage of punches to Perry's face. Once the footage emerged, the CPS sensibly dropped the prosecution.

Other officers are slightly more attuned to the pros and cons of BWV. There is no requirement that cameras be switched on at all times; it is largely a judgement call for the officer. So it is that we see cases such as that of Les, a giant fifty-something with a serious anger problem and a long history of assaulting police officers. Despite being aware of his history, and of the heightened risk of a confrontation, when five police officers kicked Les's door down to arrest him over a suspected burglary, all five mysteriously decided to switch their cameras off on entry. Les emerged from their encounter a battered, bleeding mess, and was charged with five further police assaults. He had, the unscathed officers unanimously attested, assaulted them all the minute they walked through the door, and they had been required to subdue him with a handful of proportionate stunning techniques, which were absolutely not gratuitous revenge for Les's previous misdeeds. Les's account of what happened was somewhat different.

Many people – and I would have been among them – might cheer the thought of a lout like Les receiving fisty summary justice at the hands of the boys and girls in blue. It's the only language people like him understand. The police shouldn't be pussyfooting around criminals, worrying about their human rights. They should be teaching Les and his ilk respect for the law. But even if you are intensely relaxed about agents of the state using unlawful violence against individual citizens – and having seen it in action, I'm very much not – aside from a fleeting shimmer of satisfaction that Les 'got what he deserved', what is actually achieved here? What lesson is it supposed to teach Les, other than reinforcing violence as the default mode of communication between him and anybody in uniform? How is this supposed to instil in Les, his friends and his family anything other than contempt for the legal system and its anointed authority figures? How does it help the next police constable or prison officer or paramedic whom Les encounters? When Les or someone he knows is in possession of information which could assist the prosecuting authorities, because his estate is a melting pot of serious organised crime – the drugs cartels which fuel the addictions which spawn the burglaries of houses like yours and mine – what sort of cooperation can the state reasonably expect?

I think the answers suggest that the perception of Les and his brethren as existing in a criminal silo, and their treatment at the hands of the authorities as something to which right-minded people can afford to turn a blind eye, harms all of us more than we may realise.

The first jury trial

My first jury trial is an overnight return from a senior colleague in chambers. He helpfully phones me at 8 p.m. after learning that I have inherited the case, and distils his lawyerly assessment of the evidence against our mutual client, Paul – 'He's fucked. He's absolutely fucked. I've told him he's fucked, but he refuses to accept how totally, utterly fucked he is.'

Accused of a racially aggravated section 4A* in a Co-op, Paul allegedly took umbrage when a black security guard looked at him the wrong way, and responded with a salvo of racist abuse. Paul's instructions for trial, as he told the police when interviewed, are that he was not in the shop that night, and has never spoken aggressively or racistly to any security guard, whatever his three previous convictions for racially abusing security guards might suggest about his proclivities.

As I watch the CCTV from the shop, two things leap out. One is the security guard, minding his own business in the corner of the screen. The second is Paul – and it is so absurdly, obviously Paul – walking up to the victim, his face contorted in rage, gesticulating wildly and saying something which is inaudible on the footage but causes all the other customers to turn around and stare in shock.

Surely when Paul sees this, he will have to plead guilty? Apparently not. 'I've seen it. Don't prove nothing. You can't say that's me. And you can't hear what I'm saying anyway.' I raise an eyebrow.[†] 'I'm not guilty. I'll take this to the jury.' With that, he stomps out of the tiny court conference room and heads out for a cig.

My instructions are clear, and, in many ways, this is the perfect starter trial. It is unwinnable. There is as little pressure as there can be.

The case is called on. The judge, who has read the papers and watched the footage, asks whether, really – I mean *really* – this

* Section 4A of the Public Order Act 1986 = using threatening, abusive or insulting words or behaviour, or disorderly behaviour, with intent to cause harassment, alarm or distress. The racially aggravated version carries a maximum of two years' custody.
† I can't actually raise one eyebrow, so I probably wiggled both, in the way that Mr Bean does as a come-on. This might be why Paul wasn't particularly keen on taking my advice.

is going to be a trial? In light of the CCTV, is my client *seriously* suggesting he wasn't there? I reply in the affirmative, my organs a knotted ball as the inevitability of the trial is sealed, and with a theatrical roll of the eyes, the judge tells the clerk to call for a jury panel.*

By this point, the compounded terror of the past fifteen hours has built to a climax. I am functioning on no sleep, having been up all night reading every statement a dozen times, considering and reconsidering every possible legal argument that could arise and drafting and re-drafting my cross-examination, and pestering my junior pals all morning with texts and phone calls seeking advice over the most minor facets of the case, just in case I've missed something. And then – poof! – it is all gone. The courtroom is enveloped in a thick, warm serenity, as I realise that this trial is going to happen, and there is nothing I can do to stop it. It is time. As the jury panel march in and assemble, it strikes me that this is what it has all been building to. This is my moment. I am about to become a jury advocate.

I'd like to tell you that, despite the overwhelming evidence, my forensic dissection of the prosecution witnesses and ingenious legal application to exclude the damning CCTV footage lays the foundations for what the judge describes as 'probably the best closing speech I've ever heard come out of a human mouth', and that my meticulous preparation is rewarded with a unanimous acquittal within minutes of the jury retiring.

And that might have happened. I cannot rule out that, on some parallel plane, I banked this as an astonishing debut victory which proved the catalyst for all manner of precocious professional success that has, in this reality, chosen to elude me.

---

* A panel of typically fifteen prospective jurors is called into court, out of which twelve are selected at random to be the jury.

But on this plane, as the clerk rises to read out the names of the jurors, the star-bound propulsion of my career is interjected by a panicked voice from the dock.

'Oi! Oi! Barrister! I wanna plead guilty!'

Branded

Patrick was the landlord of the Frog and Frangipane,* a quiet local in a suburb just close enough to the city centre to guarantee a healthy footfall, but far enough away to buffer it from the threat of regular trouble. That reputation was defied one balmy summer night when a pre-wedding party descended, and the two families-to-be decided to settle a silly quarrel over the bar tab in the time-honoured fashion of smashing ash trays, pint glasses and chairs over each other's heads.

A police riot van was scrambled and a dozen officers stormed the pub to a scene of anarchy – bridesmaids putting shirtless best men in headlocks; fathers of the bride and groom channelling Inigo Montoya and the Man in Black using snooker cues; the groom spinning around with a stool in each arm, sending random patrons flying like a Jägermeister-charged cyborg haymaker. Unable to distinguish friend from foe, the police took the decision to arrest pretty much the entire pub, including Patrick.

Upon arrival at the police station, Patrick was detained in a cell, interviewed and hours later charged with obstructing a police constable, three officers having made statements attesting that Patrick had been swearing, shouting and trying to stop the police arresting the protagonists. This came as news to Patrick, who had done nothing more than stand behind the bar and let the police take care of the chaos.

* It could be a real pub. Shut up.

Obstructing a police officer is one of the less serious offences, triable only at the mags. It carries a maximum sentence of one month's custody, which is almost never imposed. However, while one of the least serious cases in the eyes of the justice system, to Patrick, this was his life. He had never been in trouble before, and a conviction would be ruinous: it could mean the loss of his licence, and with it the loss of his livelihood and his home.

I don't think I've ever seen as much work go into such a 'small' case. My solicitor arranged multiple conferences, trawled hours of CCTV and bodycam footage from every available angle and traipsed the locality to take fourteen witness statements from regulars who were there on the night, all of whom swore that Patrick had done nothing to obstruct the police. After three months of letters to the CPS going ignored,* a duty lawyer finally agreed to review the case, and accepted that the police evidence couldn't be right. There was no suggestion of malice or collusion; the most likely explanation was that they confused Pat with somebody else wearing similar clothing. Honest and confident eyewitnesses, it might easily be forgotten, can be mistaken.

But perhaps the brighter cut-out-and-keep lesson for my memory bank, something which I think lawyers risk losing sight of the longer we do this job, is the significance of a criminal conviction in itself.† So often our conversations around

---

* In the magistrates' court, it is remarkable if you receive any response from the CPS to any written communication.

† The Court of Appeal certainly has, with its appalling track record of accepting that appellants are probably innocent but refusing to quash convictions on the basis that the punishment has been spent and all that is left for the wrongly convicted are 'unpleasant memories' – see e.g. *R* v. *Ordu* [2017] EWCA Crim 4.

criminal justice centre on the nature of the punishment that follows; if a person doesn't go to prison they 'walk free' or are 'let off with a slap on the wrist'. But the conviction itself, particularly where it is a person's first – where they have 'lost their good character', in legalese – is momentous. You bear the official mark of the criminal; your humiliation, and the vicarious shame of your family, will at best be the subject of points and whispers, at worst circulated in local, national and social media for the edification and judgement of the community, possibly the nation. Friends, work colleagues, business clients and complete strangers can with a simple google find not only editorialised takes on your wrongdoing, but the live-action twenty-first-century fruit pelting taking place below the comments line.

Even if it's a tiny matter that ends in a fine and is spent in a few years, it nevertheless remains formally on your record for ever; a permanent branding as one of society's fallen which can subvert in an instant the entire trajectory of a human life.

Dillon (Part 2)

Within seven months of his last appearance, Dillon and I find ourselves before the Crown Court. He celebrated his eighteenth birthday by getting plastered, stealing a BMW and, having taken the police on a merry eight-mile, 85-mph dance, ploughing the car into a residential garden wall. He pleaded guilty before the adult mags, and has been committed to the Crown Court for sentence. He is accompanied at court by his girlfriend Hanna, a sensible young woman* who impresses upon me her

---

* One of the unspoken electrostatic laws of attraction in the criminal courts is that the more insensible the male client, the more sensible the woman who chains herself to his unroadworthy wagon.

determination to keep Dillon on the straight and narrow. The Crown Court judge, reluctant to send to custody an eighteen-year-old on his first appearance at the Crown Court, follows the recommendation of probation in the Pre-Sentence Report and imposes a suspended sentence order with unpaid work and various rehabilitation programmes. This prescription doesn't seem to have worked wonders when the Youth Offending Team attempted to administer similar treatment, but Dillon confirms his intentions to do better, and strides out of court with his liberty intact.

The Magic Circle

An unseasonably icy day in April sees me rummaging through the dozens of coats piled behind our flat's front door for my Big Winter Overcoat, before mounting a two-hour expedition to the magistrates' court where my private-paying client (drink driving, naturally) is waiting to meet me, decked head to toe in couture and anxious to see how much justice her American Express Black can buy.

Her instructions are familiar to those who have watched a few 'excess alcohol' trials. She wasn't drunk behind the wheel when she careered her Jag into a wall and legged it home before the police arrived, oh no. She was sober as a judge when she careered her Jag into a wall and legged it home before the police arrived, but, shaken by her ordeal, had immediately chugged two bottles of Malbec to steady her nerves. Which is why, Your Worships, when the fuzz turned up on her doorstep twenty minutes later and breathalysed her, she was six times the legal limit.*

* This is known affectionately as 'the hipflask defence'. Like most drink-driving defences and Everton FC, its glory days are firmly back

As soon as the legal advisor hears the name of the firm instructing me, she transfers my case to the courtroom next door, in front of a fearsome District Judge who insists on personally dealing with all road traffic cases so that he can minimise defence gamesmanship.

The Big Winter Overcoat is feeling slightly more snug than usual, and I wonder how long it has been since its last outing. The answer arrives when I confidently stride into court, determined to give my client the gold-standard professional service she has paid for, and reach performatively into my coat pocket for a chambers-branded pen. In so doing, I accidentally dislodge the Christmas cracker novelty that I'd popped in there four months earlier as I left a work do. As I pull out my hand, a deck of miniature playing cards shoots up in the air, cascading a confetti cloud of fifty-two hearts, clubs, diamonds and spades over myself, my client and the bench in front of me.

I later learned that, for her legal representation in that hearing and our subsequent (ultimately unsuccessful) trial, my client had paid my solicitor over £20,000.* I will never forget the look upon her face as her barrister dropped to their knees and scrabbled frantically to pick up fifty-two tiny playing cards from that courtroom floor. It was the fixed stare of bafflement and vicarious humiliation that only an obscene amount of money can buy.

---

in the 1980s, but its aficionados valiantly persevere, notwithstanding the tragically low likelihood of modern-day success.

* I, of course, did not receive £20,000. My solicitor generously valued my contribution, as the person actually attending court and doing the trial, at a total of £400 for three days' work.

Siri

When I first got an iPhone, one of my friends who prides himself on being a tech-savvy early adopter thought it would be hilarious to program the Siri function* to refer to me by a nickname. I tend not to use Siri in my day-to-day life, so working out how to undo this mild act of electronic vandalism has never been a priority.

It should have been. During particularly tense legal submissions in front of a furious judge one afternoon, I quote from a witness statement the phrase 'Seriously, say my name.' Apparently my pronunciation of 'serious' sounds sufficiently similar to 'Siri' for him to spring into action, interrupting my submissions to boom around the echoey courtroom: 'You're SB, but since we're friends I get to call you Sweet Cheeks McGee.'

Lock! Him! Up!

Andre considers himself something of a dab hand at fruit machines. He wins more than he loses, he tells the Probation Service in his Pre-Sentence Report. Which is why, when he found himself £40 down on the fruitie in the Feathers, he deduced that it must be rigged. And why, with alcohol, he concedes, clouding his judgement, he responded by pulling down his trousers in full view of his fellow punters and urinating all over it. Why he felt the need to turn his stream towards the bar staff and, upon completion, to throw chairs at the other patrons, is more difficult to rationalise.

He is already subject to a community order, so by committing this new offence is in breach. It follows that custody is a very real prospect. While the PSR has gone through the motions

---

* For non-iPhone users, 'Siri' is the voice-activated assistant on Apple products.

of proposing an alternative to custody, Andre's performance on his current order – what I might describe in mitigation as 'disappointing progress' and what Andre's probation officer might describe as Andre's point-blank refusal to even pick up the phone, let alone turn up for unpaid work – means that I will have a tough time convincing the judge not to lock him up.

'Please don't,' Andre replies. 'I can't do it. Just ask the judge to send me down. I can't have probation pecking my head every single week. I've got two hundred and forty hours of unpaid work to do – that's gonna take, like, two years' worth of weekends.* I've already been on tag for three months. It's a headfuck. I'll just do my twelve months.'

This is the first time (although it will be far from the last) that a client has found a community penalty so onerous that he would rather go to prison than endure the intense attentions of the probation service, and so the first time I have found myself with the presumably straightforward task of inviting the judge to send my client down.

This judge, however, is not so obliging. Having heard my succinct mitigation ('Your Honour, he accepts that he has not progressed on the order, and invites the court to impose immediate custody') with a stony face, he turns to my client and, with his lips curling up, he purrs:

'Well, I have rather more faith in your client than you, SB. I'm sure if he put his mind to it he could *thrive* on this order. So I'm not going to impose prison today. Instead, I'm going to mark the breach by extending the length of the supervision order from two to three years, thus giving him more time to do

---

* You can normally knock off seven hours a week, so 240 hours would in fact take around thirty-four weeks if you got your head down. At Andre's current rate, two decades would not be enough.

the sixty extra hours of unpaid work I'm imposing. He has successfully completed his three-month curfew, yes?'

'Yes, Your Honour.'

'Excellent. Then for the new offence, I impose a further curfew of three months, starting today.'

Outside court, Andre is a broken man, shaking his head in disbelief. Whether it is at the judge driving a nail with laser focus into Andre's Achilles heel, or the barrister seemingly incapable of getting their own client locked up, Andre is polite enough not to specify.

Kinder surprise

A childhood joy in our household was a Kinder Egg. The excitement of unwrapping and devouring the sickly sweet two-tone exterior to reveal the small plastic egg housing a surprise collectable toy was the rarest of treats, but all the more delectable for it.

Sadly, in the criminal courts, their ubiquity and function are both at the other end of the scale. Should you have a few hundred pounds' worth of class A that you're minded to secrete about your person, a Kinder Egg container's size and smooth edges renders it the perfect dimension and sensation for the average drug user's rectum.

Not just drugs, in fact. Anything that can be folded into a four-centimetre ovoid. As I learn while in the cells with a freshly sentenced burglar, Alvin, who, after a quick rummage, produces and carefully unrolls two 'herbal cigarettes', nudging one towards me. 'Thanks, I don't smoke,' I stammer.

Three strikes and you're out (in eighteen months)

Burglary of someone's home is far more than a property crime. Of that much I was sure before I became a lawyer, of that much

I was sure a year into junior tenancy when my caseload was at least 50 per cent burglaries, and of that much I remain sure now, having prosecuted and defended what must be approaching a thousand of these offences.

It is not merely the loss of items of personal or sentimental value, although that can inflict the most unspeakable cruelty (I think, in particular, of cases where recently bereaved partners or parents have had their last, precious remaining physical memories of their beloved ripped away, such as irreplaceable photographs saved on stolen computers). The lasting harm is in the violation of sanctity; the intrusion into a person's most private spaces. The muddy, carefree footsteps on your carefully hoovered stairs, the casual ransacking of your daughter's bedroom, the strewn clothing across your bed a vivid marker of a stranger's hand having been through your underwear drawer. The Victim Personal Statements provided to courts for sentencing hearings repeat the same buzzwords – *nightmares, terror, unsafe in my own home* – a bingo card of misery whose familiar entries risk desensitising the justice system.

Desensitisation, I think, is the right word. The ubiquity of burglary gives rise to a way of dealing with it that exposes the truth that I suspected as an outsider, a suspicion that has been confirmed with the benefit of professional experience: the criminal justice system does not take burglary seriously. Or at least, not as seriously as it should.

The sheer volume – there are hundreds of thousands of domestic burglaries in England and Wales every year – means that, even with squeezed police resources resulting in the vast majority going unsolved, there are hundreds of burglary prosecutions coming before the courts each week. And the approach of the system appears very much tailored to managing this volume, rather than tackling the underlying scourge. For instance, burglary appears in the lowest categorisation of offences for the purposes of the CPS instructing counsel, meaning that burglary is generally prosecuted in court by the least-experienced advocates. Burglary pays less, both for defence and prosecution, than almost any other criminal offence in the Crown Courts.

And, although the lengths of prison sentences have increased for burglary (as with all offences) over the last two decades – in no small part due to the mandatory minimum three-year sentence that the courts must now impose for a third domestic burglary offence* – they still, in real terms, probably don't reflect the retributive element that the public might expect. If a passing burglar opportunistically smashes your kitchen window, climbs in and steals something of relatively low value, the sentencing guideline provides a starting point of a community order. The highest category of burglary on the sentencing guideline – such as where occupants are at home, or violence is used, or where there is professional planning – has a starting point of three years, and sentencing range of up to six years, some way below the statutory maximum sentence of fourteen years.

And of any custodial sentence, the burglar will only serve half before automatic release on licence, under laws passed by Parliament in 2003. So even a minimum three-striker is out in eighteen months. To put it in context, if you defraud the taxman out of £50,000 – a significant sum to an individual, but roughly 0.000005 per cent of the Treasury's annual expenditure and unlikely to leave the Chancellor and his children too afraid to sleep in their own beds – you can also expect a starting point

---

* If a judge thinks it is 'in the interests of justice' not to impose a minimum three years, they have a discretion not to. But this is, in practice, very rare indeed.

of three years.* If you sell a few wraps of cocaine, you can expect a starting point of four and a half years. Quite what the victim of a traumatic, life-defining burglary is expected to make of this, I have no more idea now than when I penned my 'sheep in Woolf's clothing' green-ink missive to the student paper.

The nuance that practice has exposed, however, is the profile of most burglars, as revealed in the predictable content of the Pre-Sentence Reports for these defendants: drug and alcohol addiction; mental ill health; lack of stable accommodation; lack of employment. The four horsemen of the burgocalypse, none of whose steeds respond to whatever whispering is available in our overcrowded, understaffed prisons. It is easier to score class A in many jails than it is on the streets, and training and education programmes have been increasingly replaced by twenty-three-hour lockdowns as prisons struggle to cope. Against this backdrop, it often is the case that more can meaningfully be achieved in terms of rehabilitation by enrolling an offender – particularly a first-time offender – in a drug or alcohol treatment programme as part of a community order or suspended sentence, and dragging them under the supervision of the probation service towards stability and employability. And it was this point, I think, that Lord Woolf was trying to make, despite the determination of many, including me, to misunderstand him as unrolling some sort of burglars' amnesty.

But that context allowed, I still wonder what we are hoping to achieve with the way we deal with the burglars who we do imprison. The sentences are far too short to have any deterrent

* Sentencing Council, 'Fraud, Bribery and Money Laundering Offences Definitive Guideline', p. 21, https://www.sentencingcouncil.org.uk/wp-content/uploads/Fraud-bribery-and-money-laundering-offences-Definitive-guideline2.pdf

effect, they do nothing for rehabilitation and are wildly misaligned with the punishment deemed proportionate for other, less harmful, crimes. No doubt, returning to my earlier theme, this is in large part because of numbers, and of the extortionate cost the public purse would incur were we to begin imprisoning so many burglars for a greater length of time.

At its height, our penal policy for burglary appears to amount to offering communities temporary respite from a small percentage of the minority of burglars that the police can actually catch, and defining that as success.

Cracking

There are many reasons why a trial might crack on the day. A helpful intervention from a judge paving the way for an agreeable compromise; a change in counsel eliciting more sensible instructions from the defendant (or the CPS); the surprise attendance of the battered girlfriend whom the defendant thought he had successfully manipulated into not attending ('Fucking hell, I gave her money for a hotel and everything,' a client once bemoaned, apparently expecting sympathy that his cynical attempt at witness interference had seen his ex-partner simply pocket the bribe and turn up to give evidence anyway).

But one reason a trial should never be cracking – really, really never – is the prosecution waiting until the day of trial to produce a photo of the knife that the defendant is charged with having in public, and for it to be immediately obvious that, contrary to the description given by the police in their witness statements, the offending article is a small penknife, which is something that anybody is allowed to lawfully carry. Yet, somehow, I have found myself in this position twice inside the first year of tenancy. What a time to be alive.

Family values

As my confidence incrementally grows in my Bambi-on-ice barristering skills, so too does my sense of identity as a permanent member of chambers. While there is formality and structure among the people we employ, with the clerks and staff all reporting to our chambers manager, among the barristers the minimal hierarchy and wild overfamilarity render it a familial environment in its truest sense: few social niceties, absolutely no deference and frequent outbreaks of unrestrained emotional incontinence.

Accordingly, we all conform to our nearest stereotypical role. There's sensible mum and dad trying to keep the peace; angry wine-soaked uncle raging at the universe; kindly grandfather dozing away the hours till retirement; protective aunt anxiously looking out for the welfare of the angsty junior nieces and nephews; and the kissing cousins who everybody pretends not to notice.

I find that I slot most comfortably into geeky grandchild quietly reading a book in the corner. As well as playing to my natural timidity in social situations, it also permits shelter from some of the fiercer arguments that blast like a chill wind through our department. The politics are difficult to escape. They are the product not just of personality clashes – unavoidable given the brontosaurus-sized egos involved – but the professional jealousy that I first experienced as a pupil. Envy at colleagues' practices, and suspicions that other members of chambers are getting preferential treatment from the clerks in allocation of work, frequently bubble to the surface. Usually the temperature can be lowered by reassuring hugs* from the clerks, but sometimes the boil-over tips somebody to up sticks for the green grass of another chambers.

* Metaphorical.

For me, any pangs of jealousy are kept in check – and any pretensions of throwing my weight around are modulated – by the knowledge that no other chambers has the slightest interest in adding my alleged talents to their books.

Thugs and scrotes

I meet Dev around eighteen months in. He pleaded guilty at his first appearance before the mags and has been committed to the Crown Court for sentence. His offences are burglary and having a knife in a public place, and this is not his first Crown Court rodeo. Three years earlier, he was sentenced to a year's custody after 'borrowing' a car while in thrall to a cocaine addiction and driving it through residential areas at absurdly dangerous speeds until he brought it to an abrupt stop with the help of an obliging tree.

This time around, he entered somebody's home in the dead of night, stole a large kitchen knife and made his escape. The terrified householder, awoken by Dev's noisy entrance, called the police and Dev was arrested a hundred yards down the road, knife in hand.

Aged twenty-four, Dev is now facing another spell inside. And, no doubt, anybody reading those facts would expect a functioning justice system to teach a yahoo like Dev a severe lesson by imposing a prison sentence running into years, not just months.

So why does Dev walk free from court?

To explain, we need to rewind four years, to the time of his first offence. He was twenty-one, and a huge cocaine aficionado. Couldn't get enough of it. His enthusiasm reached its zenith one evening when he decided to take his dad's Nissan Micra for a spin. What followed was a burst of short-lived but incredibly dangerous driving, which Dev was fortunate to survive and for which he was rightly imprisoned. When he emerged from his sentence, Dev resolved to put things right. He moved home and kicked the drugs. He found a job. He devoted his evenings to taking on caring responsibilities for his mum, who had multiple sclerosis, an act which meant that his dad could obtain part-time employment for the first time in a decade, and together they formed a well-oiled family unit, making just enough to get by.

What his family didn't know, however, was that Dev was living with severe, at times paralysing, depression. He functioned at work and around the home because he had to, but despite the outward signs, he was spiralling, haunted by intrusive thoughts and dark, sometimes ferocious, urges. He rattled between increasingly strong medications prescribed by his GP, and a year later found himself late one night standing on a railway bridge staring into the waters below. The jump, miraculously, didn't seriously injure him; he was able to clamber out, sopping wet, and in a daze walk to a nearby house. The door must have been unlocked, because a trail of wet footprints led from the point of entry to the kitchen, from where a knife was taken. Dev has absolutely no memory of any of this, but the mental health professional who later assessed him was certain that Dev had taken the knife with the intention of using it on himself, only to be thwarted by the prompt arrival of the police.

In the eighteen months* it has subsequently taken to bring this case before the courts, Dev has stabilised. He has found a

* Twelve to eighteen months is standard for many types of police investigation. Years of funding cuts mean that there are just not enough resources, either in the police or the CPS, to process the workload any quicker.

prescription that works, and is managing well with his job and family responsibilities. The probation service express strong concerns that a custodial sentence will undo the progress that Dev has made, as well as placing an intolerable burden on his parents, who will struggle to afford the rent without his income, and in particular on his father, who will be forced to give up his own job to care for Dev's mother.

Having heard the background and read the reports, the sentencing judge finds that it would not be right to send Dev immediately to prison, and suspends the sentence.

And so. On the one hand, Dev is a paradigm case of a society in disarray; young thugs being indulged by a dysfunctional justice system. A knife-wielding, coke-sniffing burglar is spared jail – despite having been imprisoned before for stealing a car and driving in a way that nearly killed someone.

But equally, Dev is a paradigm case of a justice system working. A young man who has worked hard to reform himself following the errors of his youth, and who now juggles weighty responsibilities at work and at home, is given support when he makes a serious mistake in the throes of a mental health crisis, and is dealt with in a way that marks his record with a prison sentence, but avoids causing disproportionate hardship to him and his blameless family.

My tendency to assume the first perspective was shaped, at least in some part, by the news reports and commentary I grew up with. It is an influential perspective which divides our society neatly between law-abiding citizen and criminal, and holds that the character of the latter is fully and permanently defined by the wrong(s) they have committed. There is a beguiling simplicity to the equation that a person who commits a crime = a criminal = a bad person, around which it is easy to construct an entire belief system about criminal justice. If criminal justice is concerned solely with bad, irredeemable people, of course its primary, if not unitary, function should be incarcerating those people wherever possible, and for as long as possible. Of course we shouldn't be wasting public time and resources remedying the irremediable. Of course we should fear and loathe the bad people, because they intend us – the good people – nothing but harm. Of course when we talk about justice, we mean punishing those people as heavily as we can; making them hurt even more than they hurt us.

And it's a tempting, comforting view to adopt, because it follows that if you are not a criminal, you probably don't need to worry about criminal justice. That world exists on a separate plane, where the terrible and irredeemable are given their just deserts. Your stake in it demands only that you monitor the quotient of punishment, and lend your voice to the throng if it's suspected to have fallen short.

But it's a perspective which, perhaps more than any other I hold, is being shattered by experience. Because most of the people I represent are not the caricatures I have been bracing for. If you'll forgive the facileness of the observation: people are complicated. Even those – especially those – who are accused of, or who have committed, criminal offences.

Many are people we would happily talk to in a pub or at the school gate without giving their personal history a second thought. They are pleasant and chatty and charming and good company and caring, and distinguishable from us solely by the rules that they have broken. Others have backgrounds that cast their choices and their actions into a context that is probably unimaginable unless you have been directly confronted by it. Most are capable of being courteous and polite and displaying insight into their conduct and their problems. Some can act rude and threatening and thoroughly ungrateful. All have explanations – not necessarily excuses, much less justifications, but explanations – for why they have acted as they have. None is defined solely by the snapshot impression that might be gleaned from a court appearance.

And I know, when I write these things – because I can hear the rejoinders in my own twenty-something voice – that it sounds as if I am minimising the criminality of my clients, or romanticising their stories in a way that downplays their blame-worthiness and attempts to shift their responsibility onto 'the state' or 'the system'. But I think it's possible to tread a middle ground. I think you can fully believe that people are responsible for the choices they make, while acknowledging the circum-stances that might allow for nuance, and the complex factors that can nudge or propel people towards certain decisions. I think you can believe that people can break our social code, even repeatedly, without being irredeemable.

Ours is not the binary world of criminals and law-abiding citizens, with nothing in between.

People are generally better than the most negative retelling of their actions. We are all more than our own worst acts.

Our own worst acts

In the early years of criminal practice, I find that I am largely shielded from the most serious crimes and the most dangerous offenders. Unsurprisingly enough, I do not find myself pros-ecuting and defending murder, rape or terrorism cases straight out of pupillage; instead, the types of criminal allegations piled up in my pigeonhole are those considered less serious by the system, although very much not so for those directly affected or accused: burglaries, affrays, ABHs,* street-level

* ABH = occasioning actual bodily harm. More serious than common

drug supply, low- to medium-value fraud, carrying weapons – that sort of jazz.

But in the course of covering hearings for senior colleagues, I get the occasional glimpse into the world that awaits me a few years down the line.

One such case involves the prosecution of three cocaine addicts who, walking the streets in the early hours, decided to break into a random flat. Once inside, they approached the sleeping occupant, gagged and bound him, and, for the eight hours that followed, systematically tortured him using a Stanley knife and a steaming iron. Just for kicks. His injuries covered every inch of his body – from his eyeballs to his toes – and the effects were life-lasting. One of the defence solicitors tells me that it is the one case in his whole career that he had refused to discuss with his wife after he was called to the police station at 3 a.m. when his client was arrested. The harrowing details spelled out during the police interview stopped him from sleeping. They remain with me, vividly, a decade later.

Another concerns allegations by three sisters against their stepdad who, a jury would later find, raped and sexually abused them from childhood through to adolescence; hundreds and hundreds of the most vile and depraved violations, committed on a near-daily basis, against vulnerable children in their own homes, in their own beds, by a man they trusted to protect them.

More than your own worst act. More than your own worst act.

In such cases I try to avoid too much introspection, lest I find a well of hypocrisy where my newfound conversionary zeal runs dry.

---

assault/battery, less serious than inflicting grievous – i.e. really serious – bodily harm.

(Very) cross courting

When I'm not in a trial, my day is usually filled with shorter hearings, both my own work and other people's returns. Mentions, sentences, plea hearings, bail applications – each in isolation pays a meagre fee* but if the clerks cram a few into my diary, I might just earn back my parking. The hitch is that rarely will all my hearings be before the same judge; I am often 'cross-courted' and find myself frantically dashing from courtroom to courtroom trying not to keep anybody waiting. Even if the clerks work miracles negotiating with court listing officers to line up my cases in a formation that gives a realistic hope of getting to all of them, a favourite trick of listing is to switch cases between courtrooms at 6 p.m. the night before without telling any of the counsel involved.

Generally, judges understand and give a little leeway, especially as we are ultimately doing the court a favour in ensuring cases are covered notwithstanding the court's wholesale disregard for anybody's convenience. My first encounter with a judge who was not so disposed arrives a couple of years in. Having kept him waiting a whole five minutes after my previous hearing has overrun due to the court recording system breaking down, I speed into the packed courtroom, take my place on counsel's row and immediately apologise.

All hell breaks loose. The judge screams – literally, hysterically screams – at me for over ten minutes, in a tone that I haven't heard since I was five. I am insolent. I am selfish. I am treating the court staff with contempt. I have no respect for my

---

* Nowadays, £91 is the 'standard appearance fee', which covers all preparation and court time, of which I take home around £35. Prior to 2018, the rate was as low as £46.50, which for a full court day worked out at a take-home rate of around £3 an hour.

colleagues. He mimics the way I speak. Mimics my accent. Asks me (apparently under the impression that I am still in pupillage) what my pupil supervisor would have to say (an image flashes into my mind of Alan drawing on a fag and describing this man as a 'Free Range Cock', which is the only thing stopping me from dissolving into crying). He tells me that I owe the court an apology, although then shouts down my every attempt to offer one with further mimicry ('Oooh, *I apologise! I apologise!* That makes it acceptable, does it?'). I am his captive verbal punch-bag, silently taking blow after blow after blow in full view of my instructing CPS caseworker, the defendant, the public gallery and around ten other barristers, and there is absolutely nothing I can say to make the pummelling stop. When it eventually subsides, I stumble my way through our short hearing – simply refixing a trial date – and then walk out in a daze.

Back in the robing room, I am reassured by others who witnessed my deconstruction that I've done nothing wrong. This particular judge just happens to be a notorious bully, but he was actually quite a nice chap when he was in practice, and is a nice chap when he is off the bench.

You hear this quite a bit. And after a decade, I have to say that I've rather had enough of encountering these men who are actually quite a nice chap in private, but just happen to be a vicious misogynistic bully when on the bench, because, I'm afraid to say, if you're a vicious misogynistic bully in the workplace, you're probably actually *not* a very nice chap in private, you're just somebody capable of not being a vicious misogynistic bully when the mood takes you, and so by definition somebody who *chooses* to be a vicious misogynistic bully when in a position of utmost power and privilege. And it's a choice that most judges manage to avoid; the majority are polite and kind and wise and civil, and even if – and I speak from extensive direct experience – they think you're a wally whose arguments and ability leave much to be desired, they still speak to you with basic courtesy.

The judicial bully's traits are universal. They take delight in humiliating junior counsel, especially women. You rarely see this breed try their macho routine on men of forty years' call. Shouting, name-calling ('Are you even a real barrister?' I've seen one type howl at a female pupil, in front of her client, after she made an entirely proper legal submission), picking pointless fights, asking irrelevant questions that they know counsel cannot answer and then berating us for 'being unprepared', insisting on relisting cases at dates or times when they know we can't attend – all just for sport. Standard playground bullying, just topped with horsehair.

The judge on this day did ultimately receive his comeuppance, in the same form as has been visited upon several other judicial bullies I have known: he was promoted. It happens time and time again. Sometimes up to the highest echelons of the criminal judiciary. We don't talk about it because it's not the done thing. Complaining about judicial bullying feels like making a rod not only for your own back, but for your future clients' should you appear in that courtroom again. So tactically, we stay schtum, or a senior colleague will offer to 'have a quiet word', or we'll tell ourselves that maybe we're being over-sensitive, or need to *handle the situation better next time*.

And then we wonder why the cycle continues.*

---

* Recently, the Bar Council has introduced 'Talk to Spot', an online tool for barristers to confidentially and anonymously report inappropriate behaviour and concerns about bullying, harassment and discrimination. Which is undoubtedly a positive move. But I can't say that I've seen much of a change among the judges whose behaviour is in need of it.

Doppelgänger

One of the more intriguing defences I've been instructed to run involves twenty-three-year-old Arthur, who has allegedly attempted to mediate a dispute between his mum and her anti-social neighbour by arming himself with a tennis racket and giving the neighbour, à la Basil Fawlty, a damn good thrashing. Arthur's defence is the Shaggy Defence* with a twist: he has an identical twin. The neighbour must have mistaken Arthur for his brother, Steve. Surprisingly enough, Steve is not willing to attend court to give evidence for us, so the best we can do, I have advised, is provide a birth certificate and photograph of the twins so that the magistrates can assess for themselves the likelihood of mistaken ID.

On arrival at the mags, Arthur proudly hands me the photograph he has dug out. It shows two toddlers in romper suits, side by side. 'See?' he enthuses. 'You can't tell us apart.'

Notwithstanding my counsel, Arthur instructs that we proceed, and after a trial in which the magistrates actually laugh out loud when presented with the photo, and in which the neighbour, when cross-examined, confirms that not only does he know Arthur's twin, but can recite in detail the physical distinctions ('Steve's not half as fat as Arthur, he's bald and he wears glasses'), our hero is convicted.

Illegal

Charmaine has worked as a carer for three years when we meet. She has lived in the UK for a decade, arriving on a student visa in her twenties having qualified and practised as a nurse and a midwife in Malawi.

Over five years, she completed further qualifications in

* aka 'It Wasn't Me'.

London, working part-time in hospitals and schools to support her studies, before becoming pregnant with her daughter. After Charmaine's daughter was born, she decided to re-enter the world of work, and obtained full-time employment as a carer. Her agency couldn't believe their luck – Charmaine's wealth of care and medical experience meant that they were getting a qualified nurse for the minimum-wage price of a carer, a position they struggled to fill. She soared through the induction process, proved hugely popular among staff and clients and quickly established herself as one of the agency's most valued employees.

A random immigration check brought it all screeching to a halt. The French passport that Charmaine had used to prove her right to work and to secure her employment was revealed to be a forgery. When her student visa had expired five years earlier, she had not applied for leave to remain, instead accepting the offer of a foolproof shortcut from a friend offering a £500 'identification pack', complete with realistic forged passport and valid National Insurance number. Everything else about Charmaine – her qualifications, her experience, her abilities, the taxes she paid – was unquestionably genuine. Just not the document she had used to work in the UK.

Possessing a false identity document with improper intention is a serious criminal offence, carrying a maximum prison sentence of ten years.* Representing Charmaine at her sentence at the Crown Court, I have to advise her that the law is clear: offences of this type are always met by immediate custody. It doesn't matter that she is of otherwise impeccable character, nor that she has contributed thousands of pounds in tax performing a vital job that British workers apparently do not want to do,

* Section 4 of the Identity Documents Act 2010

nor that she is a mother, nor that she poses absolutely no risk to the public. The Court of Appeal has for decades made it a point of sentencing principle that cases involving the use of false passports 'will almost always merit a significant period in custody'.* Charmaine receives eight months' imprisonment.

I understand the official rationale. False passports undermine immigration controls and the integrity of our borders. They provide an illegal shortcut to people who 'jump the queue' ahead of others who apply for permission to work in the UK through the official channels. The purchase of false identity documents, like the purchase of drugs, fuels demand in a shadow market run by organised international crime groups, which causes very real and direct harm to an inordinate number of vulnerable people.

I get that. I understand why it is a serious criminal offence. But the need for automatic imprisonment?

Every day, in Crown Courts across England and Wales, defendants who have beaten, maimed, sexually abused, threatened, burgled, defrauded, robbed, stabbed or shot their fellow citizens are made the subject of suspended sentence orders, where the courts, carefully weighing the individual circumstances of the offence and the offender, decide that justice does not require custody to be immediate. I know this because I have defended or prosecuted offences of all of those types where that has happened.

But obtain a false identity document to get a job that no

---

* See *R* v. *Kolawole* [2004] EWCA Crim 3047 and the authorities discussed within. Where a passport is used to obtain work, rather than enter the UK, the sentence 'can justifiably be less', but should still be immediate custody – *R* v. *Ovieriakhi* [2009] EWCA Crim 452, at [16].

British person wants, and perform it to an impeccable standard so that you can support your child and pay taxes towards our public services? In every single case I have ever seen, it is deemed So Serious That Only Immediate Custody Will Suffice.

Every single time.

Driving Miss Daisy

Arriving at court to meet my client, George, who is facing sentence for dangerous driving, I am greeted not only by the client but by his familiar-looking friend. Recognition strikes after a few seconds. George, a disqualified driver, has led the police on a lengthy pursuit, travelling at speeds of 90 mph through 30 mph zones, veering onto the wrong side of the road, through red lights and over roundabouts, until his innate satnav failed him and he drove into a dead end. Like most dangerous-driving cases involving police chases, there was dashcam footage from the pursuing police car, which captured not just the driving but George and his passenger frantically disembarking and running away – fruitlessly in George's case, fruitfully in the case of his passenger, who had the presence of mind to pause to give a middle finger to the police dashcam as he leaped across the car's bonnet and danced off into the great beyond.

Which brings me to George's companion at court, who, having successfully evaded the attentions of the police, is here because he's been told that prosecution is likely to play the dashcam footage during the hearing, and 'I want to see myself on the big screen.' I advise George that the one thing guaranteed to secure him the maximum two-year sentence is his fugitive accomplice gurning appreciatively from the public gallery, and the wisdom of their lads' day out is swiftly reconsidered.

This is George's third conviction for dangerous driving, and he's looking not only at custody, but a lengthy disqualification from driving. The thing is, George has been disqualified from driving on eight previous occasions. And every single time he simply gets back behind the wheel, typically borrowed without the owner's consent, and keeps on driving as carelessly or dangerously as he pleases.* Sometimes he's caught and given a few weeks inside, more often he's not. As with career burglars, the odds of detection are very much in his favour, and the occasional stint in prison is simply written off as a business expense. The systemic delays – it has taken fourteen months to get to this sentence hearing, despite George admitting the offence in his police interview and pleading guilty straight away – only serve to further distance in George's mind the eventual punishment from the crime.

Cases like this ram home the blunt limitations of the criminal justice system. What can actually be done with people, like George, who simply refuse to cooperate? Short sentences of imprisonment – the maximum sentence for driving while disqualified is six months, and George would be automatically released on licence after three months at most† – have acted neither as a deterrent, nor done anything to dissuade George from driving while banned. When convicted of dangerous driving, which carries a longer maximum sentence, the effect has been the same. The courts have exhausted non-custodial options

---

* The legal distinction: careless = driving which falls below the standard expected of a competent and careful driver; dangerous = driving which falls *far* below that standard.

† It is often thought that release on licence is contingent on 'good behaviour' or similar – it's not. Parliament in its wisdom has legislated so that, apart from dangerous offenders and those convicted of serious sexual or violent offences, all prisoners serving a standard determinate sentence must be automatically released after serving half.

– his record is littered with breaches of community orders and suspended sentences which make clear his reluctance and/or inability to engage with the probation service.

Once upon a time I might have rashly suggested that the way to deal with George is to impose increasingly severe sentences, without limit, until he sees sense – and indeed, some of our more simplistic politicians have proposed this very thing.* There's an understandable urge, when faced with such recalcitrance, to turn the punishment dial up to eleven, seeking sadistic comfort in inflicting as much retribution as we lawfully can. For these ingrained recidivists, with their incessant low-level criminality that ruins the lives of their law-abiding neighbours, there is an undeniable superficial attraction in simply throwing away the key.

But the insanity of this approach is obvious: clogging up our already overcrowded prisons with non-violent offenders for decades on end is the ultimate counsel of despair. A key principle of justice is that punishment is proportionate to the crime. Any mechanism which results in someone being jailed for a single incident of disqualified driving – even if it is their thirtieth such offence – for a longer period than somebody sentenced for serious sexual violence feels utterly perverse.

So if short sentences don't work, and community options don't work, and increasingly long sentences won't work – where does that leave us? What can we do, and what can we achieve? Prison reformists often voice the criticism, and I have articulated

---

* See Matthew Scott's excoriating blog on the so-called 'Sentence Escalator Bill' – 'Phillip Hollobone and Peter Bone: Could they be the stupidest men in Parliament?' 30 November 2013, https://barrister-blogger.com/2013/11/30/phillip-hollobone-peter-bone-stupidest-men-parliament/

it myself, that our jails are too densely populated with non-violent offenders. But what choices remain where somebody refuses the alternatives offered by the courts? Should judges keep imposing non-custodial sentences regardless, in the faint hope – and it cannot be more than that – that the fourth or fifth prescription of the same marvellous medicine will yield miraculous results? At what point does optimism end and give way to the nihilism of prison sentence after prison sentence after prison sentence, on the basis that we can think of nothing better?

These questions trouble both my pre- and post-conversion canon: it's all very well decrying prison for relatively minor, non-violent offences, but what else is out there?

The disqualification poses a similarly tortuous question. The courts are discouraged from imposing disproportionately lengthy disqualifications from driving. The minimum ban for dangerous driving is one year, but it is rare indeed that a disqualification will exceed five years. Even in cases where serious injury or death is caused, lifetime disqualifications are uncommon. This is something I could never understand before starting practice, and it's something I still instinctively struggle with today. Driving is a privilege, not a right, and if you repeatedly break the rules of the road and put others in danger, why should you not permanently forfeit that privilege?

The Court of Appeal's answer is that excessively long driving bans risk impeding rehabilitation. The reality of our country's public transport infrastructure is that access to private transport is essential for many types of job, and for many people living in areas ill-served by the state. If George decides one day to turn it all around and look for gainful employment, his options will be severely limited if he is for ever prevented from using a car, and forced to rely on an increasingly reduced and unreliable bus service or increasingly expensive rush-hour trains. Lifelong bans also increase the chances of somebody who is otherwise rehabilitated relapsing and finding themselves dragged back into a cycle of offending.

We may retort that these are the breaks: this is part of George's punishment for his repeated criminal behaviour. If you can't do the time, etc. But George's rehabilitation is not simply a matter of private interest – we all have a stake in maximising his chances of success and keeping him away from a life of misery-spreading crime.

So this is the balance the courts try to strike with the sentences and disqualifications they impose. I'm not confident that they always, or even often, succeed. But I'm equally confident that I don't know what else in the court system would. It seems to me increasingly obvious that a more potent deterrent for those like George would be increasing the chances of being caught and dealt with swiftly; investing political and public attention in the policing and technology that might improve detection rates for driving offences, rather than expecting deterrent solutions from a court passing sentence years after the event.

God rest ye merry, barristers

A few years in, and I am truly embracing the working culture of the Bar. The entrenched impossibility of anything in the criminal courts running efficiently guarantees not only a steady stream of returns to plump up my diary, but also that no day of the year is truly my own. Trials almost always overrun, whether due to witness difficulties, or sick jurors, or judges needing to take days out of the trial to attend to other work, or interpreters forgetting to attend, or prisons omitting to bring prisoners to court, or basic technology not working for days on end. Usually the overrun is only a matter of days, but in long trials it can be weeks, even months. Every barrister has stories of holidays cancelled, weddings not attended, funerals missed or honeymoons postponed, and I am quickly accumulating my own.

On the occasions I am fortunate enough to snare myself a week's holiday, I can bank either on the court arbitrarily relisting one of my cases in the middle of that week without consulting me, or on other people's overruns encroaching. The 5 p.m. phone call from the clerks on the eve of my week off is always the same: 'SB! You know you're marked down as "away" next week – are you *away* away? Only Ms Smith's trial has overrun and next week she has a five-day affray that needs covering . . .' The inexplicable dynamic between clerk and barrister, by which we pay the clerk's wages yet meekly obey their every command, means that unless my body is physically out of the jurisdiction when that call comes through, I will find myself murmuring assent without even computing it.

Even when the courts are closed, my time is not my own. The long-held belief among many judges that barristers' evenings and weekends are just itching to be filled with unnecessarily time-limited (and unpaid) written work means that judicial demands for skeleton arguments overnight or lengthy written submissions to be drafted between close of play on Friday and 9 a.m. on Monday are par for the course. Bank holidays, weekends and religious festivals are spent preparing written advices for the CPS (demanded within ten days of instruction, notwithstanding that it will typically take two months for the advice to be read, six months for the police to act upon it and eighteen months for the case to come to trial), or drafting documents, or fielding calls from my opponents to discuss upcoming trials.

After four years, I have worked three Christmas Days out of four. The other year, Christmas was the sole day of December that I wasn't either in court – usually ploughing through Jingle Bails* – or doing paperwork. In the years that follow, I will find myself going stretches of fifteen months without a week off. My honeymoon sees me responding to work emails on average every other day. I don't think any of this is unusual; it's normalised within a year or two of starting out. It is also, self-evidently, deeply unhealthy. If the perks of self-employment are supposed to include being your own boss, most of the criminal Bar need to be raising grievances with management.

We've had enough of experts

Expert evidence – such as DNA, medical evidence and cell-site analysis – falls outside the ordinary experience of a jury, and is tightly regulated in our criminal courts. The circumstances in which it can be received are limited, the qualifications required of experts are likewise strict, and where expert evidence is permitted, the expert's duty is to the courts – rather than the party instructing them. The infrastructure is designed to ensure that the court is provided with the most robust and reliable evidence when considering complex matters beyond its everyday experience.

A late return from a solicitor advocate of local renown is an appeal against a conviction for failing to provide a specimen of breath.† Upon opening the brief it becomes clear why the client was convicted by the magistrates, and why the appeal to the Crown Court has been hastily briefed out to chambers. The

---

* Every year, the Advent period heralds a never-ending stream of optimistic bail applications from remanded defendants.
† If you are suspected of having driven with excess alcohol or drugs in your system, and refuse without reasonable cause to give a specimen of breath, you are guilty of an offence.

High Court has long held that expert evidence is required if your 'reasonable cause' for not cooperating with a breath test is a medical complaint. Our defence, it appears, relies on the word of the client that he has an enigmatic breathing condition that isn't mentioned once in his forty-seven years of medical records, along with a printout of the 'breathing' entry from Wikipedia.

Names without faces

Some of the most affecting clients are those I never meet. The turnover of cases each year offers thousands of fleeting glimpses into people's lives, few of them blessed with fortune. If you are a party to criminal legal proceedings, it is usually fair to assume that something in your life has not gone to plan. As the legal professionals charged with representing that party, it is our responsibility to try to avoid or to minimise the damage. But often we don't get to know how the story ends; our involvement is temporary, brought to an abrupt halt by another case overrunning or court listings shifting a hearing forward by a day, or, if we are just covering, the case returning to a colleague. Many clients will be forever just names on a page, their entire existences reduced to narratives sketched by the authors of prosecution case summaries and Pre-Sentence Reports.

Raheem is twenty-two. He pleaded guilty to ABH before the magistrates and has been committed to the Crown Court for sentence. Reading through the papers, I note that I will be covering his fourth hearing. For all the previous hearings, Raheem has been in hospital. His story contains a number of familiar hallmarks, but their coalescence has been especially devastating. Raheem grew up in a home where his alcoholic father beat everyone in the household on a near-daily basis. Amid the unremitting violence, Raheem's most basic needs went unmet. His disruptive behaviour at primary school led to a Child and

Adolescent Mental Health Services (CAMHS) referral which stalled when his mother was unable to keep the appointments. His undiagnosed autistic spectrum disorder and coexisting ADHD rendered mainstream schooling a predictable disaster, and exclusion was the first recourse of his failing school. The 'friends' he met hanging around outside the Pupil Referral Unit introduced him to cocaine at sixteen, marking the start of regular appearances before the Youth Court. He met a girl, Joni, and when she fell pregnant Raheem saw this as an opportunity to build a future. Her miscarriage at fourteen weeks undid them both. Raheem started to cut himself with razors, the scratches deepening into flowing crimson wounds as the months passed. He experimented with ligatures, and overdosed on paracetamol on three occasions, in between the flashes of violence that now punctuated his daily social interactions.

He suffered regular auditory hallucinations, subsequently confirmed by prison doctors as symptomatic of schizophrenia. The assault on Joni that has brought him before court on this occasion has resulted in his remand in custody for his own protection, the magistrates fearing that, if bailed, Raheem poses a serious risk to himself. In prison, they reasoned, there will at least be constant oversight to ensure he takes his medication and is protected from his urges.

The magistrates' optimism has been defied by prison reality. Somehow – and one might think that prisons would be capable of preventing this, but apparently not – Raheem keeps getting hold of batteries. And the night before each hearing, he panics, his paranoia convinces him that he is going to be imprisoned for years, and he swallows them. He is transferred to hospital, and his sentence hearing has to be adjourned. We are stuck in this loop, waiting in vain for the prison to do its most fundamental function: keep somebody in its custody safe from harm.

This, evidently, is too much to ask. Not deemed sufficiently unwell to qualify for a more permanent residence in hospital, Raheem is one of thousands of prisoners with severe mental ill health who are warehoused in cells and then temporarily shipped out to hospital when they become unmanageable. This, equally evidently, is the best that the state feels it can do. Or should do.

One of many, many tragedies of his situation is that Raheem's fears of a custodial sentence are misplaced – the Crown Court judge who has hold of this case is desperate to get Raheem out of prison and into the supported accommodation and community mental health treatment programme that probation have lined up in consultation with the psychiatric experts. We just need to get Raheem to court, and he can then be released with the appropriate supervision. He has been advised by his solicitor of all of this, that if he comes to court he will get out of prison for good, but the counsel of his lawyers is losing the battle with the voices in his head.

At 9.30 a.m., I walk down the court stairs to the door to the cells and ring the rusty buzzer for attention. At 9.31, I walk back up the stairs, to kick my heels for twenty-nine minutes until I can tell the judge that, once again, Raheem is in hospital, and we will have to adjourn.

The public interest

Cases of domestic violence often fit a miserably predictable pattern. Police will respond to an emergency call, placed either by a terrified complainant or concerned neighbour, to find a bloodied and bruised woman – often a cowering toddler too – sitting in an upturned living room with her partner ten minutes down the road. All too often, fear prevents her from giving the police a formal account of what has just taken place, but if she does, and an arrest follows, everybody in the criminal courts knows what comes next.

At the police station, the defendant gives a no comment interview. After charge comes a bare-bones Defence Statement advancing either a straight denial of any assault or an improbable claim of self-defence. On the day of trial – which can be anything from six months to four years later, depending on court delays – if the complainant is sufficiently mollified or terrified into not attending, the prosecution might throw their hand in. If she turns up, the defendant pleads guilty and gets their 10 per cent discount on sentence for a late guilty plea.

The cynicism of defendants was for some time matched by police and prosecutors. Domestic abuse was for decades underplayed and dismissed as somehow 'lesser' violence; its inherent complexities often too much trouble to bother prosecuting. Case-hardening – the incremental desentisation caused by the ubiquity of male violence* – morphed into this cynicism. I remember vividly the shock I felt as a pupil reading the evidence in one of Alan's cases; the matter-of-fact witness statement charting the relentless barrage of punches to the face, kicks to the stomach, bites to the arm, blows with whatever heavy blunt object he had to hand. The horrendous hospital photographs of a face swollen and purpled beyond recognition, of a jaw wired shut and snapped limbs in plaster. The printout of his previous convictions showing that this casual, sickening violence is just what he did. And the Pre-Sentence Report revealing, predictably, that this brutal misogyny was the language he learned

* Domestic violence is not, of course, unique to one gender or one type of relationship. But the overwhelming majority of cases that come to the attention of the criminal justice system involve allegations of male violence upon women.

from his father or stepfather as a young boy. I remember the surprise I felt at Alan's lack of reaction; his businesslike assessment of the merits of a case the likes of which he had seen a thousand times before. I hope I have not yet reached that level of immunity. But people do. And certainly, among police and prosecutors, there often prevailed a jaundiced view of the merits of pursuing such cases where a complainant's reluctance – or terror – presented a complication. Much easier to chalk it off as 'a domestic'.

A sharp – and sorely needed – revision in the 2000s saw the CPS and police treat domestic violence with something proximate to the seriousness and care it warrants. Meaningful consideration is now given to the ways in which complainants can be supported through the criminal process – from the initial report to the police through to the ways in which evidence is given in court, which can include measures such as screening the complainant from the defendant. Novel ways of proceeding to trial even without the complainant giving evidence have been identified by prosecutors and approved as lawful by the courts.* Another important corrective is an emphasis under current policy that the public interest will almost always weigh in favour of prosecuting any allegations of domestic abuse.†

Policy is not, however, a substitute for judgement. One miserable Thursday, I'm prosecuting an early guilty plea in a domestic violence case. The facts, as I open the case, are straightforward: jealous boyfriend, long history of violence, drinks to excess and punches and kicks his girlfriend, before

* Such as adducing audio or video recordings of the account given by a complainant during a 999 call or to the attending police officer.
† Subject to the evidential test – 'is there a realistic prospect of conviction on the evidence?' – being satisfied.

throwing a glass at her, narrowly missing her head. She retreats to the safety of the bathroom, and half an hour later walks downstairs and tells him she's going to the police, slapping him before she leaves. Police are called, arrest and charge follow, as does guilty plea before magistrates, before committal for sentence to Crown Court as the offence was committed during a suspended sentence.

The first question out of the judge's mouth is the same as mine when I picked up the papers the previous evening.

Why on earth is this woman the one standing in the dock?

Video killed the barrister

A CPS in-house barrister phoning in sick leads to my clerks greedily accepting, on my behalf, a bag of nine PCMHs* in the Crown Court. With barely an hour to prepare the lot, I have stirring evocations of my days doing prosecution lists in the mags. All is going well until around case number six, when the judge asks for the facts of the allegations against the defendant, who is watching from custody over the video link. As I read the police summary, a shout rings out from the TV screen.

'It's all bullshit!'

'Be quiet,' the judge booms.

I continue, but only for a line.

'You liar! I didn't do it!'

The judge intervenes once more. 'Mr Lyons, I'm not going to tell you again. I've asked the prosecutor for the prosecution facts – we know that you deny them, now sit there in silence or I'm cutting the link.'

---

* Plea and Case Management Hearings. What we used to call the first hearing in the Crown Court, where a defendant is arraigned (asked how they plead to the charges).

He motions for me to carry on. I get as far as listing the items stolen in the burglary before the heckles resume.

'Fucking lies! Lies!'

True to his word, the judge leans forward to his clerk, and the video link is severed.

'I'm so sorry, SB,' he says politely. 'Now where were we?'

The brief cessation in hostilities has afforded me a minute to review my nine-file stack of papers and reach a sickening realisation.

'Umm, Your Honour? I was reading from the wrong file.'

Deckchairs

I wait all morning at court for my client, Deanna, to attend for her breach hearing.* She did not attend when the case was first listed last week, so optimism is not high. At midday, no explanation having been provided for her absence and the judge's patience exhausted, a bench warrant is issued for her arrest. As I walk towards the courtroom door, the usher runs in. A panicked Deanna has just phoned the court to explain that she is on her way. Reliant on public transport to travel the fifty miles to this court (her local court centre having been shut under recent cuts), her door-to-door journey has a three-hour estimate by bus and train. Her first train was cancelled and she is now stuck. She has no credit on her mobile phone so has been waiting in the rain for a passer-by to lend her their phone so that

---

* When a defendant is sentenced to a community order or a suspended sentence and they fail to comply with the requirements of the order – usually by not turning up to their probation appointments or by going out on a bender during the hours of their curfew – they are dragged back to court and 'breached'. They will either have the order made more onerous or, if enough chances have been afforded, they will be sent to prison.

she could call the court. The judge withdraws the warrant and we resolve to wait.

At 3.30, Deanna arrives, out of breath and heavily pregnant. The leniency of her sentence for supplying class A – two years' imprisonment suspended for two years, for an offence where at least three years' immediate imprisonment is usually unavoidable – becomes self-explanatory. My frustration at having spent six hours waiting at court is obviously still lined on my face, as no sooner have I introduced myself than she bursts into tears, begging me not to send her to prison. I promise her that my job is to try to achieve the opposite, and we take a seat on the benches outside the courtroom as I try to take instructions from her as to why she has not been attending meetings with her probation officer.

Shaking through her tears, she explains that her prescription medication for bipolar disorder has been causing complications with her pregnancy, and so she has had to come off the meds entirely. Only twenty-three years old, she has bounded from violent relationship to violent relationship, the authorities seemingly impotent to bring any of the perpetrators to justice, and was ultimately coerced into selling cocaine for her (now imprisoned) ex-boyfriend. Her first child, her seven-year-old daughter, is currently in the care of said ex's new girlfriend at the other end of the country. Deanna is desperate to bring her home, but doesn't know how to even begin going about this. Social services have tried to help Deanna, but her transient lifestyle – a year spent on the run from a different thuggish ex – means that she is slipping through the social-services safety net. Her present temporary accommodation is a sofa at the bedsit of her infirm mother, who last week was hospitalised after falling down the stairs, thus explaining Deanna's non-attendance at the first court hearing. Her pregnancy and compounded mental health problems mean that paid work is off the table. She is broke, and her weekly benefit has now been exhausted by today's train fare. Amid the chaos, she accepts that attending probation appointments has fallen down her list of priorities.

Having heard all this, the judge sensibly agrees to keep Deanna out of prison and directs that her suspended sentence order continue, with stern words of warning and 'last chances' echoing around the courtroom.

I hope she doesn't come back. But she probably will. How do you even begin to suggest, with any sincerity or humanity, that a person with this sort of life – this sort of state of bare *existence* – should prioritise above all else a fortnightly meeting with an agent of a state which has proven itself incompetent at offering the most basic level of protection? How is a judge emphasising how important *he* considers compliance with a court order supposed to help one lone damaged woman to reorder such intractable turmoil? As so often with this job, and with these types of orders, I feel blindly impotent; acutely and terrifyingly aware that we in our wigs, hugging our legalistic mottos, are often simply going through the motions; shuffling the deckchairs on the dipping ships of other people's lives.

Only human

Riley was in the local area to offer a quote for a paint job. He found that his prospective customer was out, but, keen to show willing, decided to leave a note to say that he'd been. He knocked on a neighbour's door and asked if he could borrow a pen and paper. The elderly occupant obliged, and Riley perched on the doorstep and started to write.

What happened next will, I expect, haunt Riley for the rest of his life.

The phone rang, and the little old lady trotted off to answer.

Peering inside the address, Riley saw a handbag, unattended, on the hallway dresser. The temptation was too much; he nipped in, grabbed the bag and ran as fast as he could.

When the police arrived, they asked the shaken victim for a description of the burglar. 'I can't remember what he looked like,' she replied, 'but he did drop this.' She handed them a crisp handwritten note:

SORRY I MISSED YOU.
RILEY ANDERSON, 4 CROFT WALK, NEASDON.
0745622143.
EMAIL: RILEYANDERSON4@GMAIL.COM.

The lamp that shows that freedom lives

Some courts have separate entrances for jurors, to ensure they don't bump into defendants, witnesses or lawyers as they enter and leave the building. Other courts, less attached to fusty old notions of minimising the risk of jury nobbling, make no such provision, and force jurors to use the main entrance and stand in the freezing cold for thirty minutes with the rest of us while a single G4S security officer prods through the bags, coats and pockets of each of the hundred people queueing. The enhanced risk for barristers of such arrangements is that anything you say about your trial as you leave court is liable to be overheard by the very last people in the world you want overhearing it. Cautionary tales abound of careless counsel spouting off to colleagues or solicitors about their frustrations towards the judge/witnesses/client, unaware that jurors are standing behind them, leading to disaster (and potential professional sanctions) when the jury had to be discharged and the trial restarted. The solution is obvious: follow the basic rules of professional conduct and don't discuss your case anywhere where you are at a risk of being overheard. But for a profession of rampant egotists and self-described raconteurs, such restrictions on grandstanding can be hard to abide by.

A secondary risk is that a juror might try to talk to you about your case. One morning, Anil, the barrister I am talking to in the security queue, notices one of the jurors from his trial stood behind us. Clocking the lady in question, he smiles politely and goes to resume his (non-trial-related) conversation with me when the juror decides to make small talk.

'So what's going to happen today?' she asks.

The cogs are obviously whirring as Anil tries to work out how to straddle 'ending this conversation immediately' and 'not offending someone who will decide the guilt or otherwise of my client'.

'Well,' he says, 'there will be closing speeches from the prosecution, and then from me, and then the judge will sum up the case to you. If there's time, you might retire later this afternoon to decide your verdict.'

'Thanks,' says the juror, as Anil turns back to me with a relieved look that says, *Well, that could have been worse*. When she retires to deliberate the fate of his client, she will at least not be harbouring any subconscious resentment towards defence counsel for being rude or aloof. She will go into the jury room with an open mind and no preconceptions about his client's guilt.

Alas, it isn't over. She taps Anil on the shoulder again.

'And the judge, will he sentence your defendant today?'

Visionary

'*An easy one for you tomorrow, SB. A two-day prosecution Crown Court trial, theft of a handbag from a nightclub.*

Issue is ID, and it's all caught on CCTV. You can't lose!'

One of the skills of clerking barristers is knowing the idiosyncratic secrets to persuading the egotistical prima donnas in your charge to agree to cover somebody else's work, at very late notice and for very little money. Paula has already identified my catnip as an easy Crown Court trial that I have a fighting chance of actually winning.

Sitting down for an evening of trawling CCTV of interminable length and variable quality – a particularly thankless (and unpaid) part of the job – I expect to struggle to make head, tail or handbag out of what I am watching. When prosecuting, I usually ask the police to add graphics to the footage – some helpful arrows or annotations, to assist the jury, and the barristers, to identify the key players. In this case, my predecessor as prosecuting counsel has had such a request knocked back – the theft of a handbag was insufficiently serious to warrant the attentions of the overstretched police digital editing department.

Salvation arrives in the form of a police memo: 'This is high quality footage and the defendant is wearing a distinctive and clearly identifiable sailor's hat.'

Reassured, I load the disc. I squint closely at the stilted images on the screen; the scores of mingling drunken bodies swarming past the camera, and I loudly swear. I zoom in on a sign above the bar, and then slam my laptop shut in defeat.

THEME NIGHT: DRESS AS A SAILOR,
COCKTAILS FOR £1!!!

Head meets desk
I receive a police memo after a judge orders an explanation for

a two-year delay in charging an allegation of serious domestic violence:

'I, DS White, inherited this job. I was told we were going to NFA* the suspect. Upon reading the file, it became clear that the wrong person had been arrested and interviewed. We had accidentally arrested and interviewed the suspect's brother. This caused an unexpected delay.'

Firm instructions

The morning of trial has been spent chasing the CCTV, listed as disclosable on the prosecution schedule of unused material but, naturally, never actually provided to the defence. As I tell Phil, my alleged thieving client, this could potentially prove vital in showing that, as per his instructions, he was not one of the gang of three who had broken into a scrapyard and driven out with twenty grand's worth of copper piping.

'Of course,' I advise, 'I don't know what the CCTV will show. But your instructions are that you weren't there, so it could be very helpful. However,' I add pointedly, 'if *you* don't think it's a good idea, Phil, I of course will not pursue it.'

'Nah, get the CCTV!' Phil insists excitedly. So I chase the prosecutor, and after a chain of phone calls a police officer is tasked with digging the disc out of the police storage room in which it has been inexplicably archived.

The judge, having been made aware of this outstanding issue but conscious of the need to avoid delay, directs that the prosecution open the case to the jury while the CCTV is being couriered to court. My opponent duly does so, and an hour later the jury are sent out for a break as a breathless officer runs into the courtroom brandishing a DVD.

---

* NFA = take No Further Action.

'Well, come on then,' says the judge. 'Let's watch it. Might as well play it on the nice big screen so that your client can see what it shows, yes?' I turn behind me towards the dock, and Phil gives a confident thumbs up. After the standard twenty-minute fumble to get the court DVD player to work, the footage begins, and we sit back and watch as a man, unmistakably Phil, walks up to the security camera and stares down the lens, before walking over to the yard's wire fence with his bolt-cutters and getting to work, chomping a hole big enough for his accomplices to drive their Transit van through moments later.

'I suppose,' the judge says with a wide grin, 'that you'll want a few minutes with your client, SB?'

Down in the cells, Phil is beside himself.

'YOU TOLD ME THAT CCTV COULD HELP ME!' he shouts as I enter the consultation room.

'Phil,' I say, struggling not to talk to him as you would a toddler, 'you told me you weren't there!'

Realisation dawns. 'Oh yeah. I didn't think, did I?'

Justice delayed

When the judge demands to know why it has taken six months for a burglar who had pleaded guilty before the mags to appear at the Crown Court for his sentence, I am happy to provide the following chronology:

— 26 September – First appearance before the mags. Court did not know defendant was in prison and had not arranged for him to be produced at court. Adjourned to 24 October.

— 24 October – Prison missed the case off the list. Defendant not produced. Adjourned to 8 November.

— 8 November – CPS record for this hearing is blank, but seemingly defendant not present.

— 7 December – Defendant not produced. Had been transferred to another prison which was not told about the hearing. Adjourned to 4 January.

— 4 January – Defendant produced at magistrates' court. No interpreter attends. Adjourned to 2 February.

— 2 February – Defendant produced and pleads guilty. Committed to Crown Court for sentence on 1 March.

'That brings us to today,' I conclude, 'when, as Your Honour knows, the video link to the prison has gone down.'

You've got mail
An email from a CPS reviewing lawyer lands in my inbox:

Good morning, just doing the reviews and I see you're prosecuting this trial tomorrow. Major problems – youth arson with intent* where defendant deliberately set fire to the AP's† flat. Not reviewed since first appearance. Real concerns over prospects of conviction. No statement from AP, no statement from neighbour, only statement is from social worker who overhears threats but we haven't warned her to attend trial. May be worth a chat with defence to see if they'll offer anything??
   Best of British!

 I reply to politely inform him that I'm defending.

---

* Arson with intent to endanger life.
† AP = aggrieved party, or complainant.

Marshall

It is probably around three or four years in that I become conscious of quite how far I have departed from some of my earlier beliefs. Marshall stands out as a case in point, because had twenty-one-year-old me been told that, in less than a decade, I would not only be arguing professionally for a court to impose a four-month sentence for the sexual abuse of a seven-year-old boy, but personally believing that outcome to be correct, I would have found it inconceivable.

When Marshall was fifteen, he orally raped* a six-year-old boy. The victim was a family friend, and Marshall abused that child's trust in the most terrible way. The young boy told his mum, the police were called and Marshall, after pleading guilty, was sentenced to five years' detention with an extended licence period of three years – an Extended Determinate Sentence, as it's known, designed for dangerous violent and sexual offenders. The sentence would have been much higher had Marshall been an adult – it was his youth that meant the judge was required to significantly reduce the starting point.

While serving his sentence, Marshall undertook various sex-offender treatment programmes. He was assessed as having made good progress – he was compliant and cooperative, and talked openly about his childhood and the warped attitudes towards sex that he had been inculcated with from a young age. Four years into his sentence, during a group therapy session, Marshall announced that he wanted to share something with the course leader. He told her that, a few months before he committed the offence for which he had been sentenced, he had

---

* Oral rape occurs where a defendant inserts his penis into a victim's mouth without their consent, and without reasonably believing that they consented. A child of that age cannot consent as a matter of law.

sexually touched another boy, this time a seven-year-old. This victim was, again, a family friend. The offence was not as serious as rape, but still a grave offence against a very young child. Marshall was disclosing this, he said, because 'that boy hasn't told anyone, and he deserves justice'.

A police investigation was immediately launched, and the child in question – who had never mentioned the assault to anyone – confirmed what Marshall had said. Marshall was charged with sexual assault on a child under thirteen,* he promptly pleaded guilty and was committed to the Crown Court for sentence.

The sentencing exercise was unusual, and it was complicated. Although now aged twenty, and so an adult in the eyes of the law, Marshall had to be sentenced as if he were still fifteen, his age at the time of the offence. This was an extremely serious offence which had wrought devastating psychological harm upon the victim; however, but for Marshall's unprompted confession, it might never have come to light. Sex offenders admitting their crimes is extremely rare – to offer admissions to offences about which the police are completely unaware is almost unheard of. It was a sign, I submitted to the court, of genuine remorse and of the significant progress that Marshall had made in prison towards rehabilitation. He was due to be released from his current sentence in less than a year, and had volunteered information that he knew would inevitably keep him behind bars for longer. This, I urged the judge, was an exceptional case, and

---

* Thirteen is a significant age for sexual offences. A child under thirteen cannot consent to any sexual act, and the penalties for sexual offences against under-thirteens are significantly higher than for young people aged between thirteen and fifteen.

the judge could properly reflect that by imposing a significantly lower sentence than he otherwise would.

The judge was required to follow the sentencing guidelines. It was agreed between the prosecution and the defence that, on the guideline for this offence, the categorisation gave a starting point, for an adult, of two years' custody, with a range of one to four years. It was also agreed that the judge would have to increase that starting point to reflect the aggravating features of the case. That gave a starting point of three years. The judge was persuaded to reduce that by one third to reflect the fact of Marshall's youth and his remorse, which gave a figure of two years. Giving Marshall full credit led to a sentence of sixteen months, of which he would serve half – eight – before being eligible for automatic release. The most significant decision the judge made was not to make that sentence consecutive to Marshall's existing sentence – it was to start today, running concurrently. In real terms, it meant that Marshall's time in prison would only be extended by four months.

The judge's analysis of the facts and of the relevant guidelines was, in my professional opinion, unimpeachable. And the decision not to significantly extend Marshall's sentence, to reward his candour and his progress by allowing the sentence to begin today, rather than tacking it onto the end of his current sentence, was an act of mercy that, as Marshall's lawyer, I felt met the justice of the case.

But it's also where I think the norms of the justice system may collide violently with the expectations of the public. Because much as I would like to suggest that my support for the decision in this case is simply the product of my informed and detached professional understanding of the issues, and that anybody thinking rationally about this case would inevitably reach the same conclusion, when I step back I can also see that this may be the part of the book where I reveal myself to have gone unquestioningly native. It may be that, as a reader, you find it impossible to reconcile Marshall's sentence with the seriousness of his offence. It may be that this is the bit where you close the book in disgust, shake your head and mutter to your partner lying next to you in bed, *Y'know, I was with the barrister up until this point, but they've lost me now.* Maybe this case is a paradigm not of a system dealing correctly with a highly sensitive case posing delicately balanced competing arguments of punishment and rehabilitation, but of a system radically and irreconcilably detached from its public; from its starting points – *the guideline suggests two years for sexually assaulting a prepubescent child???* – to the weight that the judge placed on the mitigation ahead of the aggravation. I don't know. I really don't know.

I don't know what the family of the victim, sitting in court to hear the judge pronounce sentence, would have made of it. Was this justice for them? Is their pain, and the pain of their son, in any way assuaged by the knowledge of the perpetrator's remorse and reform? Would hearing my mitigation – delivered, I hope, with sensitivity – and the judge's sentencing remarks, cement in their minds an impression of a justice system concerned more with criminals than with victims? Or would they accept, at least academically, the efforts made by the courts to juggle, calibrate and reconcile the multiple competing aims that comprise our systemic definition of justice? Does that definition meet with wider support outside our echo chamber of lawyers and judges? The deeper I find myself in the burrows of the system, the more difficult it can be to hear the voices of the real world up above.

5. All Falls Down

A few years in, and I'm settling into a comfortable Crown Court practice, weighted slightly in favour of prosecution work and kept afloat almost entirely on the toil and goodwill of the clerks, who ensure that, if solicitors aren't beating down the door to instruct me specifically, I'm still getting work funnelled into my diary when somebody calls to instruct 'whoever you've got available'. As I learned during team sports at school, mediocrity need not be a disqualifier to somebody passing you the ball; if there is literally no other option, simply being a human body in the line of sight can guarantee you at least a few touches. If asked at a job interview to describe my greatest professional strength, my honest answer at this stage would be 'Availability.' And I'm fine with that.

I should probably qualify the use of the adjective 'comfortable'. My practice is comfortable in the sense that I have enough work to warrant being in court every day and can afford to pay my rent. It is comfortable in the sense that, thanks to the particular brilliance of my clerks, the permanent anxiety of the self-employed that work is only a day away from drying up for ever is kept at a tolerably low hum. The work itself, however, is anything but comfortable. To the contrary, the job is becoming more and more difficult, and not necessarily in the way I had anticipated.

It is not just the subject matter. It's not simply because I'm becoming exposed to more complex and involved cases, although that no doubt contributes to the mounting heaviness I feel on my shoulders when I put on my wig. Instead, it's a fast-growing feeling that a job which even in ideal conditions is unique in its peculiar combination of pressures – high stakes, unpredictable human behaviours, fiendishly technical subject matter, a succession of split-second judgement calls and intellectually brilliant colleagues whose job is literally to ensure that you fail – is being pushed to the brink by its environment.

I'm finding that the chaos of the magistrates' court is gradually being replicated in the Crown. Not just replicated, but magnified. Cuts to the police – 21,000 from 2010 to the end of the decade – and cuts to the CPS – a quarter of their budget and staff – are biting hard. More and more of my prosecution briefs are coming in incomplete, missing documents as basic as the indictment or the police summary or the statement from the key witness. Half my cases are wildly overcharged, the other half correspondingly undercharged, with virtually none falling within the Goldilocks sweet spot. Goldy is finding herself charged either with simple theft of porridge or aggravated burglary with a firearm, instead of the correct offence of burglary of a dwelling house (subject to the untested argument of whether a building occupied by bears is legally a dwelling).

If this stream of consciousness sounds like my brain is spluttering and faltering, it's because it is. More and more of my evenings and weekends are elongated by poring over cases littered with elementary errors or lacking the fundamentals. After I've painstakingly picked the bones out of a brief and sent a detailed (unpaid) written advice offering a step-by-step guide on how to rescue the case, I then spend months chasing a response as I'm ghosted by the overburdened CPS lawyer. Because we are paid a single fixed fee for each Crown Court case, irrespective of how long we spend preparing it, it means that we are an instant source of free labour for those who instruct us, with overstretched CPS, police and defence solicitors shunting their overspill onto counsel to sort out. Judges add to the burden by demanding that we produce written documents, gratis, by unrealistically tight timescales. All of these small things mount up, stealing the pockets of time we carve out for a personal life and extending a sixty-hour week in the direction of a regular seventy to eighty hours. I barely see my partner, whose patience with this existence must, I constantly worry, have a breaking point. It's a good thing I don't have children as I have no idea how they would hope to get a look in. I could possibly spare them half an hour every second Tuesday, at a push.

The vagaries of the courts themselves intensify the storm. Because the government continues to cut the number of days that courts are allowed to sit, trials are frequently and repeatedly adjourned. The immediate impact is felt by the parties – witnesses, police officers and defendants spend days hanging around court only for their trial to be booted into the long grass at 4.30 p.m. But there's a knock-on for the advocates: counsel's availability is rarely taken into account when the court fixes a new date. It means that my diary is a jumble of trials listed on top of trials, and I am forced to return case after case that I've fully prepared. Preparation for trial paying, as I might have mentioned, the princely sum of £0 per hour, I am losing track of the number of weeks each year I am working for free – or, once I've factored in travel, the number of weeks I am paying to work. Both legal aid and CPS fees are being cut – again – taking the overall reduction to something close to 40 per cent in real terms over fifteen years, just to ensure we know how much we are valued.

While no doubt my waning support for austerity politics has been accelerated by self-interest – like many people, I suspect, cutting your cloth and making sacrifices are all well and good as long as it's other people's cloth and other people's altars – my feeling of betrayal goes beyond the personal. Irrespective of what is happening to the lawyers, the edifice of criminal justice itself is just not working. The system is running on empty, to the detriment of anybody and everybody unlucky enough to be dragged into its rusting gears. The current tenor of political debate about justice is two-note – we spend more on legal aid than anybody else in the world,* and we need to be tougher on criminals. Thus it ever was, but while as an outsider it was easy to swallow the favoured political prescription, as somebody on the ground witnessing the impact on victims, witnesses and defendants first-hand, I feel a constant swell of anger. How can anybody who sincerely cares about criminal justice not see the real problems? How can those in power have so little interest in fixing them?

Meanwhile, all around me, I see people leaving. Friends abandon legal aid for privately paid areas of law, seduced by the proposition that if you're going to sacrifice all semblance of a personal life, you might as well do it for ten times the fee. Bright, promising criminal pupils are burning out within a few years of practice, leaving the job they poured years of their lives and tens of thousands of pounds into pursuing. The tired refrain of *whatever you do, don't do crime* is as much a deterrent on law students as it was on me; while there is an overall decrease

---

* We don't. We never have. Politicians love saying this, but it's a lie. Our spend has, at its highest, only been average. See *The Secret Barrister: Stories of the Law and How It's Broken*, Chapter 7, and *Fake Law*, Chapter 6.

in the numbers looking to enter criminal law, there are still hundreds of applicants for each pupillage. Seeing them enter chambers, full of fervent optimism and enthusiasm for a job they are sure they will love, feels like watching lambs gambolling towards an abattoir.

And yet. And yet. I'm still here. And I have no intention of going anywhere. I'm far from alone. While there is attrition, there is a majority who, like me, simply can't envisage a life doing any other job, and who, importantly, are trained for literally nothing else. As long as we remain, with our stoic idealism, resolute lack of imagination and pugnacious refusal to change, we will continue to whinge and moan and stamp our feet and demand better, and dutifully keep on keeping on when absolutely nothing improves.

Setting the tone

Cases continue to surprise. For months, the police have insisted that there was no relevant CCTV at the prison. The mystery of how my client Joshua and the complainant prison officer sustained their respective injuries – two black eyes for the prisoner, a broken jaw for the PO – will have to be litigated on the evidence of the parties alone. Despite Joshua's insistence that the altercation took place directly under a CCTV camera on the first-floor landing of the prison block, and that the footage would prove that it was the officer who threw the first punch before Josh responded in kind in lawful self-defence, no such footage, the solicitors have been assured, exists.

A modest shift in position occurs the week before trial, in the form of a statement from a junior police officer, who confirms that there *was* a CCTV camera, that he *did* download and seize the footage from the prison, but that he has only remembered this because last weekend when he was at the gym he found the labelled DVD at the bottom of his sports bag, broken in half. 'I'm not sure how this has happened,' he helpfully adds.

The prosecution's failure to preserve crucial CCTV can, in exceptional circumstances, be ruled by a judge to amount to an 'abuse of process' – a failing so serious that the defendant cannot have a fair trial, or alternatively that it would not be fair to try him. If successfully argued, the indictment is 'stayed' and proceedings come to an end. So we lodge a written application to be argued on the morning of trial.

The ingenuity of the hardball negotiators at the Ministry of Justice has resulted in long-standing and generous contractual arrangements with private companies to transport prisoners to court, the terms of which impose absolutely no meaningful incentive or penalty to ensure that prisoners actually arrive in time for court to begin. So it is that come the day of trial, Josh arrives not at 9.30 a.m. to meet his fresh-faced counsel for a 10 a.m. court start, but at 12.45 to meet his irritable, stale-coffee-breathed counsel for a 2.15 p.m. start. The tone of the day having been well and truly set, we proceed to lose the legal application, but the argument and judge's decision absorb the rest of the afternoon. This would mean the trial having to start tomorrow, except the judge announces that he can't sit on Friday and the court won't let the trial go into the following week, so the whole shebang has to go off, the earliest date being in five months' time. It's a date which I absolutely cannot do, as I have two other (adjourned) trials starting that day, so the case will have to be returned. My day of legal argument and hours spent preparing for an ineffective trial yield a take-home fortune of around £28.

As I put in my headphones for the train ride home, some talk-radio shock jock is inciting his listeners to share his outrage at 'fat-cat legal-aid lawyers milking the system'. I am sorely tempted to phone in, but, while a part of me is intrigued by what it might be like to go viral, the Bar Standards Board has pretty strict rules about shouting 'ignorant disingenuous shithouse' on national radio.

Gun for hire

While my ungainly scramble up the ladder of criminal offences is exposing me more regularly to the darkest recesses of the human condition, I like to tell myself that my dinner party stump speech, viz. 'How I Can Defend Somebody I Think is Guilty of Doing Something Terrible', remains steadfastly faithful to its original text.

The truth is a little more complicated. While I do believe that adversarialism – arming prosecution and defence with equally competent legal representation to robustly present their respective cases and challenge the case of their opponents – is the best model to minimise the risk of wrongful convictions, that is not to say that its practice is without difficulties. Suggesting to a police officer that they are mistaken about their identification of a shoplifter is plainly not the same as suggesting to a teenager that they are lying about being sexually abused by their uncle. If my client is lying about the first, my cross-examination of the police officer will be brushed off as part of the job. If my client is lying about the second, my public interrogation of the victim could carry devastating consequences.

There is no easy answer. I've written before about why, on balance, I think adversarialism is the lesser evil compared to the inquisitorial system adopted in many other European countries.* Instead of the state, usually a single judge, taking responsibility

* See Chapters 8 and 9 of *The Secret Barrister: Stories of the Law and How It's Broken*.

for assessing a file of evidence and reaching a decision on guilt (inquisitorialism), we opt for independent advocates fearlessly testing and dissecting all of the evidence, which is supposed to ensure that, when a person is convicted, we can be sure that any state errors have been rooted out and that the court has reached the right decision. That is (a ruthless bastardisation of) the theory, and I think it just about stands up.

But academic justifications don't change the fact that, when standing in court and advocating on behalf of my client, I may well be compounding the already unbearable suffering of an entirely innocent victim of the most hideous abuse. When I put to her that her complaint is vindictive, and deliver a speech to a courtroom packed with press, public and family deriding her evidence as a fabrication, I am giving voice to her worst fears. I am fiercely and publicly disbelieving her and inviting the assembled courtroom, and the watching world, to do the same. Even though a not guilty verdict does not necessarily mean that a jury thought the complaint was false – 'not guilty' only means 'not sure of guilt', nothing more – a victim may carry that verdict, and my words to her, for ever, as a vindication of what she suspected all along: that there was no point, because the system was never truly going to believe her.

That is the cost of adversarialism. To minimise the risk of wrongfully convicting the accused, we accept that the pain of victims will in some cases be amplified exponentially by the process. And while there is an argument that the greatest suffering is inflicted by a not guilty verdict, which will occur in every model of justice system, it would be too easy for us, the lawyers, to ignore that adversarialism vests us with enormous power to cause direct and lasting harm.

I think this is the more interesting question – not 'How can you defend somebody you think is guilty?' (Easy answer:

'Because they might be innocent'), but 'How does it feel knowing that you are often instrumental in causing harm?'

We loathe such questions, of course. We dismiss their premise as betraying a misunderstanding of the role of a lawyer. And we may be partly right. But that is not an answer; it is evasion. An honest answer, for me at least, would be 'terrible'. The knowledge that I might, through my words and deeds, have caused lasting pain to another person is something I consciously avoid dwelling on. I don't think I'm alone.

But I think, in answering that question, there is a need to zone in on the word 'instrumental'. Because that is the key. Lawyers are not their clients' cause; we are instruments. We give voice not to our beliefs, not to our stories, but to those of our clients. They feed in the information, we process it and spool it out in the most legally persuasive language.

That fundamental principle is often forgotten, including by lawyers. In crime, you sometimes meet those hardened defence-only advocates whose mask of objectivity has slipped, who become their client's cause, not just their counsel. That's not why we're here. I don't do this job because I believe in my client's innocence, or because I believe that the man I'm prosecuting is guilty. I do it because the rule of law requires that the prosecution be adequately represented in legal proceedings by an advocate who will ensure a strong but fair prosecution, and that defendants be represented by somebody who will fight their corner, without fear or favour and irrespective of their own personal views on the issues of guilt or innocence.

Something which I worry does enormous harm to public understanding of the role of lawyers is the behaviour of celebrity defence attorneys in the US, often reflected in true crime documentaries on popular streaming sites. The way in which criminal trials in the US are litigated in the media as much as in the courtroom – something alien to England and Wales with its strict laws on contempt of court – results in episodes such as were seen with Donna Rotunno, lawyer for convicted sexual abuser Harvey Weinstein. In the build-up to Weinstein's criminal trial in 2020, Ms Rotunno regularly made media appearances in which she expressed disbelief in Weinstein's accusers, making observations such as: 'If you don't want to be a victim, don't go to the hotel room'* and 'I would never put myself in that position'.† After Weinstein's conviction, she declared that men 'have no power any more' in sexual assault cases, and 'a woman can say anything she wants and they're going to be believed.'‡

Aside from the grotesqueness of these statements, this apparently personal adoption of a client's cause is to me an egregious distortion of what it means to be a lawyer. When I defend an alleged rapist, it is because I believe he is entitled to be properly legally represented when accused by the state; not because I believe the complainants are liars, or that women have too much power, or were asking for it, or that rape is no big deal. I do not enjoy causing distress to complainants, any more than when prosecuting I revel in the tears of a man whom I am publicly

---

* S Carlin, 'Harvey Weinstein's lawyer questions his accusers, rape accusations ahead of trial', Refinery 29, 8 December 2019, https://www.refinery29.com/en-gb/2019/12/8988173/harvey-weinstein-lawyer-victim-blaming-nightline-abc-times-up-response

† P Melendez, 'Weinstein's defense lawyer: I would "never put myself" in a position to be sexually assaulted', The Daily Beast, 7 February 2020, https://www.thedailybeast.com/harvey-weinsteins-lawyer-donna-rutonno-says-she-would-never-put-herself-in-position-to-be-sexually-assaulted

‡ A Walker, 'Harvey Weinstein's lawyer: His accusers are guilty of a lot of things', Sky News, 11 March 2020, https://news.sky.com/story/harvey-weinsteins-lawyer-his-accusers-are-guilty-of-a-lot-of-things-11954976

accusing of raping his own child. Likewise, I don't choose to prosecute him because I believe he is guilty, or that everybody accused is guilty; I am bound to prosecute him, if instructed, because a fair trial requires legal representation on both sides. That – the rule of law – is our cause; not, however much sympathy certain cases might engender, the humanity, or otherwise, of our client.

It follows, and this is perhaps the most difficult question of all to reckon with, that when we grandiosely style ourselves as warriors for justice – my Twitter biography states 'Wears a black cape and fights crime. Not Batman' – we are entitled to be asked: What justice are you fighting for? We can't possibly be fighting for the 'right' outcome, for an identifiable truth to emerge, because in any given case we can't know what the truth is. As an advocate for hire, some days we will be the good guys, some days we will be fighting for the opposite. For bad. Either way, we will almost never know. To the extent that we are fighting for justice, it can only be justice of the procedural kind. We are warriors for process, placing our faith in the notion that if we perform our part as best we can, the machinery will, at the end, spit out a result that we can wrap up and label 'justice'. And we have to keep that faith, even if, as has happened on more than one case, we pack up our wig and gown and drag our trolleycase away from court with a quietly needling suspicion that, in the name of our definition of justice, we have just helped to acquit a guilty man, or to convict an innocent.

Blessed are the caseworkers
A straightforward violent disorder trial – community elders decide to mediate a commercial dispute in a restaurant after hours, which quickly turns into a competition to see who can

throw the most furniture/who brought the biggest machete – which I've prepared fully, and for which the witnesses and defendants are all here on time, takes two and a half hours to get off the ground.

Why? It's largely because the diligent CPS caseworker covering my trial is also expected, by her managers who never attend court and so are gloriously insulated from the consequences of their budgetary decisions, to cover two trials in two separate courtrooms. Caseworkers are invaluable when you are prosecuting. They are the glue that holds everything together. They have access to the CPS's digital Case Management System (CMS), which is off-limits to independent counsel, and so are the first port of call for any queries that either I or my opponent may have about evidence in the case, or what material has been received from the police, or where the hell our witnesses are. They also hold the door code to the CPS room at court – again, barristers are apparently not to be entrusted with such secrets – so admin tasks such as having documents copied and printed for the jury fall on the caseworker.

Covering a trial as a caseworker is a full-time job. The dynamics of trials are such that new issues spring up at every turn; a comment by a witness can generate an urgent line of inquiry, the answer to which may lie in one among a thousand documents on CMS. A judge's impromptu ruling on whether a piece of evidence is admissible can mean suddenly needing to edit or redact documents that were ready for the jury. The prosecution's duties of disclosure persist throughout trial (and beyond), and ensuring that there is nothing in our possession that the defence should have had and haven't had is essential to avoiding miscarriages of justice. The caseworker must also accompany counsel to speak to the witnesses before the trial starts, to give them copies of their witness statements to refresh their memories, to explain the likely course of the day ahead, and to check that there are no unexpected hitches.

Sadly, these realities do not trouble management, who blithely expect caseworkers to cover multiple trials at the same time. So in one trial, when the court DVD player won't play the CCTV and we need to call upon the equipment locked in the CPS room, the entire ensemble – judge, jury, defendants, counsel and witnesses – have to wait one and a half hours for my harried caseworker, who is stuck in another courtroom dealing with a highly vulnerable child witness in a sex case, to sensitively extricate herself and burst breathlessly through the courtroom doors brandishing our Panasonic saviour. It takes another hour for the court clerk to track down IT support to confirm that the DVD produced by the police is not compatible with this model of machine.

Bad news bear

As I queue for the video-link booth to speak to my remanded burglar before his sentence today, a tearful woman grabs my elbow. 'Are you here for Eddie?' I nod. 'Can we talk somewhere private before you see him?'

I look around and gesture impotently. In this court building, there are no conference rooms for lawyers to hold private discussions with clients or their families; or rather, there are a dozen conference rooms, but eleven are permanently locked and the other has been in use all morning. This is ubiquitous across the court estate; perfectly serviceable court and conference rooms, all mockingly locked so that nobody can use them. It drives me fucking crackers.

As a result, the most intimate details of a person's life – histories of drug addiction, mental ill health, physical and sexual abuse – are spilled to strangers in bustling foyers amid shrieks of tannoy announcements. If fortunate, your barrister may find a quieter corner on a top-floor corridor, but in general the dignity that the system affords to defendants and their loved ones is equal to that of cattle.

Her name is Fiona, and she is Eddie's wife. She introduces herself as I lead her, gown flapping behind me, down the stairs and towards the cells. We stop on the ground floor, where the din subsides and, trying not to be overheard by the congregating security guards to our left, we scrunch up against a wall.

Fiona explains, her voice cracking, that due to recent staff cuts the prison visits have been cancelled this past week, so she hasn't had a chance to see Eddie. The earliest she can book is over a week away. 'You're allowed to see him over the link, right?' she asks, a hopeful lilt in her voice. I nod, but pre-empting her next question I add, 'But I'm afraid you're not allowed to come in. It's lawyers only.'

The sudden violence of her sobbing takes me aback. She clings on to my arm for balance as I try to make sense of what seems, with respect, a gigantic overreaction to not being able to see your husband for a week. When she regains her composure and starts to explain, it all makes horrible sense.

Yesterday, Fiona attended her doctor for the results of an MRI scan, the final in a gruelling series of medical tests, which confirmed a diagnosis of vascular dementia. She is forty-two. While Eddie is inside, a not infrequent occurrence, she is responsible for their three children. Their lives, as of twenty-four hours ago, have now changed for ever. She needs Eddie home, but, more immediately, she needs him to know. More specifically, she needs me to tell him. Me, an idiot in their late twenties who less than forty seconds ago was silently dismissing her as an emotionally incontinent encumbrance on my very busy and very important morning. She needs me to pack away my prattish ego, walk into that video-link booth, meet her husband for the very first time and deliver the sort of news that I am in no way, medically or emotionally, trained to give. We have a ten-minute slot allocated for our conference. *Hello, I'm your barrister. You're probably staying in prison for a while, and your wife has just found out she has vascular dementia and needs you home desperately. Anything else I can help you with? No? Great. See you in court, buddy.*

I hope my delivery is more sensitive than that. Eddie takes it as well as I suppose anyone could. I obviously can't answer any of the questions that he – obviously – asks, and it's fair to say that he isn't particularly focused on the contents of his Pre-Sentence Report as I try to talk him through it. But he bears the news stoically, far more so than I would in his circumstances. He doesn't shout, he doesn't cry. I don't think that I would ever stop.

In mitigation, I tell the judge about the diagnosis, and she mercifully passes a suspended sentence that allows Eddie to return home this evening. Fiona grips me in a bear hug as we step out of court. I hug her back.

The loneliness . . .

'I really can't thank you enough.' Peter grabs my elbow and effusively shakes my hand, his wife brings in the hug from behind, and for a five seconds that feels like forever, we stand entangled in the court foyer, a triple-headed something or other.

His case has been bizarre. It has dragged on for three years: an allegation by a stranger that Peter, who has never been in trouble before, had randomly lain in wait with a hammer to attack a man he'd allegedly been talking to in the pub. The prosecution could ascribe no motive, Peter had a rock-solid alibi and the identification by the complainant was flawed in the extreme. It was every inch the sort of case that a competent defence lawyer should win, but infinitely more pressurised for that. The acquittal was delivered by the jury within twenty minutes, and, just like that, Peter's life is now unpaused. He will momentarily stride out of the doors into the dazzling July sunshine bursting with what I am told is the greatest feeling in the world – the mixture of vindication, relief and freedom that accompanies a not guilty verdict. And I don't kid myself, he will probably not remember my name in a few months' time, but right now, as we awkwardly extricate our limbs from this barrister sandwich, I am a hero. I have saved him from the injustice of a wrongful conviction. Me. My hard work. My ingenious cross-examination. My barnstorming closing speech. Me me me.

Such are the stories we tell ourselves. Although we strive to remain distant, it can sometimes be tricky not to become personally invested in the outcomes of cases. We cheer these victories as our own – chambers' websites will talk of Mr X 'securing' an acquittal or conviction – the vindication of our individual professional brilliance and the purity of trial by jury. And while our precious ego's self-preservation mechanism kicks in when we lose, reminding us that *you can never tell with juries, those mad fish are a law unto themselves, I'd do away with the lot of them tomorrow*, we carry some of those losses too. We of course don't bear the consequences, but the outcomes define us, if only for a moment. *What could I have done differently? Should I have asked that particular question? Did I strike the wrong tone with my closing speech?*

This solipsism is linked, I think, to the peculiar concentration of responsibility vested in a barrister. It often falls on you, and you alone. While you are notionally part of a team – instructed by a solicitor instructed by a lay client – you are the public face.

In numerical terms, the lack of caseworkers and funding for defence solicitors to attend court usually leaves counsel as a team of one, if prosecuting, and two if defending, albeit with a teammate who doesn't understand the rules of the game and stands to be locked up for life if we lose.

Either way, you are the one taking all the strategic and tactical decisions at trial – which questions to ask of witnesses, which legal applications to pursue, what to include in your speech and how to deliver it. The vaunted comradery of the Bar engenders a sense of interdependence in chambers and the robing room, everybody bustling and scrabbling for advice and/or consolation, but peers don't share the burden. When you've put down the phone to your oracle of a colleague at 10.45 p.m., it's just you. You, your client and the giant machine of the legal system. And while you will damn sure be held responsible if something goes wrong, credit for something gone right is vanishingly rare. There are no performance reviews for the self-employed. No CheckATrade comparison sites for criminal barristers where grateful clients can post five-star reviews and upload photos of our courtroom handiwork. When thanks or compliments are given, by judges or by clients, they are cradled close, wrapped in tissue paper, carefully put away in a box of treasures and gently reopened for a peek on the bad days.

This is why, I suspect, the myth of our own importance is not something we thrive on, but the thing we survive on. Without it, there is usually only criticism or silence. This job is an almost Grecian punishment for criminal lawyers. Take a nation's most self-involved egotists, dress them in their most pompous regalia and give them stage after stage after stage, performing day after day after day, to a silent audience which cannot react and never applauds. Of course we're going to write our own reviews.

The reality – again, one that is difficult for us to admit – is that in the vast majority of cases we probably don't make a difference. Most cases, I expect, are destined to go the same way, irrespective of the lawyer. As long as they act within a wide margin of competence, the evidence is usually not capable of vast improvement or diminution. Could anyone competent have secured Peter's acquittal? Yes. Are there any cases in which I believe, hand on heart, I was personally responsible for an outcome that another barrister would not have achieved? A handful, perhaps, lying in that dusty box of treasures, and I'm not about to take them out and expose them to the destructive blanch of the light. I need them.

Arguably, we shouldn't make a difference. In an ideal world, there would be parity of ability across the legal profession. Your success should not depend upon the wit of your lawyer, but on a fair and balanced assessment of the evidence. We should be the functionaries, not the stars. The instruments, as I've mentioned, not the musicians. Equality of arms, our raison d'être, should, surely, necessitate equality of lawyer. The strongest arguments that can possibly be made should be made, for each side. The best evidence, and the right conclusions, should organically emerge. No court victory should arise because one lawyer asked 'better' questions of the witnesses or gave a more 'persuasive' speech.

Such is the theory, anyway. It's why we are banned from advertising our 'win percentage'. Justice as process, remember. The virtue is in taking part. We sustain no wins and no defeats. Except we do. Especially the defeats.

. . . and the darkness

I also carry the subject matter. More and more heavily, the longer I do this. Sealing off the trauma of the lives we pick through in court is something that is just presumed to come naturally. If you are the 'right type of person' for criminal law, you will arrive with, or quickly develop, your coping mechanisms. There are no content warnings, no CPD training days on 'How to Pick Yourself Up After Your Client Commits Suicide' or 'What to Do at Weekends to Take Your Mind Off Child Rape'. For most of my practising life, there has been no institutional support whatsoever for the lawyers, judges or juries tasked with each day listening to the most harrowing details and viewing the most traumatising images of what human beings can do to each other. The recent efforts by members of the profession to address this, while undoubtedly welcome, will for many have arrived too late.

I find myself hardening. Sometimes it leaks out in performatively crass and flippant comments about shocking cases, just to show How Fine I Really Am With This Sort of Thing. The darkness oozes in the jokes I tell out of court, the offhand remarks which can stun a group conversation into awkward silence. Most often, though, I carry my cases in my paranoia.

Crime, for me, is everywhere. Any sense of perspective was years ago warped. When my partner is five minutes late home and not picking up their phone, it is not because they're round the corner and can't hear their ringtone over the traffic; it is because they have been viciously attacked and abducted, in the identical manner of that horrible street robbery I prosecuted last week. That bump in the night is not the plumbing, or a restless cat; it is an intruder. The sound of those car doors slamming means there is more than one; probably a professional gang. Which means weapons. If they've mistakenly targeted us believing that we have jewels or a hidden safe, I, my partner and my children might be moments away from being sadistically tortured for answers we don't hold, like last month's horrendous case in the Court of Appeal.

Even out in broad daylight, expressing any sort of disagreement with a stranger is wholly out of the question. They probably carry a knife and would think nothing of plunging it into my ribs for the most innocuous of perceived slights. That, in my world, is just what people do. I religiously avoid lorries on the motorway, ensuring there is at least one lane and two vehicles between my tiny car and them. I have seen too graphically, too often, the consequences when tiredness or distraction causes 7.5 tonnes to slip the leash. Every day, I find myself war-gaming for widowhood, whether mine or my partner's; planning the contingencies of an arson attack on our home or a future where we lose a child in a car crash caused by the dangerous driving of one of the thousand stupid, reckless youths I have defended on such charges.

I don't suggest that this is universal, or even common; it's possibly just me, and my brain's way of maximising my innate talent for catastrophising. I imagine, and I hope, that cases don't stick with other people in the same way, clogging their filters and infiltrating their nightmares. But I do know that all of us, in our own way, struggle. And I know that we don't ever talk about it. And I wish we would. Because it is exhausting. It is too much for one person to carry.

Delay delay delay

Another thing I am witnessing increasingly often is the snowballing systemic delay between date of alleged offence and date of trial, and the direct effect it has on the outcomes. The currency of the criminal courts is oral evidence, and it is on a witness's words that the jury will make their assessment of truthfulness, deceit, reliability and accuracy, and from there reach their verdicts. The passage of time corrodes memory, diminishing its quality and increasing the chance that an honest mistake is misconstrued as sinister, and that the wrong verdict is returned. This applies equally to defendants as to prosecution witnesses, although with significantly higher stakes for the former. When I started at the criminal Bar, it was commonplace for a Crown Court trial to be held a year after the event. Writing in 2022, after further cuts to court sitting days combined with a global pandemic to restrict court capacity even further, a delay of only a year is the stuff of fantasy. Currently, we are often experiencing somewhere between three and four.

Delay also impacts on how guilty defendants are sentenced. Time spent in custody on remand awaiting trial counts towards any custodial sentence imposed, as does (to a lesser extent) time spent on bail if you have been made subject to an electronically monitored curfew restricting your liberty for at least nine hours a day.* Even if a defendant has been on unconditional bail,† a sentencing court can still take into account a delay not caused by the fault of the defendant as a mitigating factor that warrants a reduction in sentence.

The sentence of Francis is one among thousands of identikit examples we see every year. Decades of alcohol abuse and a vicious temper had contributed to an offending history stretching back four decades, the latest instalment of which opened with him being disorderly in an A & E waiting room and concluded in him punching a police officer and being charged with assault with intent to resist arrest. A year later, he appears at the Crown Court for sentence, having spent six

---

* One day on a 'qualifying curfew' counts towards half a day in custody.
† Meaning the only requirement imposed is that you turn up to court when required.

months on bail with a curfew. The sentencing guidelines provide a starting point of six months' imprisonment. Even taking the maximum sentence of two years once time on curfew and automatic early release were factored in, Francis wouldn't spend more than a few weeks inside, during which time absolutely nothing constructive would be achieved with him. So the judge decides instead to impose a two-year community order, packed with conditions, to ensure the system had a more enduring grip on Francis than custody alone would offer. I have no doubt that, had I read about this sentence in the newspapers, I would once have lined up fully behind the complaints of the Police Federation that judges are failing to protect front-line officers through their soft sentencing of recidivists like Francis. Context usually teaches that if judiciary's hands are not tied, they are at the very least bound between a rock and another rock.

There is a wealth of academic research that shows that immediacy and certainty of punishment is a greater deterrent than severity.* This plainly makes sense – believing that you are likely to be caught and immediately punished is going to weigh heavier on your mind than an airy confidence that you are unlikely to be caught and that, even if you are, your fate will be kicked several years down the road. Yet whenever our politicians talk about deterrence, it is only ever in terms of longer prison sentences. The intuitive notion that more might be achieved by improving things pre-sentence – the actual criminal justice process – never seems to occur. Nor does the idea that the Francises of our society, thrashing around in a chaotic

---

* See, for instance, this summary by the US National Institute of Justice: 'Five Things About Deterrence' (June 2016), https://nij.ojp.gov/topics/articles/five-things-about-deterrence

state of day-to-day survival, might not be rigorously guided in their decision-making by the Home Secretary's stern pledge to increase the maximum sentence they *might* serve by a few months.

There is always money and political support for more prison places. Rarely so for the less headline-catching resources to ensure that offenders are detected and prosecuted timeously; to put in place an efficient framework that effectively prevents the acts that are filling those prison places.

Full house

Prosecuting a plea hearing for a section 18 GBH. Papers received the night before, as per. Checklist:

— Alleged offence over two years old ✓

— No evidence served on defence or court ✓

— Count 1 on the indictment states wrong date of offence ✓

— Count 2 is wrong in law ✓

— Count 3 misspells the complainant's name ✓

— Count 4 is missing ✓

— Count 5 replicates an offence the defendant pleaded guilty to in the mags ✓

— No witness availability provided ✓

— Defendant not produced from custody ✓

— Interpreter doesn't attend anyway ✓

Bobbies on the beat

A memo lands from the police officer in charge of our case. It is a messy, paper-heavy fraud, which falls in the sour spot of being insufficiently high value to trouble the specialist, better-resourced fraud unit, but much, much too factually complex and time-consuming for a single police constable to manage alongside front-line duties. Hence the terse reply to my prolix, twenty-page advice pointing out something close to a hundred areas of the case where we need to obtain or improve the evidence:

'I do not have time to attend to the file as a front-line officer. A 2-2-2-shift pattern* unfortunately does not easily provide me opportunity to get file work completed.'

And that, it seems, is that. It's a familiar refrain, and there is absolutely no criticism at all of the officer. Front-line policing does indeed make it extremely hard to stay on top of the paper side of investigations. Faced with a choice between apprehending the living, breathing criminals on the streets and having trained officers shuffling papers in a back room, I can fully understand why those in charge of allocating resources lean towards the former. It's what we tell them we want, after all. It's what *I* wanted. Our politicians, our media, our vox-pops on local news – *more bobbies on the beat*. Since 2010, police numbers have been cut by over 20,000. Strained resources must be poured into thickening the thin blue line, not behind desks drowning in needless bureaucracy.

The problem is that it's in the needless bureaucracy that criminal prosecutions live and die. The notion that the police's work is done when a copper nicks and charges a scrote, and that

---

* Two consecutive days on shift, followed by two days off, followed by two days on.

further resources should be taken out of the backroom and allocated to the front line, is one that captures the political imagination more than perhaps any other fiction. And it makes me want to scream. Because as one of the people trying to transform these cases from a police file into a healthy court prosecution, what I need more than ever is police officers at computers, with time to engage with me and the CPS lawyer in order to ensure that viable prosecutions don't collapse because we haven't served a key piece of continuity evidence, or an important piece of disclosure has been missed. I need police officers trained fully on disclosure, because the number of junior officers who routinely mark obviously disclosable material as 'does not undermine or assist the defence' is increasing, not diminishing. I need cogent and comprehensive witness statements, and clear MG5 summaries, and dated MG6 memos so that I can see clearly the chronology of the investigation and where the gaps might be.

Given how often material gets lost between the police and CPS computer systems – because the first rule of government IT procurement is that no two interdependent systems should be compatible – I need officers who aren't made to feel that keeping on top of files and emails is just 'red tape' and that real policing only takes place in the open air. In any case involving electronic evidence – such as mobile phone or computer downloads – there is usually a queue of a year due to lack of resources at Digital Investigation Units. I need this to change, because the number of complainants, especially in sex cases, who simply can't wait a year for a charging decision and then two years for a trial, is one of the main reasons we have such an appalling attrition rate.

None of this, I emphasise, is a criticism of the police. I am acutely aware of their burdens. It is a criticism of the fetishisation

of Bobbies on the Beat as the be all and end all of modern policing, and the unrealistic cargoes that it loads onto divisional
officers.

If I were standing for elected office, my manifesto would
pledge More Bobbies Behind Desks.* Because that, overwhelmingly in my experience, is where the battle against crime is most
often lost.

Friday feelings

When I started out, I was promised that Friday afternoons
would be pub time. This, the myth ran, was sacred time for the
criminal Bar; courts would move mountains to ensure that all
business was finished by Friday lunchtime, thus ensuring everybody got an afternoon off to drink heavily on the Strand before
spiralling into a weekend of paperwork and marital acrimony.

That, like so much else that made the criminal Bar just the
best job in the 1980s, is a mirage. One typical Friday morning
is spent in court dealing with a burglary sentence in which the
police have failed to obtain a Victim Personal Statement or any
information as to the value of the stolen goods, which leads to
me darting in and out of court all morning making frantic
phone calls to the police (there being no CPS caseworker to
assist) to answer the judge's many, many questions. All the while
my phone buzzes furiously with emails and missed calls for my
other hearing, a prosecution mention I inherited the night
before.

Glancing at my phone as I run in and out of court, I see that
defence counsel for this afternoon wants to talk about the pleas

---

* Or, at the very least, a reinstatement of the vital civilian support jobs
that have also been the focus of sweeping cuts, ramping up the
administrative burdens placed on officers.

that his sex offender client wishes to enter. Apparently, the CPS in-house advocate at the Plea and Trial Preparation Hearing (PTPH) made an offer which the defence now wish to accept. The problem is that the CPS lawyer was not consulted, and has very different views. She has been furiously emailing me all morning, asking why the defence have written to her about the 'agreed pleas' when none have been signed off by her, and demanding to know if I have been unilaterally striking deals behind her back.

I call her at intervals throughout the morning, but her voice-mail is full. There is no option to leave a message. I email her, but the CPS email server is rejecting all incoming emails. The judge, anxious that the case resolve today, puts the hearing back until the afternoon for me to confirm my instructions. The CPS servers are back up by 3 p.m., but my email provokes an out-of-office response averring that the lawyer will be away until January of the previous year. At 3.30 p.m., having wrangled a caseworker, I finally manage to get through to the person who sits at the next desk, only to be told that my instructing solicitor doesn't work Friday afternoons.

I apologise to the defence and tell them I can't help. 'Your client will have to plead to all charges, I'm afraid.' He doesn't, of course, because, we learn at 4 p.m., the private contractors decided – for reasons presumably pertaining to their own convenience – to take the defendant back to prison at lunchtime.

The gravy train

Sitting in a busy Crown Court list, I watch as the next defendant steps through the double doors and is guided by a kindly faced usher towards the glass-walled dock. He is here for a committal for sentence, having pleaded guilty at the mags' court to possession of cannabis with intent to supply. The prosecutor takes to her feet to make the standard introduction (usually 'May it please the court, I prosecute this case, my learned friend Mx X defends'), but instead informs the judge that the defendant is unrepresented. He is prosecuted by counsel, but not defended. The judge, concerned that this young, smartly dressed man is at risk of a prison sentence and is without any legal help, addresses him directly.

It emerges that the defendant is twenty-one years old and of previous good character. He has a full-time job in a call centre, on a gross salary of £13,000. Once he's paid his tax, rent, food, clothing and travel costs, he is left with around £290 a month to live on. Due to ever-tightening restrictions on who is eligible for legal aid, this is deemed the sort of lavish wealth that excludes a defendant entirely from publicly funded assistance. If he wants legal representation, he has to pay privately.* Due to the volume of paperwork in this case, which includes hundreds of pages of mobile-phone evidence, the private commercial rate he has been quoted is £2,000 plus VAT, a figure he simply cannot afford.†

This case sends me hurtling back to all those cases I prosecuted in the mags involving bewildered litigants in person. The legal-aid means test is so strict that virtually nobody in full-time

* If, after deductions for tax, National Insurance, housing, childcare and a so-called 'adjusted annual living allowance', your annual income is more than £3,398, you are not eligible for a penny of legal aid in the magistrates' court, or if you are then committed to the Crown Court for sentence. Ingeniously, if this man, instead of immediately admitting his guilt, had pleaded not guilty and had been sent to the Crown Court for trial, and had then pleaded guilty at the Crown Court, he *would* be eligible for legal aid. This is where our national conversation about legal aid leads. Utter moronity.
† To put this in context, legal-aid rates for this offence would pay around £200 for the solicitors and £150 for the barrister.

employment qualifies, and even those who satisfy the means test have to meet the Legal Aid Agency's arbitrary interpretation of the 'interests of justice' test, which effectively licenses refusal on a whim. So it was that I found myself prosecuting confused and vulnerable individuals like the man whose defence was – I promise – 'I committed this offence after being hypnotised by aliens', and who refused to give evidence in his own defence unless the prosecutor – i.e. me – went into the witness box first.* While the court can do its best to neutrally assist litigants in person (LIPs), it cannot advise or counsel, or argue their corner.

Being accused of a crime that was being tried at the Crown Court used to automatically qualify somebody for legal aid, with the sensible proviso that, if you were convicted and had the means, you could be later required to reimburse the tax-payer. In 2014, that all changed. The government removed legal aid in the Crown Court from anyone whose joint *household* disposable income – i.e. the combined income of you and your partner – is £37,500 or more. Which is not a particularly high threshold.

It means that if you are wrongly accused, say, of involvement in a complex fraud perpetrated by your employer, you could find yourself embroiled in a complex and lengthy Crown Court trial lasting many months, the private legal costs of which could

---

* In case it's not immediately obvious, giving evidence is the very last thing that advocates are allowed to do. We call the evidence, and ask witnesses about evidence, and make speeches about evidence, but we are obviously not witnesses ourselves. If we ever found ourselves in the position where we thought we might inadvertently become a witness to something relevant at trial – let's say I go out for a smoke mid-trial and overhear the defendant confessing to his wife – we would have to withdraw from the proceedings.

run into hundreds of thousands of pounds. So either you have to represent yourself, or you plough yourself into six-figure debt. The kicker? If you are found *not* guilty, the government will not reimburse your legal costs. It will pay only a tiny fraction, equivalent to the legal-aid rate – the one that the state said you weren't eligible to receive.*

None of this is reported in regular scare stories about our 'legal-aid gravy train'; the kind of tales that foolishly led Teenage Me to believe that a criminal barrister's wig and gown conferred a licence to print money.

War on knife crime

Dennis walked into his local police station and up to the front desk. Fighting back tears, he opened the Tesco carrier bag in his hand and took out two kitchen knives, which he placed on the desk. 'Please, please take these,' he said to the officer on duty. 'They're from my kitchen. I can feel myself escalating, and if you don't take these I think I'll walk straight home and stab my flatmate to death.' The knives were removed to safety, and a clearly unwell Dennis was taken to one side. His unusual behaviour, evident mental health needs and plaintive cry for help called for only one course of action: he was arrested and charged with possessing a bladed article in a public place and making threats to kill.

This is how I came to be prosecuting him. 'Is this prosecution really in the public interest?' I ask the CPS lawyer. 'It's knives,' he replies. 'We can't be seen to be dropping anything weapon-related in the current climate.'

---

* If you are as outraged about this Innocence Tax as I am, you can learn more in *Stories of the Law and How It's Broken*, Chapter 7.

How the other half

I turn through the Pre-Sentence Report. Jenny's mother was a heroin addict, and when she was born Jenny spent the first months of her life being medically weaned off methadone. When Jenny was three, her mother died. When Jenny was five, her father went to prison for murder. She lived in the care of her grandmother, until being taken away into care aged ten because her grandmother was a drunk who alternated between neglecting and beating her.

Jenny only knew how to interact with people through conflict, because that was all that she had ever been taught. Her inability to control her emotions and explosive outbursts led to exclusion from school in Year 5. Aged twelve, she started smoking cannabis and drinking spirits. She left school altogether at fourteen. Throughout her teens, she self-harmed, both cutting and overdosing with regularity. On one occasion she was found tying herself to a railway track. At sixteen, she was raped. She miscarried the baby that resulted. She was belatedly assessed as having learning disability and an IQ of seventy, and her multiplicity of mental health needs – PTSD, depression, ADHD – were obvious to the local authority, but the referral to CAMHS slipped through the cracks. There was one support worker to whom she appeared to respond, to whom Jenny would listen and under whose supervision small, tentative steps were made towards stability. After two years, the support worker was made redundant due to cuts. She was substituted in Jenny's affections for cocaine and LSD. When Jenny turned eighteen and left the supervision of Children's Services, there was no transition plan put in place to help her adjust to independent living. She was dumped in 'supported accommodation' and the sharp reduction in supervision saw her misbehaviour escalate.

This is how she came, one evening, to be drinking with another eighteen-year-old with a similarly dysfunctional history, and, when an argument over trainers caught alight, how Jenny came to take a large kitchen knife from her studio apartment and bring it down between the girl's shoulder blades.

The report went on for pages and pages. All of its contents had been independently verified. Custody was inevitable; a case of wounding with intent of this severity carried a starting point of twelve years. Jenny had lost her trial, the jury disbelieving her claim to have been acting in self-defence. But the report made a plea: while on bail for the eighteen months awaiting trial, Jenny had made some very real progress. She was in meaningful assisted accommodation, which was meeting her desperate need for consistent support figures. There had been an improvement in her mental health, as she was engaging with counsellors and drug workers, and although still a high risk to herself and to others, she had attained a plateau of relevant stability. Her coping strategies, however, remained limited, and she would present a high risk of self-harm and suicide if sent to prison. Furthermore, she would lose all of the support structures – her accommodation, her support workers, her counselling – and when released would find herself in the exact same position as when she committed the offence.

What a court is supposed to do in a case like this, I have absolutely no idea. Truly. I don't know how you begin to wrestle with the complexities of the lives involved, how you properly assess a person's culpability set against a childhood like this, how as a judge passing sentence you define, let alone deliver, justice for the young people involved.

These cases also lay bare the chasm between the justice system and those most affected by it. I have written earlier of my feelings of otherness at the Bar, my realisation, as a state-schooled, non-Oxbridge legal outsider, that I was a minority. But the truth is that I have no fucking idea. I am in a tier of unimaginable privilege, as are nearly all of my colleagues. I may well be a totem of a class divide, but not in the way I like to tell myself. I exist in an ivory tower whose height cannot even be imagined by the people I am paid to represent, the people for whom I speak, and the people who I prosecute. I swoop onto their estates and into their lives on a patrician poverty safari, and back out again to the safety of the suburbs. And I dare to style myself as an establishment outsider?

I have not experienced even a fraction of the hardship visited on Jenny in her two decades on this earth. Nor even the more mundane, 'everyday' hardships that we see in case after case after case that is churned through the criminal justice system, into our diaries and out again, neatly wrapped and billed. I have not had to feed children on minimum wage, or less. I have not had to raise a baby on benefits, on the run from debt collectors and an abusive partner. I have not had to jump from refuge to refuge, from insecure tenancy to sofa and back again, while hounded by the state to attend court. I have enjoyed the exquisite privilege of a loving upbringing, good education and the material and social buffering that my class and professional status confer, as have almost all of my legal brethren.

And yet it is us, festooned in horsehair and sitting in judgement, who are charged with assessing the merits of our fellow citizens' decisions, forming summary views and imposing life-defining consequences without having so much as dipped a toe in their shoes.

Dillon (Part 3)
Five years since we first met, Dillon is getting worse. The violence he suffered growing up is now being replayed in his own

home, with his girlfriends the victims of his controlling and sadistic behaviour – cigarette burns are, several partners attest, his current weapon of choice. His combination of charm, ruthlessness and recklessness has seen him soar up the hierarchy on his estate, and a growing illusion of invincibility – not helped, I'm sure, by the frequency with which police investigations and prosecutions against him falter, or compromise at court with vastly reduced sentences – is spawning grave consequences. His latest trial is for robbery and wounding with intent – horrific machete attacks on teens on the estate; some acquisitive, some purely punitive. On remand, he has prison officers in his pocket, smoothing the passage of contraband from the outside into his cell as he reinforces his empire.

Again, the complainants fail to attend trial. Although the prosecution succeed in presenting their witness statements as hearsay evidence, the jury, presumably not keen on the idea of convicting a young man of life-defining offences on the say-so of witnesses who haven't come to court, acquit. Dillon grins and offers his fist as he emerges from the court cells, his swagger perceptibly enlarged by his latest improbable victory. Any notion that his horizons might be tempered by his whisker-thin escape from a double-figure sentence is immediately dispersed. He will return home emboldened, his aura enhanced and his ambitions higher than ever.

What can stop him? Probably only prison. Or death. Or both. One day, I have little doubt, he will kill someone, or be killed. The prosecution hope that they will be able to make one of these cases stick before he inflicts or sustains that preordained fatal blow, but even incarceration may just postpone the inevitable by a few years.

The realisation that some people simply cannot be 'fixed' by criminal justice may sound like an overdue disabusement of naivety. Maybe it is. Dillon causes me to wobble uncontrollably between pessimism and idealism; between the hard realism I espoused before coming to the Bar, and the dewy, stupid, stupid optimism that creeps in between the cracks when we're sitting in his cell and he is chatting brightly and articulately and grinning goofily and is the same damaged-yet-promising seventeen-year-old I met at the Youth Court all those years ago, the one whose potential I was going to unlock, and whom I was going to save from himself with my talented lawyerliness and home-spun bourgeoise wisdom.

What *could* have stopped him? I don't know. But I doubt it was anything that exists in the criminal justice system. The fault in his stars was fixed long before he received his first referral order in the Youth Court. There has been no lack of effort by dedicated youth justice professionals, no shortage of second, third, fourth chances. They just didn't work. Looking at the aims of criminal justice – punishment, reduction of crime (including by deterrence), rehabilitation, compensation, public protection – how many of these have actually been achieved? Possibly the first, in increments. The fifth, in short-term bursts.

And maybe the problem is that we expect too much of the criminal justice system. We kid ourselves that the small box of blunt tools available at a sentencing hearing is capable of undoing decades of damage, effectively erasing the experiences of a lifetime. More often, a criminal conviction and sentence is simply an end result. It's the official stamp as the product leaves the warehouse. Another notch on the criminal record. How much can it realistically change? How can a judge, dealing with a case years after the event, reverse the toll of an abusive childhood, a failing care system, an absent education and a decade of being modelled in the image of a violent criminal gang? How could any court, or any youth justice professional, have counteracted those forces moulding him as he grew? How could YOT workers, even with intensive orders requiring Dillon to spend forty hours a week under their direct supervision, neutralise the malign influence of those who control him for the remaining 128?

The gloomy answer may be 'they can't'. That the best we can hope for in cases like Dillon is reactive justice; catch him and punish him, ad nauseam. But it may also expose the truth that criminal justice does not exist in a vacuum. Crime reduction is not simply a matter of catching criminals, processing them and having them sentenced. Responsibility for preventing the conditions that nurtured Dillon extends far beyond the court walls. But it is perhaps easier, for those who configure and run our social infrastructure, to confine responsibility for crime to the courts, instead of looking wider towards, to evoke a phrase I once mocked as hopelessly naive and woolly, the actual causes of crime.

Choose hope

My sixteen-year-old client, Nadeem, had been remanded in detention by the Youth Court at his first appearance, the magistrates concluding that the prosecution allegations – a string of late-night knifepoint robberies in which other teenagers had been badly wounded – gave rise to substantial grounds to fear that, if granted bail, Nadeem would commit further offences or fail to surrender.* Given Nadeem's lack of previous convictions, the Crown Court judge hearing the bail appeal has agreed that, while there is a risk, it can be met by Nadeem being remanded into local authority accommodation – a care home, rather than a young offender institution. Credit is owed not to my bumbling

* i.e. Do a runner.

submissions, but to the commanding contribution of Nadeem's local authority youth worker, Mohammed, who has assisted the judge with Nadeem's troubled upbringing and made a forceful argument as to why the risk he posed would be better managed under the watchful eye of Mohammed and his colleagues rather than amid the *Lord of the Flies* pastoral ethos of youth custody.

As we leave court, I thank Mohammed for his invaluable help. He shakes my hand and asks, almost as an afterthought: 'Is Judge Evans still sitting in this building?' I confirm that Judge Evans retired a few years ago, and Mohammed offers a rueful smile.

'Have you been in front of him before?' I ask. He nods. He then tells me how, twelve years ago, he was the one in the dock. He'd been carrying drugs and knives for older lads, rebelling against his unhappy home life in the all-too-familiar pattern. His Honour Judge Evans had 'given me the fright of my life' with his sentencing remarks, but had at the last second drawn back from sending Mohammed to prison. That judicial dressing-down, while probably formulaic to judges and practitioners ('This offence is so serious that ONLY custody will suffice . . . [DRA-MATIC PAUSE] However, I can suspend that sentence' is the usual cliffhanger), had a transformative effect. With the help of the Youth Offending Service, Mohammed turned his back on crime entirely, channelled his energies into voluntary work and eventually found his calling in helping to divert teenagers away from the path which he himself had managed to reverse out of. He was now happily married with young children, and in every respect a model citizen.

This story sticks out for its rarity value, but I like to think it's much more common than we realise; that the revolving door is not as jam-packed as it's easy to presume. Barristers, of course, only see the failures; the Dillons of this world, breaching their court orders and hurtling straight back into reoffending in defiance of all systemic attempts to save them from themselves. No doubt it would help our perspective if we reminded ourselves of this once in a while. And, I dare say, not just us but the wider public. We see and rail against soft rehabilitative sentences and the irrepressible criminals indulged by foolish judges, but the tabloids don't do follow-ups with the success stories. I sometimes wonder how the tone of our national discussions about justice would sound if, in place of some of the rancour at judges 'letting criminals walk free from court', we swapped in the more optimistic stories of those who then never walk back in.

Cash crisis

I do know, when I put on my tin hat to receive a judicial whacking for the prosecution's most recent failure to comply with court directions/serve key evidence/obtain key evidence, that it's not actually my fault. I know that the judge knows that, and that I know that, and that we are both ultimately performers dancing a practised, choreographed routine in which counsel apologises *on behalf of the Crown* and Her Honour delivers the standard soliloquy peppered with *unacceptable*s and *outrageous*es and *inconceivable*s. I know that these familiar adjectives are directed not at me, and often not even at the police or the CPS, but usually at those responsible for such things being a regular feature of a starved, limp justice system. I do.

But it is still hard to shake the feeling of personal shame. I always struggle to quash the sensation of regression, of being at school and receiving a stern telling-off for failing to do homework or for shitting in the sandpit. One memorable blast of judicial wrath is entirely justified: I have to deliver the news that we are dropping an armed robbery prosecution because the police cannot obtain budgetary authorisation for an expert report from a footprint analyst, in a case which hinges on footprint evidence. We know that the footprint from the scene matches the shoes that the defendant was wearing that night. The police just can't afford to pay for the formal report to make it admissible evidence. Even writing it down, it sounds ludicrous. And unacceptable, outrageous, inconceivable, etc. Yet even as I internally douse the dragon flames with a chill blast of rationality to remind myself that I am not to blame, the flickers of guilt don't easily dampen. Long after the hearing has ended, the case is over and the files are archived, the embers still glow. I carry them everywhere, accumulating heavy pocketfuls with each unsuccessful case; a smouldering taunt that somehow, I could – and should – have done more.

Ill-gotten gains

The Proceeds of Crime Act 2002 is often described as the most draconian legislation in English and Welsh criminal law. If you commit a crime and benefit financially from it, the state can swoop in and recoup your 'benefit' – a legal term which means not merely your direct financial gain from the offence, but, depending on the offence, includes an assumption that all money and property flowing through your hands over the past six years has been derived from crime, unless you can prove otherwise. You will only be forced to pay what you actually have, but – and this is the fact omitted from the tabloid favourite 'MILLION POUND SWINDLER ONLY HAS TO PAY BACK £1' headline – that (often artificial) benefit sum, which can be six or seven figures, hangs over you for the rest of your life until it's paid off. If you obtain legitimate employment and work hard to accumulate savings or buy a family home, the state can come back at any time and try to take it away.

One afternoon, I find myself prosecuting such a case, where a defendant who was convicted of supplying class A ten years earlier has seen an increase in the equity in his home. Cue the Financial Investigations Unit bringing him back before the court for an order that he realise that equity and pay it towards the outstanding six-figure benefit. The main dispute between the prosecution and defence is the value of the house – the defence say the equity is £25k, based on a full valuation survey; we say it's £50k based on a quick browse of Zoopla for average house prices in that postcode. Fairly quickly, defence counsel and I arrive at a middle ground which the financial investigator is happy with.

Getting this putative agreement signed off by the CPS lawyer sadly proves impossible. There is no caseworker allocated to my court, so I'm left to track down a duty caseworker who today is based in Leeds, despite that city having no link at all to the case or anybody involved in it. The Leeds caseworker does his best to get hold of the lawyer, who didn't pick up when I dialled the London contact number on my brief (this is also not a case with any links to London). The Leeds caseworker eventually snares somebody at the Southwark office who informs us that the lawyer in question is today working in Newcastle-upon-Tyne (also not a Newcastle case), and passes me two possible numbers. Both numbers ring out with no voicemail facility enabled.

We adjourn to try again in a week's time.

Deus ex machina

'We're dropping it,' the prosecutor says, thrusting a statement into my hand. I scan through it, expecting to see a retraction from the star witness who, although at court to give evidence against my client, Jayden, has been calling my solicitor daily to ask how she can 'drop the charges' because she wants him home for Christmas.

Instead, it is a statement from the private company that fitted the electronically monitored tag that Jayden was wearing at the time that he allegedly chased his ex-girlfriend's new beau down the street with a baseball bat. We've been asking for this information for a while, and at the last it has emerged to ensure a dramatic and satisfactory conclusion, to wit: There is no indication of the tag having been interfered with, meaning Jayden was definitely wearing it. There is no electronic record of the tag having left Jayden's address, meaning that he could not possibly have chased anybody down the street. And there is no question at all over the integrity of the technology. It was an impossibility, the statement averred, that Jayden could have left his address without the equipment being triggered.

The offence just could not have happened. It was a proven false allegation, bringing Jayden's five months on remand to an abrupt finish. As I break the news to him in the cells he seems somewhat perplexed. After being formally acquitted, he walks out of court with the same look of semi-bafflement and makes his way to the Tube.

A week later, I'm talking to Jayden's solicitor about a different case, and he mentions that, after court, Jayden had called the solicitors to thank them for their help, and casually mentioned that he *had* actually been running down the street, baseball bat in hand, in pursuit of his love rival. He had also been wearing his tag. The company's determination to protect its reputation and deny the possibility of error had handed him the best Christmas present he could have asked for.

Other countries' problems

Joe has a pretty dreadful criminal record. Robbery, affray, violent disorder – a familiar potpourri of semi-serious offending which has seen him serve multiple prison sentences before he hit his mid-twenties. But the offence for which he is in custody when I meet him is slightly more off the beaten track. His crime is refusing to apply for a passport.

Joe is a South African national. He came to the UK at the age of four with his mother, who arrived on a work visa, and they were both later granted indefinite leave to remain. His childhood was, to put it decorously, difficult. Joe had special educational needs, and his disruptive and aggressive behaviour resulted in multiple exclusions from multiple schools. From there, it was a hop and a skip to lower-tier criminality, which quickly accelerated into the bigger leagues.

Since his eighteenth birthday, Joe has been in the sights of the Home Office. They, perhaps unsurprisingly, have assessed Joe as an undesirable presence, and, because he is not a British citizen, have informed him that he is liable to be deported back to South Africa. Joe won his first appeal against the Home Office's decision, but when he received a four-month prison sentence a few years later, the Home Office seized the cherry and took a second munch. This time, there was no reprieve. It didn't matter that deportation would separate Joe from his partner and his young children, who are all British citizens. Those human rights laws that we are often told allow the worst foreign criminals to stay on our shores – they haven't worked. Joe is a repeat offender and the courts have concluded that, in law, the Home Secretary is free to deport him.

The only hitch is that Joe doesn't have a passport and, in order for him to be able to fly to South Africa, he needs to apply for a South African emergency travel document. And he won't. He refuses to sign the paperwork, which in itself is a criminal offence carrying a maximum sentence of two years.* He keeps being convicted, and keeps being imprisoned. And just as his sentence is about to expire, Home Office officials visit Joe in his cell and thrust the paperwork under his nose, and Joe refuses to sign, and he's charged again. And sentenced again. On and on and on. But Joe isn't budging – if he goes to South Africa, a country to which he has no ties aside from accident of birth, he won't see his partner or his children or his mother or his friends for years, if ever. They don't have the means to visit, and there's little chance of Joe being let back into the UK for a holiday, even if he could afford a return ticket. At least while he's in custody here, he gets to see his family and friends on prison visits. It's not life as he'd wish it, but it's something. It's everything.

On the one hand, I can comprehend the Home Office's perspective. Joe's is exactly the kind of case I would have railed against as a student. A foreign national who has been granted the privilege of an invitation to live in our country, and who has thrown that opportunity back in our faces. Offence after offence after offence. Ingratitude after ingratitude.

But on the other hand, Joe is a product of our country. We made him. He went through our education system, our social services, our criminal justice system. Without absolving Joe of responsibility for his bad decisions, to the extent that his environment played a role in his behaviour, it was an environment created by us. When he stole a pedal cycle aged twelve, we chose to put him through the criminal justice system. Our institutions failed to stop him offending and have repeatedly failed to rehabilitate him.

---

* Section 35(1) of the Asylum and Immigration (Treatment of Claimants, etc.) Act 2004.

For us to now seek to return him to South Africa, a state which has had absolutely no input into his formation – even if your sympathy is limited for Joe – hardly seems fair on the South African people.

But it's also unfair on Joe. Yes, he's an unrepentant criminal, but he's *our* unrepentant criminal. I can feel my twenty-year-old self's unsympathetic glare burning into me as I write. *He chose to commit crime. He chose to put his children in this position. His children are probably better off without him.* And those things may – certainly the first two – be true. But the punishment that we are visiting on him – transportation 6,000 miles away and estrangement from everything and everyone he's ever known – is a punishment that we can't impose on any of the other unrepentant criminals, with records equal to or worse than Joe's, who had the fortune to be born on our shores. If I were in Joe's shoes, I too would cling on to my foothold in the country I'd grown up in, however precarious my grip and however hard the state tried to shake me loose.

And that's now where we are, stuck in this loop. Joe is bouncing from custodial sentence to custodial sentence, and there is no sign of an exit, for him or the Home Office. Because as long as Joe is here, the Home Office will keep trying to deport him. And as long as they try to deport him, Joe will break whatever law he needs to if it means he can see his children. Even if – and this, I fear, is how this story ends – he remains in our prisons, for failing to sign a document, for the rest of his life.

Plus ça change

Another day, another sign of cuts in action.

'I have heard enough,' says the judge, raising his hand. 'I would like you, please, to take a note of what I am about to say, and to ensure that it is communicated directly to the CPS lawyer. I appreciate that this is not your case, and that you are helpfully stepping into the breach today, but this is a very, very serious firearms case, the preparation of which has been nothing short of shambolic. There has been a series of unexplained delays with the prosecution obtaining the obviously key evidence. I am particularly astonished by the suggestion that the prosecution did not serve their expert evidence because, I am told, they "couldn't find the address for the defendants' solicitors". The trial date is in three weeks' time and is in jeopardy. Given the numerous prosecution delays, if that trial date is lost, there is little prospect of an extension to the custody time limits being granted, meaning that two potentially very dangerous men will be released onto the streets.'

Listings

A nasty assault outside a nightclub. A second trial listing. After the young complainant, his family and two witnesses spend a full day in one Crown Court witness suite, we are told at 4.15 p.m. by the listing officer that the trial will begin tomorrow in an entirely different city. I break the news to the witnesses, who agree – far more graciously than I would – to rearrange their college, childcare and work plans, and reattend the following day. We all turn up at 9.30 a.m. the following morning to be greeted in court by an overwrought judge, furious that the listing officers haven't consulted her, because, had they done so, they would have learned that she is not sitting beyond today and so can't possibly preside over a three-day trial.

I trudge to the witness suite to ask the family for their diaries for the next eight months.

The war on drugs

The two defendants huddle in the dock, flanked by security. The man, Roy, unkempt and in his late fifties, is at the Crown Court for only the second time in his life, but it's a big one. He has decided mid-life to forge a new career producing and selling amphetamine, and was plying a roaring trade until the police had the temerity to raid his stash house and seize upwards of 40 kg of class B. The woman standing next to him, Anna, is previously unknown to the police. Also in her fifties, her Pre-Sentence Report speaks of a hitherto blameless existence, a succession of casual minimum-wage jobs as she strived to raise her children alone, a running battle against payday-loan debt defining the last five years, leading to her agreeing to let her co-accused, her long-time neighbour, store his drugs, bulking agents and equipment in her poky kitchen for a rent of £100 a month.

For Roy, custody is unavoidable, even on a guilty plea. He gets five and a half years. For Anna, in a much lesser role, the sentencing guideline would give a starting point of three years' custody. She gets a one-third 'credit' for pleading guilty at the earliest opportunity, making two years. Any sentence of two years or less can be suspended. This case has been hanging over Anna for two years, since she made full admissions in her police interview. She presents no risk at all to the public and is assessed as highly unlikely to reoffend. She has already lost her tenancy, her job and her good character. Her mental health is fragile and probation fear for her welfare in a prison environment. She is still gasping for breath as the payday-loan debt ticks up each day; immediate imprisonment would plunge her under completely. Her barrister makes a thoroughly persuasive plea for a suspended sentence. As the prosecutor, it is not my role to comment on whether I think a sentence should be suspended,* but I think it should. I don't see what purpose is served by adding custody to this woman's burden. Give her a year-long curfew and hundreds of hours of unpaid work and the mental health support she is crying out for. Her record will be marked with a custodial sentence, which is its own punishment.

The judge appears to agree. When he turns to Anna, he summarises her mitigation. He finds that the appropriate sentence is eighteen months, 'which is capable of being suspended'. Out of the corner of my eye I see Anna exhale sharply.

'However, drug offences are serious . . .' And just like that, it's over. 'Your barrister has said everything on your behalf that could be said . . .' and we don't need to hear any more. Those words are the judicial cue for immediate custody. Eighteen months is passed, and Anna is taken downstairs. The next case is called on, a sentence for an ABH committed against the defendant's pregnant partner. The defendant in that case leaves with eighteen months suspended.

Unforgivable

I rise to open the prosecution facts for Victor's sentence. He is sixty-nine years old, and pleaded guilty at the mags' court to offences of distributing indecent photographs of children. Due to the seriousness of the offences, he has been committed to the Crown Court for sentence.

The victim was his six-year-old granddaughter. Victor had taken photographs and videos of her in the bath and getting changed, and had then uploaded them to the internet, sharing these violations for the edification of like-minded strangers, and

---

* Unless it's something like murder, in which case I'd politely check that the judge hadn't been smoking the Devil's Lettuce.

trading his images for those held by others. Police intelligence led them to Victor's address, and an examination of his phone revealed what he had done. In my limited prosecution papers, there is no Victim Personal Statement, nor, my caseworker informs, are any members of the family at court today. Usually in a case involving a child victim, a statement will be provided by a parent describing the impact of the offences. The absence of any such statement is, hopefully, an indicator that the child is unaware of what her grandad has been doing. She will learn one day, of course, but it is perhaps a mercy, of sorts, that that conversation can be delayed until she is older.

As I read the details of what Victor has done for the court record, there is an audible gasp from my left, followed by a guttural howl and the sound of someone running out of court, slamming the heavy double doors behind them. The judge breaks the silence by asking an usher to make enquiries, and adjourns for ten minutes. The usher returns minutes later and gestures for me to follow him outside, whispering: 'She wants to speak to you.'

I step onto the concourse, and the woman, Maria, introduces herself. To my horror, she explains that she is the daughter-in-law of the defendant, and the mother of the child in this case. She apologises – entirely unnecessarily, I assure her – for her reaction in court, but today is the first time that she has heard the details of what Victor has done. She had not even been told by the police or the CPS that he had been charged; she only discovered today's hearing by chance, after a neighbour stumbled across a local newspaper report from Victor's magistrates' hearing which mentioned that today would be the sentence date. All that Maria knew was that there was something untoward found on Victor's phone. That it related to her little girl, she discovered from my opening three minutes ago.

I apologise profusely and repeatedly on behalf of our incompetent, callous, fucked-up embarrassment of a system, as if that can in any way begin to repair the damage. I urge Maria to lodge a formal complaint, although quite how high admin features on your list of priorities when you've just learned about your child's sexual abuse at the hands of your father-in-law, I don't know. I submit my own report to the CPS when the case is over, but what follows – what consequences, what amends – I am never told. I can hazard a guess.

Lives in hands

I can probably count on one paw the number of times I have felt genuinely fearful for my safety when alone with a client. One that sticks out was Adam, whose natural predilection for methodical violence had taken on a new vibe of unpredictability thanks to a spice addiction he'd picked up in prison.* His reaction to receiving information – good, bad or neutral – was to assume that, somehow, somebody was 'mugging him off', punch the wall and scream threatening obscenities at the messenger. After making clear to me and my instructing solicitor that, if convicted, he would 'find out where you fucking live and fucking burn yous out, you're going down in fucking flames', he had a change of heart on the day of trial when the complainant turned up.

The case was called on and Adam was rearraigned and pleaded guilty. All was going as well as could have been hoped until he saw the complainant sitting in the public gallery. The transformation from Bruce Banner was instantaneous. He

---

* For the uninitiated, Adam was not smoking nutmeg. Spice is a synthetic cannabinoid which alternately zombifies users and turns them in a flash into raging aggressive maniacs.

launched himself at the Perspex wall of the dock and with every available part of his body endeavoured to smash his way out, sending security officers flying as he thudded the panels until they cracked and screamed murderous intent at the complainant. An emergency alarm and six officers later, Adam was forcibly subdued and his sentence adjourned. The judge made a point of asking the security staff to ensure that the private contractor's management arranged for a heavy security presence in the dock on the next occasion, lest Adam react to his (inevitably lengthy) sentence with the same good humour.

Whether the message failed to reach management, or arrived but was deemed unimportant, I don't know, but come Adam's sentence date, the dock was attended by a single female security officer. Mercifully, Adam refused to get on the prison van to court that day.

The knock at the door

Martin will never see his daughters graduate. He will never meet his grandchildren. He will never again dance with his wife on their wedding anniversary – twenty-five years next week, as cynical, spiteful fate would have it. He was as generous with his laughter as he was with his praise – he would find the good and the humour in pretty much everything – and his family will never again hear that hearty, staccato chuckle that put everybody in the room at immediate ease. His brothers will never have to feign yawns as Martin sermonises about his rallying, never have to field the phone calls each year reminding them, because Martin was the designated reminder, about their mother's birthday. He will never finish the countless jobs started around the house; the alcove floating shelves sit wrapped in polythene in the garage; the two shades of green paint for the spare room that he'd vacillated over will remain streaks from a tester pot dragged thickly down one wall. He'll never have to decide.

He will never say I love you, and never hear it back. He will never walk into a room of silence and with only a few words transform it into a theatre of laughter. He'll never cradle the family beagle like a baby, as the daft hound throws back its head and tries to lick his beard. He will never take his wife, Lizzie, back to the B & B in Provence where they'd stayed on their honeymoon a quarter of a century ago – was it even still open? Neither knew, but Martin's promise, renewed with every anniversary milestone, was that one year they'd go back.

Neither Martin, nor anyone whose life shone brighter for his energy and his love, will ever get the chance to say goodbye. The overriding memory they will carry with them, for the rest of their days, is the knock on the door at 11.47 a.m., and the sombre pallor of the two young police officers in their smart uniforms, from which moment everything changed. The words that followed did not stick, only 'car' and 'accident' – and accident, they would later learn, it was certainly not. 'That knock at the door,' Lizzie said in her Victim Personal Statement, 'was the point at which my life came to an end. You,' addressing the defendant, 'brought our lives to an end.'

The sudden death of a loved one is impossible to comprehend until it has come to pass, and no two bereavements are capable of comparison; you can't attribute quotients of grief. But I think that there is a certain quality of rawness when the fault is not illness or accident, but human wrongdoing. There is something about the ceremony of the criminal courts that accentuates the depth of loss, the formal appropriation by the state of a person's last moments reminding with every beat of the process that *this is not how it was supposed to end*. It is never how any story is supposed to end.

In Martin's case, the defendant, Rikki, had been high on cannabis and three times over the limit when, hitting 80 mph in his VW Golf, he careered round a bend, onto the opposite carriageway and straight into the driver's side of Martin's Toyota. Causing death by dangerous driving carries a maximum sentence of fourteen years and, having listened as Lizzie read out her Victim Personal Statement from the witness box, the judge took a starting point close to the maximum. Allowing full credit for Rikki's guilty plea, the overall sentence was eight years.

Lizzie and Martin's two daughters had been advised by the police and the family liaison officer of the likely outcome, and they said that they were content with the sentence and grateful for what the judge had said in tribute to Martin. But cases like this, to me, merely underscore the limitations of criminal justice. As is said in every such sentence hearing, no sentence the court can pass can begin to assuage a family's grief; nor can any sentence undo the damage that has been done or reflect the true value of a person's life. Such truisms are well familiar to criminal practitioners. But with dangerous driving – in this case taking the conscious decision to drink, smoke drugs and drive like a maniac, which results in the death of another person – I can fully understand why to many a maximum sentence of fourteen years feels inadequate. My fear, however, is that as we see with sentencing for manslaughter and murder, where life sentences are imposed, it is rare that any sentence, of any length, is ever enough. The minimum terms of life sentences are too low; if it's a whole life order, the prison environment itself will be condemned as too cushy, insufficiently unpleasant. This is not in any sense a criticism of anybody bereaved who feels or expresses this; rather, again, it is a query as to whether we expect too much from the criminal justice system. Because what we want in cases where somebody takes a life is to transfer our pain, if not away entirely then onto the person responsible. And no sentence in the world can ever achieve that.

More complicated still are those cases, often involving driving, where there is irreversible, fatal harm, but minimal culpability. Not explicitly outrageous behaviour like Rikki's, but momentary inattention leading to catastrophic consequences. The pain of the bereaved is the same, but the courts, required to consider not just harm but culpability, will often pass sentences even more incongruent to the value we attach to human life. In recent years, governments have legislated to create offences where there is almost no fault at all – offences such as causing death by driving when uninsured – where the culpability of the driver lies not in a criminally dangerous or careless standard of driving, but in failing to have the correct paperwork.

And I understand the impulse, really I do. If it were my partner or my child who had been killed, I would want the person responsible to be punished. I would have little truck for gradations of culpability; if they were responsible, I would want them held accountable. I would want them to hurt.

But an important test in criminal justice is how it bites from the other side. If it were my partner on the road, who had through error let their insurance lapse – a renewal on an expired credit card not going through – and who was involved in an accident in which someone was killed, and in which everyone agreed my partner's driving was not even careless, would I be happy to see them imprisoned for up to two years? It's a question that we rarely ask ourselves, because, I suspect, we just don't think it will happen to us. If we dare to envisage a scenario in which we are a character in a road traffic accident, we are on the side of the angels. We wouldn't – couldn't – be the person in the dock, or in the public gallery praying for a sentence that, in a parallel existence, we would vilify on social media as an outrage.

A career in the criminal courts teaches otherwise. Not all defendants are like Rikki. Not all defendants who kill are like Rikki. I wonder how our conversations about justice would sound if those who speak loudest in public life were not so complacent as to assume that the course of their life – your life – will never take a sudden, unplanned diversion to the court-room door.

Weekend offender

Jemma was a fourteen-year-old girl who had alleged serious sexual offending against her stepdad, in a case I was instructed to prosecute. A few months before trial, a second stepdaughter, Steph, came forward to make similar allegations. I advised that she would need to be video-interviewed by the police and the CPS would have to make a charging decision quick smart, because whatever happened in that investigation would likely be relevant to Jemma's case.

Unfortunately, despite repeated chasing, the police had not, four months later, got round to interviewing Steph. Jemma's trial had to be adjourned for this to be done, and the enduring lack of courtrooms meant that the earliest slot for a new trial was a year away. This did, at least, give us plenty of time to progress the investigation into Steph's allegation.

Alas, at the pre-trial hearing six months later, I am standing up and reading aloud from an email in which I am advised that no interview has taken place because 'the AP [Steph] can't attend the police station on a weekday, and the OIC [Officer in Charge] doesn't work weekends.' Seemingly flummoxed by this insoluble dilemma, the police had just given up. I pride myself on my unfailing forced politeness, but it turns out there really isn't a non-passive-aggressive way to ask, 'Can the case not be allocated to a different fucking officer?'

Soft sentencing

The relentless churn of grimness continues with a week-long trial prosecuting a man for sexual offences committed against his four-year-old daughter. The video evidence of this tiny child making a gesture to show the police officer what daddy did with his willy while she was in the bath – a gesture that could only be learned by experience – is as compelling for the jury as it was horrific, and he was rightly convicted. The case sticks in the memory partly for the testy exchanges in cross-examination, culminating in the defendant declaring me 'a fucking nasty cunt'. (Judge's response: silence. Opponent's sotto voce response: 'Entirely improper. You're not nasty.') But also partly for the sentence.

For two offences of causing a child to watch a sexual act, the overall sentence is three years and four months' imprisonment. This is, on the sentencing guidelines, unimpeachable from the prosecution's point of view. The judge took the specified starting point of two years, and increased it significantly to reflect the aggravating features.

But stepping back and viewing this through a non-legal lens, it is one of those sentences that jolts me back to my tub-thumping teens, impotently furious at outcomes which neither rehabilitate nor mark the seriousness of the harm caused to the victims. In my present incarnation, I spend a lot of time defending a sentencing regime which a younger me – and many people reading this – would deride as soft or illogical; I patiently* point out that the courts are bound by maximum sentences determined by

* Not always true.

Parliament and by sentencing guidelines composed by an independent Sentencing Council after much research and widespread consultation, and that too often we focus attention on retribution or punishment and overlook the equally valid sentencing purpose of rehabilitation.

But as well and good as those faithful platitudes may be, sometimes the priorities of our justice system leave me quietly aghast. A sentence of three years and four months – of which the defendant will serve half before automatic release on licence – for the most serious betrayal of his own child. A betrayal that will define the course of that innocent girl's childhood, if not her entire life. How on earth can I argue with somebody reading about this in the newspaper and feeling visceral, burning outrage? At the risk of rehearsing the media clichés that I abhor, what message does this sort of sentence send? What will spending twenty months in one of our prisons do for this man? It is insufficient time for him to undertake any meaningful rehabilitation (the sex offender treatment programmes are generally only available for prisoners sentenced to four years or more), so the only purpose of this sentence can be retribution. And when we compare it to, say, the guidelines for the supply of controlled drugs, I find it impossible to make sense of what we're trying to achieve.

If, instead of sexually abusing his four-year-old daughter, this man had sold a few wraps of crack cocaine, the guidelines would prescribe a starting point of four and a half years. Somebody explain that to me. Please. A criminal justice system which defines low-level street supply of drugs as more serious than the sexual abuse of a child. The emphasis that our system places on punishing drug pushers more severely than those who commit life-defining crimes of sexual or physical violence is something I cannot, no matter how hard I bury myself in my learned liberal dogma, bring myself to comprehend.

And maybe the problem lies in my reaction – *quietly aghast*. Maybe, because we too often find ourselves battling what we perceive as the reactionary sentiments of the tabloid press when it comes to discussing criminal sentencing, we fail to speak out about the failures we see travelling in the opposite direction. Because they exist; the sentences that, although perfectly correct in the eyes of the law, are too lenient to command public support, and can't – upon meaningful, principled inspection – withstand scrutiny on a non-legal plane.

The sentencing starting points and ranges prescribed by the guidelines are anchored to sentencing decisions approved by the Court of Appeal over many decades; decades in which, lest we forget, violence against women and children was routinely minimised or even indulged by a justice system run by men, for men. It would be unpardonably naive to deny this, yet that, it seems to me, is so often what we – in the system – do. On days like this I find myself on the side not merely of the revolutionaries but the nihilists, biting through my bottom lip to stop myself screaming for someone to burn the whole system to the ground.

Tips of icebergs

Each year, thousands of men – and it is almost exclusively men – appear before the courts charged with possessing, downloading or sharing indecent images of children. And, as police officers regularly tell me, what we see in court is only a fraction of the problem. Police numbers have been cut and digital forensic units are already buckling under the weight of the computers, mobile phones and other electronic media requiring analysis in cases of this type, and so police forces have to be selective in who and what they investigate.

A sobering reminder of the regularity of this type of offence arrives whenever a case concerns a defendant distributing images. This usually takes place over messaging apps in which groups of dozens of anonymous users trade the most vile material and engage in the most depraved conversations, glorifying and inciting acts of which most people would not be able to begin to conceive. And while sometimes the police get lucky and crack an entire paedophile network, in most cases the prosecution have identified and caught only the defendant, and his myriad co-enthusiasts for child abuse skulk undetected in silhouette. Even with those who are caught, there is often much more going on than the police can prove.

There is something in the manner in which these men talk that always strikes me as particularly chilling. Where you might expect fetishisation, you find normalisation. The shorthand, the acronyms, the overt familiarity with particular acts – all the hallmarks of community. Whereas in a pre-digital age, social norms might have a hope of repressing a person's urge to seek out such material, the internet offers instant reassurance, a plethora of shadow societies where the urge is not only condoned, but encouraged and inflamed. The term 'echo chamber' is often used in reference to social media, but it applies equally to this realm, where degenerate norms are reinforced so strongly that its members lose all sight of the real world.

Notwithstanding the serious and lasting harm caused by these offences – even 'mere' downloading still fuels the demand for the production of the images – and even though a single offence carries a maximum sentence of ten years' custody, it is more common than not that a first-time offender who pleads guilty will not receive immediate custody. The starting point for possessing a 'Category A' image – the most serious type – is twelve months' custody, which will often be suspended, or will be substituted for a lengthy community order.

This, understandably, provokes public alarm when the press report on such sentences. The idea that paedophiles can amass substantial collections of images of abuse and avoid immediate custody instinctively offends many people's notion of justice. Certainly it offended mine. The explanation – not, I emphasise, necessarily a justification – is that lengthy community-based treatment programmes (usually between two and three years), combined with intensive monitoring of the person's computer activity (in the form of a Sexual Harm Prevention Order), can offer a better prospect of successfully guiding somebody away from reoffending. The courts are often dealing with psychologically vulnerable and isolated men, frequently with mental ill health and their own experiences of childhood abuse, who have descended into a wormhole of internet offending which consumes every minute of their day. Attempting to wrench them back out is more likely to succeed if they are allowed to keep what few stabilising influences they have – accommodation, work, family ties – rather than if they are given a prison sentence of a few months, of which half is served before release on licence. In such cases, the court's assessment is that the likelihood of reoffending is greater if the defendant is sent to custody, thus offering much less protection in the long term for the public.*

As ever, though, monitoring of convicted offenders and the incidence of reoffending is only as successful as resources allow. Sexual Offender Management Units have ever-increasing caseloads, without the corresponding increase in staff numbers. Hundreds of people are convicted each year of breaching their

---

* If you're wondering why the courts can't impose a short sentence of imprisonment as punishment followed by intensive rehabilitation on release, there's not really a satisfactory answer beyond 'they just can't'. Parliament doesn't allow for it. Take it up with your MP.

Sexual Harm Prevention Orders by having secret phones or computers that they've hidden from the police, or wiping their internet histories, or by simply continuing to offend. Again, it strikes me as the height of naivety to assume that we are catching all, or even the majority, of those who, presenting a public face of conformity to the officers at the door, retreat into the familiar darkness of the web when night falls.

Firefighting

The allegations are theft and fraud. Joanna, the prosecution say, inveigled herself into the affections of the seventy-eight-year-old victim, Thomas, and over the course of a year helped herself to regular cash withdrawals from his account. Thomas, who lived alone with early onset Alzheimer's, had trusted Joanna, who had moved in next door, to help him day to day. It started with offers to tidy the house, progressed to trips to the supermarket, and culminated in her acting as a de facto carer, albeit one whose self-awarded salary – close to £70,000 was cleaned out of Thomas' account – far exceeded services genuinely rendered. When Thomas's daughters discovered what had been happening, they informed the police. Joanna was interviewed and claimed, improbably, that Thomas had handed her his debit card and told her to help herself to as much of his money as she pleased, as a 'thank you'.

Because of his age and infirmity, Thomas's evidence was not taken in a witness statement, instead he gave an 'ABE' interview – a pre-recorded video interview with a trained police officer, which would stand in place of Thomas's evidence-in-chief at any trial. This is the way that vulnerable witnesses, including children, the elderly and complainants in sex cases, typically give their evidence in court proceedings, with cross-examination taking place over a video link during the trial.

The prosecution's difficulty is that the interview is a shambles. Thomas was evidently in poor health; his answers were at times confused and contradictory, not helped by the baffling way in which he was interrogated by the officer. Most egregiously of all, the police omitted to establish the most important part of their case: at no time was Thomas asked whether he had given Joanna permission to take his money.

Two years have now passed between this first inadequate interview and Joanna being brought before the courts. Quite how it was deemed to pass the charging threshold is a mystery, but in any event, when it comes before the Crown Court for a plea hearing, it is plain that, as matters stand, the prosecution cannot actually prove the essential elements of its case. It cannot prove that Joanna was acting without Thomas's permission. To do so, it would need to conduct a further interview with Thomas and ask him directly the question that the police had failed to clarify two years earlier.

By this time, however, Thomas is in no fit state to be interviewed. His health has deteriorated rapidly. He cannot, when spoken to, even remember Joanna, let alone answer questions about their relationship from two years previous. There is simply no way for the case to be fixed. Despite the strongly held suspicions of the police, and of Thomas's daughters, there is not enough to secure a criminal conviction.

So at a dismissal hearing, the defence apply to dismiss the charges for want of evidence, and the judge agrees. There will be no trial. Joanna leaves court hugely relieved, and she might, of course, be genuinely innocent. Certainly she's presumed to be in law. But this isn't a case in which an independent jury has carefully assessed all the evidence and reached a not guilty verdict. That might have been difficult enough for Thomas's family to bear, but at least they would have the crumb of knowing that due process had taken its course. Instead, due process was aborted in infancy, denied because of basic failings that were overlooked until it was simply too late.

The value of justice

This failure, I know by now, is not a one-off. As each day passes, the obstacles I encounter are more numerous and more immovable. Whether prosecuting or defending, the inability of the criminal justice system to process criminal cases efficiently, timeously and correctly is making my job – all of our jobs – impossible. Most days I am not an advocate; I'm a firefighter, expected to douse a dozen blazes with a broken hose and a pyromaniac forever by my side. And the only people who seem to be aware of this, aside from those working in the system, are the members of the public unfortunate enough to be dragged in. By which time, as they are learning to their cost, it is too late.

It has been the best part of a decade since I qualified as a barrister; since that sun-splattered hope-drenched day at my Inn, grinning inanely under my too-big hired wig as my mother took photos of me and my Bar school friends prancing over the exquisitely manicured lawns. Although so much about my future remained uncertain, there was a simplicity that I, sometimes, think that I miss. My ambitions were uncomplicated: become a criminal barrister, using my consummate skills to prosecute the guilty and defend the innocent. I had no desire to champion reform, much less go on any sort of personal 'journey' (ugh). The assumption was that I would simply slot myself, beliefs and all, into the existing functioning infrastructure and click 'play'. The rest would take care of itself.

No prediction made on that day would have cast me where I am now. No round-the-table game of 'Where will we be in ten years?' in the pub after graduation from law school could have foreseen the gap between what I believed about criminal justice – what I was so certain I *knew* – and what I am encountering, day after aching, heartbreaking day. Looking back further, to the righteous certitude of the eighteen-year-old proudly carrying their *Daily Mail* to their first law lecture, the disparity becomes incomprehensible.

Could I have prepared myself for what was to follow? I doubt it. But if I had to try – to encapsulate everything I've learned, and everything I can identify that I still need to learn, and distil it in a letter to my eighteen-year-old self – I think I would say something like this:

Dear SB (to-be) (SB2B?),

It is almost certainly too soon, after only a few years in practice, to be reclining in a rocking chair to reveal immutable truths about the way we do criminal justice. It will probably still be too soon if I'm doing this job in another thirty. Criminal justice engulfs too much of the human experience to ever be known, let alone mastered, by any one person. Certainly not by you – me – who as we both know, is an absent-minded dunderhead at the best of times. That much, the decades haven't changed.

And so this letter, which, time-travel postman-dependent, should arrive as you step into law school, is not intended to change your views. I doubt I could, even if I wanted to. It is not words that change minds, but experiences. But in any case, I am not offering you one set of certitudes for another, because I have no such set to give. All I have, to borrow from a well-worn phrase, is reasonable doubts. And some are not even that reasonable. They are often arbitrary, capricious, self-interested, contradictory, hypocritical and nonsensical. They will be of no use at all to any academic understanding of theories of justice. But sharing them might, possibly, help to unfix some of those certainties you've proudly erected; loosen the guy ropes just a little, to prepare you for what is ahead.

What are these doubts? It's hard to know where to begin. I won't catch them all, because I'm not yet aware of them all. They lurk behind every robing room door, between every oak bench and inside every witness box, catching me off guard every day, whack-a-mole style. Just as I think I have a handle on one, another three pop up in its place.

They burrow into the heart of what criminal justice means, what my role – your role, soon enough – means, and where our collective, sincere energies to improve justice are most meaningfully directed.

Criminal justice means more than ever-increasing measures of punishments. It is more than longer sentences and more prison places for the people who hurt us. It means more than criminals, more than lawyers in wigs incanting Latin. It is more than the courts, the police, the prisons and the probation service. It doesn't begin at 9 a.m. and knock off when the court building closes at five, nor when the lawyer tidies away their papers at eleven. It doesn't start with an arrest and end with imprisonment. It is pervasive and effervescent and permeates every second of every day of every human life, whether we are aware of it or not. It is the philosophy of what we do to each other.

The justice system does not exist on a discrete plane, populated by those unlike us and hermetically sealed from Middle England. 'We' are not merely an audience; justice runs like a channel through our society, and its quality affects us all. The parties may be state (and complainant) against defendant, but a criminal case is no private matter. It behoves us not to attach our allegiance automatically to the former, no matter the sympathy that their cause may generate, and not to paint justice as the pursuit of elevating 'victims' rights' above defendants'. Justice for one side alone is no justice at all.

Most defendants, even those who have done terrible things, are not irredeemable. They may be flawed, but most criminals are not the ghouls we are urged to fear and loathe. Their stories still deserve to be heard. Few, if any, deserve for us to give up on them.

Many, we must never forget – although we do; I do – are innocent. Wrongly accused. Victims in their own right. Miscarriages of justice do not arrive with a fanfare; they are mundane and quotidian, and all the more dangerous for it. They lie in the sheet of disclosure that's been missed, or the victim thrice denied their trial who beats a bruised retreat rather than be denied a fourth.

Our role is more than I suspect you, SB2B, realise. More than I realise too, some days. Prosecuting means more than getting the bad guy. Certainly more than winning at all costs. It is about fairness and decency and humanity. When you defend, it will be not because you love criminals, or hate victims and take pleasure in their tears. It will not be because your ego – and Lord knows, that's an entry requirement – needs the dopamine hit of saving The Innocent Man. It will be because you recognise the value to all of us of justice done properly. You will not and cannot always be fighting for the morally pure; justice will require that you flog yourself in service of the unpleasant, the ungrateful, even the monstrous. It is no less important. No less noble.

Being an advocate is more than fizzing questions and soaring oratory. For every ounce of tenacity and grit, you must carry a quart of judgement and compassion. Counsel, though we are wont to forget etymology, must counsel. Not just in the advice we give, but in how we help to manage other people's pain, offering to share it even if we cannot relieve it.

The real problems in criminal justice, the viral weeping sores that transfer by mere proximity to the system, are not found in soft sentences or loopy judges or legal-aid gravy trains. They lie in its most basic functioning. Crumbling court buildings without operating lifts or working toilets or even somewhere to get a glass of water. Prosecutions collapsing for want of basic evidence, prosecutors and caseworkers stretched beyond endurance, bearing caseloads that can never be sustained, yet are always growing. Defence solicitors laying off staff and closing their doors to legal aid, the unviability of decades of cuts forcing bankrupt junior lawyers out of publicly funded work. Delays of years before cases even come to court, due to chronic under-resourcing of the police and Crown Prosecution Service, with victims and defendants waiting the same time again for a trial slot. Court backlogs deliberately allowed to grow by politicians who hack at court sitting days for a quick saving, calculating that voters won't notice. And they don't.

It's hard, SB2B. I find myself losing my optimism. And that is perhaps most important of all. A sense of gallows humour, perspective, humanity – all essentials to survival – but I think that above everything else, you need to believe that what you do makes a difference. Inevitably there will be days and weeks when the fog of cynicism makes it hard to see, but that flame has to keep flickering, however precariously; the belief that our role in the process has intrinsic value.

I'm finding that it dims, day on day. It dims because I can't do my job. However many hours I work, however hard I squeeze the air out of my personal life, I can't prosecute cases in the way they deserve to be prosecuted; I can't defend people in the way they deserve to be defended. I do my best, of course, and there's an argument from vanity that my efforts might, on occasion, be better than those of maybe a handful of my colleagues. But when I see, for instance, the way in which divisional CPS lawyers and caseworkers – those dealing with the unglamorous, 'volume' work – are expected to manage their caseloads and compare that to the resources available for the specialist Complex Casework Unit, or I contrast the capacity of legal-aid solicitors with the quality of defence that is available to individuals who can afford private market rates, I am reminded that justice doesn't have to be like this; we, or those we elect to govern us, choose to configure justice like this. Second-class tickets for all.

And while we grumble in our robing rooms and whine in our conferences and console in the pub, these problems go unobserved and unremarked upon by the public at large. Justice collapsed, and nobody noticed. This, perhaps more than any of it, is what hurts the most. People would care about this, I'm sure. They do, when they find out. They just don't know. And there seems no way of sounding the alarm. We are a profession of advocates who are incapable of making a public argument. As long as there are rabble-rousing politicians on *Question Time* draping themselves in the rhetoric of the Tough On Crime, fiddling with criminal sentencing while the justice system burns, nobody notices the smoke.

So those are my thoughts. There's an inconsistency or two, I accept. Many, in fact. But (lifts up rug and grabs broom) I think that's OK. I think, returning to where we started, that one of our biggest problems with how we talk about justice is our certainties. Because, as I have found and you will find, they are often based on incomplete information, or don't stand up to logical scrutiny, or can be confounded by a human experience that hasn't even occurred to us.

Certainty is the enemy of progress, and the enemy of discussion. By all means, be certain of your facts. Those can be verified, and a bedrock of objective fact is the foundation of meaningful debate. But there is no point debating values if we all know what we're going to believe at the end of it. Too often our conversations about justice amount to two fat men shouting at each other across a Pizza Hut buffet, one yelling that pepperoni is tastier, and one screaming blood in favour of Mighty Meaty, neither pausing to notice that the buffet cart is empty.

And yes, I am happy for hypocrisy to be added to my indictment. Because I, no doubt, when holding forth stridently about criminal justice in books and tweets passim, have been as certain in my principles as you are right now, SB2B. I have not evolved in that respect as much as I like to pretend. But I do try to listen. And that, ultimately, as you take your first step on the road to getting that wig and gown, is all I can ask of you. Listen to the people who you are sure are wrong. Open your mind to the pepperoni.

Yours,

SB

P.S. If you must still send that angry letter about prison for burglars, then so be it. But please know that 'sheep in Woolf's clothing' is nowhere near as clever, or as funny, as you think it is. You sound like a prick.

I chunter this stream of consciousness – or at least its bare scaffolding, without the florid letter conceit – as we wind down late one sticky May evening. It is far from the first time; my non-lawyer partner has endured a version of this refrain, on a loop, for some years now, talking me down from my ledge with a practised combination of patient nodding, theatrical eye rolls and shameless distraction techniques (usually in the form of a shop-bought strawberry trifle).

When we go to bed, eyes heavy and souls weary, my partner tosses me the book they were reading on our last holiday. 'This,' they say, 'is what you need to do.'

I glance at the title and then back at my partner, brow furrowed sceptically.

'Don't pull that face. You say you want more people to know what's happening in the criminal courts? There's your answer. Open a Twitter account. Start a blog.'

I hand back their copy of *The Secret Footballer*.

'My sweet summer child. Absolutely nobody, not even you, would read such a thing.'

'I think you'd be surprised. Other people – not me, but other people – seem to find what you do interesting. And at the very least – *at the very least* – it will stop you talking about it at bedtime.'

The next morning, I pour a coffee and switch on my laptop. I open the Twitter home page and click 'sign up'. My eye catches the Royal Doulton Barrister Bunnykins that my parents gave me on my Call day, and I pick him off the shelf and run my fingers over his smooth, wigged little head.

I start to type.

Acknowledgements

This book would not exist without the immense talents of Kris Doyle, Gillian Stern, Andrea Henry, Chloe May, Fraser Crichton and everybody at Picador whose skill and diligence has ensured that the book that exited the editing process is of a significantly higher quality than the half-baked manuscript presented as an alleged 'first draft'. Their continued patience through the considerable complications posed by working with an anonymous author is appreciated more than I can express. If it is any consolation, I am assured that I am even more inconvenient to live with.

On that note, a permanent debt of gratitude is owed to my agent, Chris Wellbelove, and his tireless assistant Emily Fish, for being the glue that holds my manic second existence together.

Mary Aspinall-Miles has brought not only eternal kindness and wisdom, but has once again trawled through drafts of my witterings to offer invaluable notes and suggestions. I'm sorry I left some of the swearing in.

To those friends and colleagues whose stories and cases I have purloined or bastardised, thank you. As a wise man once said, it is easier to get forgiveness than permission (although you need neither if nobody ever finds out).

And special thanks, of course, to Alan, for everything he

taught me, even if 90 per cent of it is unprintable. If he recognises himself in this book, I hope he forgives the liberties and appreciates the effort I have taken in trying to disguise him.

Finally, most importantly, and in the vain, self-serving hope that words can atone for deeds, I thank my family, without whose own sacrifices none of this wild ego trip would have been possible. I love you. Please don't leave me.

Appendix: A Note on Representation and Resources

One thing which hasn't changed since I first considered a career as a barrister is that, for somebody without any links to the legal profession, the Bar can seem an alienating place. Historically, as I observed in this book, barristers have been drawn from the narrowest social stratum, rendering the Bar woefully unrepresentative in terms of sex, race, disability, sexuality, gender identity and social and educational background. These problems persist today.

Where there has been important change in recent years, however, is in the outreach work that is carried out by those in and with links to the legal profession, aimed at improving social mobility and making the Bar accessible to people from all backgrounds.

If you have read this book and are intrigued by the idea of becoming a barrister, or of visiting that fate on somebody you know, below is a (non-exhaustive) list of charities, organisations, schemes and opportunities aimed at opening up the Bar to everybody, so that those standing up in court and representing people in legal proceedings better reflect the communities they serve.

The **Bar Council,** the representative body for barristers in England and Wales, offers a number of schemes for school and college students, including:

— The Bar Placement Scheme allows sixth-form students to spend three days shadowing a barrister and to receive advocacy training from the Inns of Court College of Advocacy.

— The Bar E-Mentoring Scheme is intended to support students from under-represented backgrounds who are interested in pursuing a career at the Bar.

— If you would like a barrister to give a talk at your school, college or university, the Bar Council has a database of barrister volunteers.

Details of these are here: https://www.barcouncil.org.uk/becoming-a-barrister/school-students.html

The **Inns of Court** each have their own social mobility programmes and scholarship schemes, summarised below:

Gray's Inn
— University Advocacy Days are held throughout the year and offer university students the chance to meet barristers and to perform advocacy under the guidance of advocacy trainers. https://www.graysinn.org.uk/joining/outreach/university-advocacy-day-0

— Griffin LAW (Law and Advocacy Workshops) is a programme introducing sixth-form students to the legal profession and teaching advocacy skills, culminating in a mock trial held at the Royal Courts of Justice or the Old Bailey. https://www.graysinn.org.uk/joining/outreach/griffin-law

— Vocalise trains law students as 'debate mentors' to train

prisoners in the skills of public speaking and debating.
https://www.graysinn.org.uk/joining/vocalise

— Details of the scholarships, prizes and other financial
assistance available to those interested in pursuing a career
as a barrister are here: https://www.graysinn.org.uk/
scholarships

Inner Temple
— The Pegasus Access and Support Scheme (PASS) aims to
improve access and to support high-achieving students
from under-represented backgrounds by securing a funded
mini-pupillage in chambers for each participant and
providing a professional and advocacy skills development
programme. https://www.innertemple.org.uk/becoming-a-
barrister/how-to-get-involved/pass/

— Insight Events are held throughout the year, in person and
online, to allow school and university students to hear
from practising barristers and judges, and to attend
networking receptions. https://www.innertemple.org.uk/
becoming-a-barrister/how-to-get-involved/insight-events/

— The In Focus series aims to have open and frank round-
table discussions, in a safe space, with barristers and
prospective barristers about issues faced by under-
represented groups. https://www.innertemple.org.uk/
becoming-a-barrister/how-to-get-involved/in-focus/

— Details of the scholarships, prizes and other financial
assistance available to those interested in pursuing a career
as a barrister are here: https://www.innertemple.org.uk/
becoming-a-barrister/

Lincoln's Inn

— InnSight Sessions are held throughout the year, in person, online and at universities, aimed at demystifying the process of training for the Bar. https://www.lincolnsinn.org.uk/becoming-a-barrister/careers-events/

— The Mini-Pupillage Grant Scheme offers financial support to students wishing to undertake mini-pupillages who would otherwise not be able to do so. https://www.lincolnsinn.org.uk/becoming-a-barrister/funding/

— The Neuberger Prize is targeted at students at non-Russell Group universities, offering funding for a summer-school placement at the Inn, a mentor and a mini-pupillage. https://www.lincolnsinn.org.uk/becoming-a-barrister/funding/

— Details of the scholarships, prizes and other financial assistance available to those interested in pursuing a career as a barrister are here: https://www.lincolnsinn.org.uk/scholarships-prizes/

Middle Temple

— The Access to the Bar Awards provide two funded weeks of work experience every summer for up to thirty undergraduates from disadvantaged backgrounds. One week is spent shadowing a judge, one week shadowing a barrister. https://www.middletemple.org.uk/becoming-barrister/access-bar-award

— The Middle Temple Open Day for Schools and Universities offers the opportunity for students to meet judges, barristers and trainees. https://www.middletemple.org.uk/joining-the-inn/access-and-outreach

— Details of the scholarships, prizes and other financial assistance available to those interested in pursuing a career as a barrister are here: https://www.middletemple.org.uk/education-training/scholarships-prizes

Mentoring and Networking

10000 Black Interns: https://www.10000blackinterns.com

AllAboutLaw Diversity: https://www.allaboutlaw.co.uk/diversity

The Association of Disabled Lawyers: https://www.disabledlawyers.co.uk/about-us

The Association of Women Barristers: https://www.womenbarristers.com

Bar None (Western Circuit): https://westerncircuit.co.uk/bar-none/

Big Voice London: https://www.bvl.org.uk

The Black Barristers' Network: https://www.blackbarristersnetwork.org.uk/our-work

The Black Lawyers Directory (Legal Gateway): https://www.bldlawyers.com/the_legal_gateway.html

BME Legal: https://twitter.com/BME_Legal

Bridging the Bar: https://bridgingthebar.org

Centre for Women's Justice Mentoring Scheme for Aspiring Lawyers from Black, Asian and Minoritised Backgrounds: https://www.centreforwomensjustice.org.uk/mentoring-scheme

City Disabilities: https://citydisabilities.org.uk

The Chancery Bar Association: https://www.chba.org.uk/for-members/mentoring-scheme/

The Commercial Bar Association: https://www.combar.com/news/25th-anniversary-scholarship-scheme-2020/

The Criminal Bar Association: https://www.criminalbar.com/resources/equality-and-diversity/mentoring-programmes/

Disability's Not A Bar (Podcast): https://twitter.com/ DisabilityNoBar

Guru Nanak Social Mobility Scholarship: https://singhbarrister. co.uk/scholarship

InterLaw Diversity Forum: https://www.interlawdiversityforum. org

The Kalisher Trust: https://www.unitydiversityinlaw.co.uk

The Lemn Sissay Law Bursary: https://www.socialsciences. manchester.ac.uk/connect/making-a-difference/equality-and- diversity/black-lawyers-matter/

Next Step Foundation: https://www.nextstepeducation.org.uk/ our-programme

Neurodiversity in Law: http://neurodiversityinlaw.co.uk

Pupillage and How to Get It: https://pupillageandhowtogetit. com

Queer Lawyers of Tomorrow: http://www.queerlawyersof tomorrow.org

Rare Foundations Law: https://www.rarerecruitment.co.uk/ foundations/law/index.html

The Social Mobility Foundation: https://www.socialmobility. org.uk

Society of Asian Lawyers: https://www.societyofasianlawyers. co.uk

Sutton Trust (Pathways to Law): https://www.suttontrust.com/ our-programmes/pathways-to-law/

Unity Diversity in Law: https://www.unitydiversityinlaw.co.uk

Urban Lawyers: https://urbanlawyers.co.uk

Women in Criminal Law: https://www.womenincriminallaw. com/mentoring

There are many, many more organisations and initiatives not listed above. Many barristers' chambers have their own social mobility initiatives, offering funded work experience/mini-pupillage placements, providing mentoring schemes and bursaries, and attending local schools to speak directly to students. A number of universities also have their own mentoring and financial assistance schemes.